The World's Great
ARCHITECTURE

The World's Great

ARCHITECTURE

From the Pyramids to Modern Times

General editor: Patrick Nuttgens

EXCALIBUR BOOKS

NEW YORK

Endpapers:
Machu Picchu, an Inca town high in the
Peruvian Andes

Title Page:
The Doric Temple of Poseidon at Cape Sounion
in Attica

CONTENTS

*The section on Colonial North America is by John Archer.

INTRODUCTION

Architecture is an expression of human experience in the creation of usable space. Like any other art and many other activities it cannot fail to express the experience and aspirations of the people who make it; it expresses them through what it is – the spaces used by people, living or dead. What makes it different from many other arts, though not from all, is that it arises not only from the wishes and ideas and visions of its designers, but from the wishes and needs of the people who are going to use it. There is no other art quite so comprehensive in requiring the collaboration of all the people concerned with it.

The origin of architecture is the challenge to a creative mind of the need for a building to exist at all. At its most elemental that need arises from simple things that lie at the very beginning of human experience – shelter, warmth and food. The basis of all architecture all over the world and at every age is what has in our time come to be known as the vernacular.

There has to be architecture in any kind of civilization, any culture which has developed from hunting and gathering to settlement and the formation of communities dependent upon agriculture. The vernacular is the range of buildings required by that simple society and required for functional reasons. It is basic architecture for everyman. Because those elementary needs do not come to an end when other more sophisticated needs are met, vernacular architecture continues throughout history and is usually undatable. Vernacular architecture is the simplest use of human ingenuity to answer the needs of the ordinary man.

It provides him with his house, his animals with a shed, his produce with a barn, his products with a workshop, his pathways with a bridge. At its earliest and simplest the vernacular is created by an ingenious answer to the problem of where you have to build and what you have to build with.

Of its very nature therefore the vernacular tends to be impermanent. It is created not for posterity or for recognition but for survival and for the straightforward satisfaction of human needs. It is subject to no aesthetic criteria until it is exploited for that purpose; the measure of its success is direct and known at first hand. If society changes or a new technology displaces the one on which the settlement was founded and the functions alter, the vernacular may disappear, like many of the houses and byres in the Scottish highlands and islands.

But it has a profound influence upon great architecture, for at least three reasons. The first concerns the places where the vernacular is found. At the earliest times they are places of agriculture and forestry. From these activities and their needs are derived the basic house types, unified or multiple, and the basic settlements, centralized or dispersed. As activities change, the places change. Commerce grows and things are moved. Houses and workplaces and settlements become more diverse and individual. The sites become more varied because they become more accessible, no longer only in valleys and river plains but on hillsides and hilltops and in places only made habitable by technology and art.

The second factor is the way in which the buildings are made. There are two basic ways of building anywhere – by laying one block on top of another, or by making a skeleton and covering it with skin. They are quite different and require a different perception. Almost everywhere people have built by assembling blocks – stone or clay bricks or dried mud or, later, concrete – piling one on another, inventing ways of turning corners, leaning the walls over, leaving holes, and finally covering the construction. In other parts of the world people have built by making a skeleton of wood or, later, iron and steel and covering it with skins of many kinds, animal hides, canvas and cloth, plaster and straw. The two methods are put together on an ordinary block building where the ordinary roof is a skeleton of timber with a skin of reeds or straw or slabs of stone or tile.

The third factor – and one that influences everything else in architecture – is the availability of materials. Almost anything can be used in building and has been, from sticks to sardine tins. But it is the readily available materials that have the most profound effect upon architecture all over the world, first through the local vernacular and then in the greater buildings. The basic materials are relatively simple – stone, clay, wood, skins, grass, leaves, sand and water. But what is not simple is the distribution of such materials throughout the world, either where they are found in nature or in what man has done to make them more accessible. It would be convenient for the historian if a country or a continent was restricted to one main material. It is rarely the case. But it is the case that one or more material will always dominate during certain periods and in certain regions.

Stone, of many kinds and subject to many treatments, is the most versatile of all natural building materials. But it is by no means alone. Apart from timber of many kinds, there are sun-dried bricks, palm leaves, reeds, rushes, terracotta, timber, adobe blocks, and almost anything which can be made or burnt with mud. Until about two hundred years ago such materials and their ready availability dictated to a large extent the local vernacular architecture of any region. What transformed the situation and effectively brought about the death of the vernacular except as a conscious style was the development of communications. Once it became cheaper to move natural materials or to make new ones and move them to the site rather than find them locally, the vernacular was effectively dead – a victim of the Industrial Revolution.

But from simple solutions to the

Trulli at Alberobello, Apulia, Italy: mainly 18th-century dry-stone walls with conical roofs and capstones.

above
Taos Pueblo, New Mexico, north-east
of Santa Fe: adobe houses originally
entered through a hole in the roof.

right
The simplest of all vernacular houses,
made by placing one block of ice on
another: an Eskimo igloo.

questions of where, how and what to build has produced a quite astonishing variety of ordinary buildings, many of which seem extraordinary only to those whose ordinary world is different – the black houses of the Scottish highlands, the igloos of the Eskimos, the wigwams of the North American Indians, the tents of the Arabs, the more elaborate timber-framed houses of the medieval English, the pueblos of New Mexico, the wood and paper houses of Japan, the elaborate timber houses of Indonesia, the stone-domed trulli of Alberobello in southern Italy.

And many more. In short, there is a basic architecture, never uninteresting, always capable of wonder and delight, to be found everywhere in the world, unlimited in its variety, and often unexplored. It is an architecture of creative ingenuity, of the use of common sense, of inherited ways of doing and making, of competence rather than concept. And it provides solutions to basic technical problems in building and the provision of space.

The history of the world's great architecture is the astonishing story of how individuals and groups have taken that basic necessity of building and transformed it into possibly the greatest manifestation of the human spirit – more profound, more lasting, more inexhaustible than any other art, a vital and truly wonderful expression of the experience of mankind, in every part of the world.

If the start of a vernacular architecture is the house, the start of the world's great architecture is the tomb. It is not the graveyard of the ordinary man; the ordinary man for most of human history has been put away under the ground without a marker. The tomb is made for someone special and in almost every part of the world it is given special treatment, implying not only the importance of the occupant, but his or her need for immortality. The tombs and the temples of the ancient world are the start of an artistic story and they record its glories and its aspirations.

That story starts in the region which was the cradle of the first civilizations – the plains and hills roughly defined by the edges of the Dead Sea, the Caspian Sea, the Persian Gulf, the Red Sea and the Mediterranean – the lands of Mesopotamia, Anatolia and Persia. There were villages from the sixth millennium BC, towns and cities from about the fourth millennium. And with the cities came the division of labour, the growth of political and religious hierarchies, literacy and the start of monumental architecture. The buildings of those alluvial plains overlap in date those of the Mediterranean coast, of the Nile Valley in Egypt and of Crete. From the Mediterranean came in due course one major strand of world architectural history. The other centres, starting rather later, were the Indus valley in northern India, the Yellow River in northern China, and across the world Central America and the Andes.

In every case the story of monumental architecture has to do with the impulse of people with power to perpetuate or glorify themselves or seek the favour of a deity greater and more permanent than themselves. Expressive architecture moves from the tomb to the temple, from man to the gods, and stays there for a long time.

Next to the architecture of the gods is, from almost as early a time, the architecture of power – of fortresses, defences, palaces and castles. Between those two poles of design, religious and secular, are to be found most of the characteristic building types of history in different parts of the world, moving closer together or further apart as they reflect the bias of a particular society. They include the pagodas of China and the castles of Japan; the temples of India and Cambodia; the mosques and palaces of Arabia; great fortifications like the Crusader castles; the vast palaces of European humanism; huge complexes enshrining government and administration; and most extraordinary of all in our time, housing.

The history of world architecture is inexhaustible in its variations, but it does reveal a few themes which most countries seem to have in common.

One is the way in which limitations have been overcome in different ways, or more surprisingly not overcome at all, without disaster. The Mayans produced some spectacular buildings but failed to discover the wheel. The Greeks of the Hellenic Age produced very sophisticated architecture but ignored the arch. The arch, the vault and the dome are some of the great themes of architectural history and inspired at least two great styles, Gothic and Islamic. But their lack did not prevent a spectacular architecture from developing elsewhere.

Roof systems, for example, stimulated the most astonishing feats of craftsmanship. Whereas Europeans developed the timber-roof truss with an ever increasing imagination throughout the Middle Ages, with king posts and queen posts and hammer-beams with fantastic pendants, the Chinese followed another line of development and created instead a longitudinal system of heaping up purlins, one above the other, with elaborate brackets. It was in some ways less flexible than the European system; on the other hand it created wonderful spaces underneath and made possible a great variety of curving roof lines and the elaboration of decorative eaves.

It seems that the most astonishing feats of architectural design do not require the most amazing technology. We have today the most advanced technology in history, but it cannot be said that we have so far produced the most supreme buildings. It may be that our best modern architecture is to be found not among buildings at all but among such things as supersonic aeroplanes, deep-sea capsules and rockets going to the moon. In contrast to them, the greatest buildings can be made from the simplest things, provided there are enough people available with the right manual skills.

No explanation other than vision, work, ingenuity and skill is required to account for the pyramids, the

cathedrals, the great temples and shrines, the aqueducts, and the railways. One of the lessons of architectural history is that the most supreme and awesome buildings have been made from materials that were won by hand.

The turning points in architectural history are caused by the exercise of ingenuity of a very high order after a lot of experiment has transformed a material into a process and ultimately into a style. Such turning points were the invention of the arch (in many parts of the world but notably exploited by the Romans), the groin vault (so that a stone roof needs to be supported only at the corners), the pointed arch (which led to Gothic), the pendentive (which made a beautiful link between a dome and a square compartment and characterized Byzantine), and the stained-glass window that opened up the possibilities of Gothic. All of those were based on materials found in nature; what has transformed the recent world has been man-made materials – iron, steel, concrete, plastics and glass – on different scales and with characteristics due to their differing industrial processes and inventions.

At the other end of such movements is the exhaustion of a style. There seems to come a point when no further development is possible. It happened with Greek Doric, which gave way to other styles; with

Gothic, by the end of the Middle Ages; with the Inca temples; with pyramids; with eastern temples and towers. It may have happened with modern flat roofs and multi-storey office blocks. There comes a point when there is little to be gained by going further. The Tower of Babel looms at the end of every architectural journey.

But that does not diminish the excitement and fun of the adventures on the way or the intellectual challenge of the buildings. The manifold architecture of the world in all its richness and variety can be looked at with the same eyes and valued with the same critical faculties. But we need to know something about it, not to change our views or lessen our wonder, but simply to see it better. To a considerable extent our perceptions depend upon our knowledge; if an object makes sense, it is also easier to see. We see it better because we recognize what it is made from, what is its form and what the people who made it had in mind.

To appreciate these factors we have to look not only at the building itself but at the social, economic, political and ideological context in which it was placed and which helped to shape it. There is seldom time for most of us to do that properly; we need guidance of the sort offered in this book. But even without it we can recognize that there is no documentary evidence to

compare with architecture as an indicator of the character of a civilization. It is all the more subtle and provocative because it does not tell a simple story. Beautiful buildings do not necessarily reveal a beautiful society; the most spectacular structures may be the products of a detestable social system. There are many layers of meaning and of confusion to be stripped away before it can be understood. For architecture is not a simple work of art. It exists at many levels and in many dimensions, and there is no one simple formula to assess it by. Ultimately it has to be seen as part of history as well as art.

But never just as a piece of dry scholarship. Architecture is profoundly moving and inspiring. Every country and every epoch has produced such things. In the end they are very personal, different for every individual, but available everywhere and at every time. A love of architecture means that one can never be bored. There is something everywhere for everyone.

For everyone there are high spots – some obvious, others less so. They include such majestic monuments as the Pyramids, Santa Sophia, the Angkor Wat and Sydney Opera House. For me, some of the most intense architectural experiences have been the prehistoric dwellings at Skara Brae in Orkney, the mausoleum of Galla Placidia in Ravenna, the cathedral of Torcello

right
On a dramatic site, with elaborate buildings and a perfect 13th-century choir: Rievaulx Abbey, Yorkshire (1132).

left
The 'Rose de France', north transept, Chartres Cathedral: a brilliant geometrical exercise in colour and light.

in the lagoon of Venice, a remote
mountain temple in south Korea,
the Pazzi Chapel in Florence, a
pueblo in New Mexico, the spaces
and carvings and windows of
Chartres Cathedral, the ruins of the
Yorkshire abbeys, the mountain
towns of Perugia and Orvieto, the
scintillating rococo interior of St
John Nepomuk in Munich, the
castle of Craigievar in Scotland and
the baroque fountains of Rome.
They include the Albert Dock in
Liverpool, with its iron Doric columns, the misty brick spaces of
Westminster Cathedral, the strange
evocative interiors of Mackintosh's
Glasgow School of Art and the
wholly original structure of the
crypt of Gaudi's Santa Coloma near
Barcelona.

They have been experiences
nowhere more intense and memorable than the modern shrine of
Ronchamp in France and the
ancient shrine of Delphi in Greece.
In all of those, but especially the
last two, I have spent many hours
and experienced a happiness which
is all the greater because it can be
shared.

right
A rich expression of Baroque with
twisted pillars and dramatic lighting in
St John Nepomuk, Munich (1735).

right
Craigievar Castle, Aberdeenshire
(1626): in the Scottish baronial style,
compact in plan and topped with
fantasy.

12

PREHISTORY
and the
EARLIEST CIVILIZATIONS

below
Stonehenge: a chiefdom culture raised these sarsens and lintels on a site oriented for midsummer ceremonials.

Ranging across Europe and the Middle East are architectural structures, dating mainly from the last three millennia BC, which are monuments to man's ingenuity in solving problems of environment, stone supply and security from invasion. Because of the geographical and chronological diversity of these buildings we can only attempt to isolate common architectural phenomena. This chapter will include early megalithic monuments whose purpose is not always explicable, temple-orientated city-states, palace-centred civilizations, fortress-citadels and various types of domestic settlement.

Megalithic monuments
No definite answer can yet be given as to the function of long stone alignments found in north-west France at Carnac (*c.* 3000 BC). Parallel rows of thousands of granite monoliths (menhirs), some of them 8 m (20 ft) high, were set up. There should be no derogatory connotation in our minds when we describe the civilization that organized these alignments as prehistoric. However we must be cautious about theories which over-complicate the simple architectural mathematics of these great stone-raisers. A feasible suggestion is that the rows led to a sacred precinct.

Even more inexplicable is Stonehenge in England, an extremely complex monument which developed into its present, third form between 3000 and 1200 BC. The architects of its second

Mycenaean monarchs of the sixteenth-century BC were buried in shaft-graves protected by sturdy walls.

Side-chamber containing a lustral basin in a megalithic passage grave at New Grange on the River Boyne.

construction phase seem to have chosen deliberately a solar orientation where the entrance roughly coincided with the sun on the horizon on Midsummer Day. The final plan involved raising 50.8-tonne (50-ton) hard sandstone monoliths (called sarsens), which had been pounded into shape, to form a circle of uprights supporting a continuous lintel. By tonguing a horizontal stone beam across the tops of two uprights the familiar trilithon of the inner horse-shoe was built. A kind of inverse perspective is achieved by the trilithons being broader faced at the top to avoid the appearance of tapering. The generations that built Stonehenge – and other circles using sarsen megaliths like Avebury, also in England – belonged to societies where manpower was expertly channelled into erecting edifices which clearly played a dominant role in their culture but whose *raison d'être* is lost to us. Stonehenge, of indigenous inspiration, probably originated from the need for a focal point for government or temple ceremonies requir-

ing some astronomical alignment.

Funerary monuments

Burials in the ancient world were frequently accompanied by monuments designed to indicate the grandeur of the deceased's role in society. In the Orkneys and Ireland are fine examples of megalithic passage-graves cut into large mounds. At Maes Howe in the Orkneys finely-split red sandstone lines the long corridor leading into a central chamber with a corbelled roof, an advanced architectural feature of these tombs. Dowth in Ireland has the most spectacular of the passage-graves the Boyne farmers built for their cremated dead. Around the huge circular mound were fixed stone markers while, inside the corridor of the major grave, orthostats support a roof of transverse blocks. A recess in the corbelled chamber leads off into two more rooms. For its time Dowth has no architectural rival in Europe.

On mainland Greece at Mycenae are later examples of funerary monuments with vaulted roofs. The

left
Mycenae's finest 'beehive' tomb – the Treasury of Atreus – has an impressive approach-road.

below left
At Skara Brae the community used Caithness flagstone to make cupboards, beds, boxes and hearths.

below right
Temple of Warka, Iraq (*c.* 3000 BC): this court's mud-brick walls are set with a mosaic of coloured cones.

pages 18–19
The Great Bath at Mohenjo-Daro and its surrounding rooms were perhaps a centre for state or religious ceremony.

most impressive of these beehive tombs is misleadingly called the Treasury of Atreus. An approach or dromos lined on each side with massive masonry met the facade, which had two semi-columns engaged to it. A monolith lintel, about 122 tonnes (120 tons), has the pressure eased from it by a relieving triangle, revealing knowledge of the areas most vulnerable to stress. Inside, the overhanging slabs of the corbelled dome are skilfully cut and polished. The burial in this magnificent tomb was insignificantly situated in a rock-cut recess off the main chamber, thereby leaving the most impressive part free for rituals.

Selection of building materials
Studying the domestic architecture of two settlements as far apart as the Orkneys and the Indus Valley, we can see how the environment conditioned the selection of building materials. At Skara Brae a village of roughly 1800 BC was preserved when it was engulfed in a dune. It shows an almost totally 'lithic' approach to houses and their accessories because timber was not available. Without using mortar, rough stone slabs were piled to form small rectangular rooms linked by corridors. Stone-lined effluences were cut to run out of some walls. Around central fireplaces the dressers, shelves and sleeping quarters were also made of stone. The small entrances with the doorway closed by a sturdy stone slab convey a general impression of the inhabitants' overwhelming fear of being plundered.

In contrast in Pakistan the late third millennium site of Mohenjo-Daro shows an exploitation of baked brick in all its structures. This suggests a social set-up able to concentrate a large percentage of its labour-force into striking and firing thousands of mud bricks. The town itself, thriving like others in the area on aggressive trading abroad, was a series of blocks formed by the intersection of main streets. Its most striking architectural conception was the great bath, with rows of rooms around it suggesting a collegiate purpose such as a complex for ritual ablutions.

Temple-orientated city-states
In Mesopotamia a city-state would be judged by the magnificence of its religious architecture. Possessing fertile lands fed by the waters of the Tigris or the Euphrates, a city could set aside sizeable resources for constructing a temple to its patron deity. However, the only native building material was clay for sundried bricks which could be embellished by polychrome glaze. There were several building innovations based on clay, such as the development of the plano-convex brick and

the ornamental device of patterning walls and columns by the insertion into their surface of coloured clay cones. Other building materials, such as limestone and wood, had to be imported from neighbouring uplands.

Against the background of a loosely-knit consortium of city-states with major ones like Ur claiming overall kingship, princes and temple officials formed the governing force, controlling laws, land and manpower. They were jealous of the prestige of their city's god and this found expression in their ziggurats, imposing temple towers rising in stages. A ziggurat symbolized a mountain containing cosmic powers and the source of life – a majestic image architecturally rendered as a residence for the god whose manifestation took place in the shrine on the top.

At Ur the ziggurat was sacred to the city's moon-god, Sin, and was built around 2000 BC by the ruler Ur-Nammu. From an oblong court the strongly-buttressed sides of the ziggurat rise; matting is built into the thick brickwork to help bind the mass together. The court itself is orientated to the points of the compass – possibly signifying the claim made by some Mesopotamian rulers to be 'King of the Four Quarters', i.e. the world. The monument is climbed to the first stage via three stairways on its north-eastern side and from there a single flight of steps reaches the second stage. Actually the best information about the shape of the upper part of a ziggurat comes from Choga Zambil in Iran, where Untash-Gal constructed one of which five tiers survive.

Palace-centred civilizations

The first millennium BC saw the re-emergence of the Assyrians as the predominant power. A ruler's residential city, in addition to having a temple and ziggurat, became an architectural reflection of his secular power. When Nimrud was the capital city under Ashurnasirpal a palace was built from which the basic form of an Assyrian royal complex can be seen, incorporating a temple area, reception hall, throne room and administrative offices. Outside this bustling nucleus Shalmaneser III improved the defence system by building a fort encompassing a palace, store-rooms and a barracks for the army and their chariots.

At Khorsabad King Sargon II resided in a city covering approximately 3 hectares (8 acres); the architectural landscape was largely the palace, temple and a seven-tiered ziggurat. The throne-room walls were adorned with orthostats or sculptured slabs forming the lower stone perimeter upon which mud-brick upper courses could be laid. The themes of the reliefs on Assyrian orthostats in general were the king's participation in sacred rituals and the glorification of the monarch by stressing his heroism as a war-leader or his prowess as a hunter. Sennacherib's 'palace without a rival' at Nineveh for example contained, as an integral part of the architectural demands of the state, a vivid depiction of his siege of Lachish.

Similarly in Ashurbanipal's palace at Nineveh foreign ambassadors would be suitably subdued when, proceeding to an audience with the monarch, they saw on the walls the panorama of a gory battle in which an Elamite ruler who opposed Assyria is killed trying to escape the field. The same propaganda occurs in narrow bronze bands rivetted in registers to massive cedar-wood double gates. Gateways could be made more impressive by being flanked with stone winged lions or bulls with bearded anthropomorphic heads. These 'lamassu' were both architectural supports to the vault across the entrance and superhuman powers guarding the palace. Approached from the front the colossi are seen standing motionless as if representing the steadfastness of the building. Passing between them,

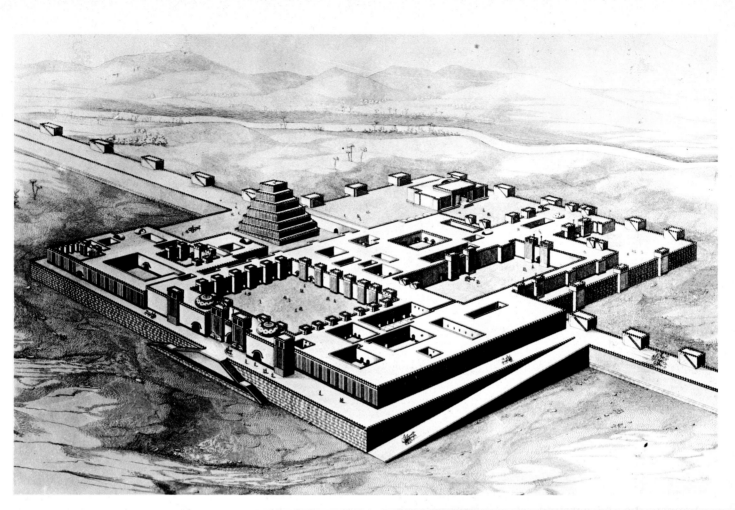

above
The citadel of Fort Sargon (Khorsabad) contained the palace and a ziggurat with a continuous ascending ramp.

above left
Ziggurat of the moon-god at Ur, built by Ur-Nammu: its staircases ascended a probable three-staged temple-tower.

right
An orthostat from Nimrud glorifies Assyrian military invincibility: a citadel's fortifications crumble.

above
At Choga Zambil near Susa in Iran the ziggurat had stairways on three sides, each leading to a gatehouse-chapel.

left
The city of Babylon's processional way left the palace and temple quarter through the imposing Ishtar gate. (Vorderasiatisches Museum, Berlin)

however, we see their four legs striding, indicative of their magical ability to become animated and pounce upon any threat to the palace.

Architecture in Babylon, under the guidance of Nebuchadnezzar, was a combination of urgent but unslovenly city-planning and an impressive defence network. The inner city's main roads ran roughly parallel to the River Euphrates on the west with intersecting streets at right angles to them. Burnt-brick tiered town houses formed a tight complex. In the sun-dried brick walls of the city was the Ishtar Gate. Its decoration in glazed brick consisted of a blue background sporting moulded yellow bulls and white dragons, symbolizing the protection given to Babylon by the gods Adad and Marduk.

Fortress citadels
The fortifications of some ancient cities are their most outstanding architectural feature. In the highlands of Anatolia stone and timber

above
The ruins of Nebuchadnezzar's city of Babylon show the use of kiln-fired bricks for ramparts and buildings.

above
Fortified Jericho (*c.* 8000 BC onwards) incorporated this imposing round tower of stones set in clay in its defences.

above
Hattusas's fortifications defended the citadel and lower town, enclosing a series of temples (here, the ruined court of one).

were plentiful so that no constraints existed to hamper architects in designing massive defences. From its commanding position at the access to fertile countryside Boghazköy (the modern name for Hattusas, capital of the Hittite empire) might seem relatively unthreatened. Attacks however could always be expected from tribes to the north. Consequently fortifications of cyclopean masonry covered the extensive acreage, taking full advantage of natural crags and rocks. As well as projecting bastions the defences had elaborate casemates and a tunnel constructed for launching sorties from within against any tribal attack from the north.

In the constantly rebuilt walled city of Troy the architects at the zenith of its prosperity (Level VI) constructed well-cut masonry gateways and towers. These contrasted sharply with the unprepossessing fortress of the later Level VIIA, disconcertingly equated with the magnificent Troy of Homer's epic. Further east the civilization of Urartu, renowned for its intricate bronzes, which flourished around Lakes Van and Urmia in the ninth century BC, leaves us in no doubt as to the excellence of its military architects. Projecting from the cyclopean masonry of the citadel of

Van, a barbican defended the water supply. But the designers of these citadels had to cope with the constant confrontations that Urartu had with Assyria and no bulwarks could be contrived to thwart the determined onslaught of the Assyrian war machine, as we know from the records of King Sargon's campaign in 714 BC.

In Palestine architects made similar efforts to reduce the vulnerability of towns sited on one of the major military highways of the ancient world. As far back as 8000 BC a stone wall encircled Jericho, with a tower in it mountable internally. Later mud-brick walls were plastered and angled in such a way as to foil direct penetration by rams. It was also necessary to protect the spring watering this citadel and its immediate environs in an otherwise arid quarter of the Jordan Valley. We find another defensive water system in a stone-lined passage leading to a spring at the foot of the mound on which Megiddo stood, controlling the routes to the south from the plain of Esdraelon. The strength of a city's strategic position in war-torn Palestine was commensurate with the ingenuity of its architects. At the Canaanite city of Hazor, commanding the best routes to Damascus and the north, were massive earth ramparts nearly 3.5 m (100 ft) wide and a brick wall 7.6 m (25 ft) thick. It fell at least three times to hostile armies.

On mainland Greece the palaces of the Mycenaeans also functioned of necessity as fortresses, securing trade-routes. The citadel of Mycenae used cyclopean masonry for its walls, which enclosed the palace, villas, the granary and an underground cistern in case of siege. From the Lion Gate and its adjacent tower troops could scrutinize the approach of strangers. The ashlar masonry of the gate comprises colossal jambs and a monolithic lintel. The pressure-relieving triangle was employed and the space it created ingeniously filled with a slab carved to show two antithetical lions. In the palace, halls follow the megaron pattern of a portico projecting from the walls of a main rectangular room with a central hearth. Derived ultimately from western Anatolia, this style became prevalent in Aegean palaces.

Palatial architecture

In contrast the Minoan hegemony of the Aegean meant that scant attention was given to fortifying Cretan palaces. Palatial architecture blossomed in the Aegean civilizations, which on the surface at any rate were free from the theocratic syndrome that produced the temple-towers of Mesopotamia. At Knossos architects had to cut into and adapt the naturally sloping knoll against which the palace complex was built. This led to the brilliant conception of the grand stairway rising two storeys with four flights of steps. Where gloominess occurred because of the hillside or heavy colonnades light-wells were devised. Columns were made of

above right
The cyclopean masonry of Mycenaean Tiryns gives impregnability to the corbelled casemate of its defences.

right
A view across the southern gateways of the palace of Minoan Crete at Knossos, defended by its naval strength.

25

left
Persepolis: 100 column bases mark
Xerxes's throne hall, beyond Darius's
audience hall and palace and the
tripylon, giving access to inner royal
apartments.

right
Xerxes's great gatehouse at Persepolis
bears two human-headed bulls,
symbols of divine protection.

above
Spear-bearers and bowmen of
Persepolis immortalized in the
sculptured staircases of state halls and
palaces.

wood and stood on stone drums,
their shafts adorned with moulded
plaster. One innovation was the use
of a column to divide a doorway.
The western side of the palace was
clearly designed mainly for ceremonial and cult purposes as we can
see from the throne room with its
sunken ritual basin. The bull-leap-
ing fresco re-creates the excitement
that took place in the central court
of the palace, which acted as the
arena for this cult-sport. Interlocking terracotta drainage pipes, bathrooms, basement granaries and
store-rooms for oil jars all add to
the picture of a culture with time
to be concerned with architectural
niceties.

There are similarities, particularly in the use of frescoes, with the
palace at Mari (*c.* 1750 BC) on the
west bank of the Euphrates in
northern Syria. This was the royal
residence of Zimri-Lim, whose coro-
nation is depicted on a living-room
wall. There were reception halls,
offices, stores and a civil-service
college. The arrangement of these
rooms around courts enabled
architects to ensure a modicum of
light and ventilation.

There is no better final example
than the architectural expression of
sheer munificence found in the royal
city of Persepolis. Founded by
Darius I, its inspiration was to
commemorate the prestige of the
Persian empire. On a stone platform rising 15.2 m (50 ft) above the
plain were palaces and columned
halls. The approach was via a stairway sloping gently enough for
horses to negotiate it. Winged bulls
flanked the entrance and the monumental gates and staircases were
decorated with reliefs of foreign
princes, guardsmen and tribute,
capturing in stone the New Year
festival at which the Persian
monarch received the homage of his
vassals and courtiers. The throne
hall or Hall of a Hundred Columns
was a treasury where gifts were
presented to the king. Its roof was
originally made of beams of cedar
wood. Some of the most intriguing
architecture is to be found in the
fluted columns themselves, resting
on bell-shaped bases. Their capitals
were designed as ornate scrolls,
clusters of palm leaves, bulls and
horned lions.

The splendour of Persepolis is a
fitting conclusion to this survey
since it borrows building styles and
devices found throughout the
Ancient Middle East. From these
cosmopolitan influences the collec-
tive genius of its designers constructed a magnificent architectural
'cocktail'.

ANCIENT EGYPT

In many people's minds Ancient Egyptian architecture is solely religious in inspiration, centred around a god's sanctuary or a burial-place. Yet a moderate amount of archaeological evidence does exist to give a general picture of secular architecture. The bare fact is, however, that religious and funerary buildings have survived far more extensively than domestic ones. Three major reasons account for this. Firstly everyday housing consisted of perishable materials like wood or reeds and friable sun-dried mud bricks. In contrast tombs and temples were predominantly made of stone with the expressed intention of lasting forever. Secondly many ancient towns are now below the foundations of modern settlements. Thirdly some conurbations were abandoned and at length engulfed by sand or by the silt left annually by the Nile flood (that is until the man-made changes in the river's regime this century). Most tombs and temples were built safely beyond irrevocable damage by the inundation on the very edge of the cultivatable area or in the desert.

·Limitless stone was available to architects from three major sources. There were the limestone quarries of the north, particularly valued being those at Tura near Cairo, which produced a fine white variety used, for example, to provide a gleaming outer casing for the pyramids. In the south the sand-stone quarries at Gebel el-Silsila supplied the building materials for temples while thousands of tons of granite, the most durable stone of all, were cut from the quarries at Aswan and floated on barges hundreds of miles northwards. All this quarrying was done by stonemasons with simple copper or bronze chisels, wooden mallets and pounders of dolorite.

With a history of inscribed monuments stretching over three thousand years the following basic terms will be necessary to show where within this time-span a piece of architecture lies:

Archaic Period	3100–2686 BC
Dynasties I–II	
Old Kingdom	2686–2181 BC
Dynasties III–VI	
Middle Kingdom	2133–1786 BC
Dynasties XI–XII	
New Kingdom	1567–1085 BC
Dynasties XVIII–XX	
Ptolemaic rulers	304–30 BC
(Greeks)	
Roman occupation	30 BC–AD 395

Tombs

Monarchs of the Archaic Period constructed for themselves two funerary monuments, both almost entirely of mud brick. One in the north, likely to be the actual burial-place, at Saqqara on the desert escarpment overlooking the capital of Memphis. The other in the south, probably a cenotaph near the origi-nal family seat of their ancestors, at Abydos. The superstructures of the Abydos monuments have not sur-vived whereas those at Saqqara have; called mastabas, they are rectangular, made of mud brick and can reach a height of 7.6 m (25 ft). They have outer walls which are panelled in a series of buttresses and recesses, a style ultimately derived from the royal palace facade at Memphis. The burial chamber is cut down into the rock beneath with a number of unconnecting storerooms around it containing provisions for the ruler's afterlife. Much of the internal superstructure is filled with rubble. Concern for the cult of the dead king's spirit moti-vated small funerary temples out-side the north wall where priests could leave bread and beer.

Kings began building pyramids but aristocrats continued the tradi-tion of mastabas throughout the Old Kingdom. These later mas-tabas had more elaborate super-structures made of stone with inter-connecting chambers, many of them decorated with reliefs. There could be a large court with rectangular pillars bearing stately representa-tions of the official who owned the tomb and his numerous titles. In designing a mastaba's interior the architect felt obliged to provide sur-faces for the draughtsmen to recre-ate the routine of daily life. The themes of wall decoration included the administration of an estate and

the leisure of an aristocrat. A walled-off chamber called the serdab contained a statue of the official, which, when animated by the deceased's spirit, could look out into the tomb through slits cut in the wall at eye-level. For security the body and valuables were buried in a sealed chamber cut out below the mastaba. However no architectural device evolved in Ancient Egypt thwarted the determined tomb-robbers.

In Dynasty III the architect Imhotep built the first pyramid, the Step Pyramid, for King Zoser at Saqqara, earning fame that was eventually to result in his deification over two thousand years later. His skill lay in employing stone on a scale unprecedented at that time anywhere in the world. Whether the desire for grandeur was the driving impetus or an attempt to encapsulate in stone the religious motif of a stairway for the king's access to the sun-god, the result was an architectural complex of such diversity that

later pyramid architects had to reduce in scale or abandon some of Imhotep's innovations. Imhotep preserved in stone the forms of contemporary architecture evolved in Egypt over previous centuries but lost to us because of the ephemeral material used. The Step Pyramid was originally a mastaba over a deep shaft to the burial chamber but grew under Imhotep's genius through several changes in plan into a monument of six superimposed layers each decreasing in size.

However no pyramid is an edifice in isolation and so around it were buildings designed to assist the ruler's afterlife. The whole complex was enclosed by a boundary wall whose recesses and bastions are the direct descendants of the walls of the archaic royal mastabas. In the entrance colonnade Imhotep used stone columns, the shafts of which are fasciculated to imitate the reed bundles which were a mainstay of secular buildings. The columns are not yet free-standing but abut onto

Engaged columns imitating the stem and umbel of the papyrus plant in Zoser's Step Pyramid enclosure at Saqqara.

adjacent walls. The gate leading into the pyramid courtyard is in the style of a wooden one but made of stone and static in an open position. Imhotep raised ceremonial pavilions and throne rooms with impressive facades but solid rubble interiors. These dummy buildings were for use by the king's spirit during the celebration of his jubilee festivals. One facade has adjoined to it three columns in the form of papyrus plants, symbolic of north Egypt. Subsequently papyriform columns are frequently used but with their shafts rounded; here, below the column's capital depicting the umbel, Imhotep has accurately rendered the plant's triangular stem.

In Dynasty IV the 'true' pyramid evolved, its four flat triangular surfaces meeting at an apex. The ear-

29

liest to survive is one of two pyramids built by King Sneferu at Dahshur – the other one being an intriguing monument where the angle of the sloping sides changes to a sharper degree about midway, earning it the description of the Bent Pyramid. Sneferu's successors constructed the famous pyramids at Giza with Cheops building the Great Pyramid – 137.2 m (450 ft) high today, base lengths 228.6 m (750 ft); Chephren the second largest – 136.2 m (447 ft) high today, base lengths 210.3 m (690 ft); and Mycerinus the smallest – 62.2 m (204 ft) high today, base lengths 103.6 m (340 ft).

In Cheops's pyramid, the burial chamber is, unusually, within the superstructure, involving an ascent by a gallery lined with high-quality limestone, possibly its most impressive architectural feature. The chamber itself is lined with granite and has a series of relieving cavities above it to avoid direct pressure on the ceiling over the sarcophagus.

Thousands of workmen hauling on papyrus ropes dragged the blocks of stone, some about 15.2 tonnes (15 tons), into position in the pyramid along sloping ramps of mud and rubble set up against each side.

Pyramids were connected to valley temples on the edge of the cultivated area by a causeway. The valley temple was where the king's corpse was received for various rituals before burial in the pyramid. Chephren's valley temple with its precise squaring of the granite

above
This court in the Temple of Amun at
Luxor has colonnades of columns which
imitate bundles of papyrus stalks.

left
The Step Pyramid, the world's first
massive stone monument, was
originally surrounded by a bastion wall.

monoliths and architraves is a
prized example of Old Kingdom
architecture at its most dignified.
Nearby, the sphinx was the brain-
child of one of Chephren's architects, who converted a natural crag
of rock into a lion's body and the
king's head. During Dynasties V
and VI pyramids were built with far
less care, especially in the internal
buttress walls which support the
casing. Consequently they appear
ungainly masses caricaturing the
clarity of line and precision found in
the Great Pyramid.

In the New Kingdom pharaohs
were buried at Thebes, which had

become the religious capital of
Egypt. Their tombs were cut deep
into the limestone cliffs in the
Valley of the Kings. The basic plan
was a long corridor, regarded as a
passageway for the sun-god, sometimes with a shift in the axis, leading to the golden hall or burial
chamber. Square pillars, ornamental rather than structural supports,
depicted the king accepted by the
major Egyptian deities. Ruses were
devised by architects to foil robbers,
such as deep pits cut into the corridor floor and false walls across the
passageway. The pits also had the
practical intention of catching any

31

above
The pyramids of Cheops, Chephren and Mycerinus at Giza, impressive witnesses to Ancient Egypt's ability to organize manpower.

left
The sphinx at Giza: a limestone crag ingeniously transformed into a lion's body with the monarch's head.

rainwater penetrating the tomb. That these rock tombs were not cut out haphazardly is known from architects' plans surviving on flakes of limestone. The burial chamber and annexes of Tutankhamun, originally destined for his vizier, are not typical of a Theban royal tomb; the best example belongs to Sety I of Dynasty XIX, containing throughout its 99-m (325-ft) length masterfully executed mythological scenes on its walls, ceilings and columns.

Temples
Egyptian temples embody the fullest architectural expressions of complex religious beliefs with huge

pages 34–35
A colossal statue of Pinudjem, high priest and *de facto* ruler of southern Egypt, outside the hypostyle hall at Karnak.

bottom
A sanctuary depicted in the Temple of Sethos I at Abydos: partly shrouded by linen, the shrine of Amun-Re stands on a gilded boat.

below
The smashed sarcophagus of Ramesses VI surrounded by wall-paintings showing Osiris and the journeys of the sun-god.

above
Skill at shaping granite blocks and architraves with pounders and copper chisels produced the restrained architecture of Chephren's valley temple.

courtyards, columned halls and sanctuaries existing solely for the god's ceremonies. Many scenes on the columns and walls of temples represent stages in rituals or festivals where the pharaoh takes the role of high priest. Other decorations magnify the superhuman prowess of pharaohs in combat. Although archaeologists have discovered shrines and sun-temples from earlier times, major temple architecture belongs to the New Kingdom or to the Ptolemaic and Roman periods.

During the New Kingdom Thebes was the centre of the cult of Amun-Re, king of the gods. On the eastern bank of the Nile were two temples to him, of which Karnak is the most complex since within its huge temenos we are surveying the results of centuries of pharaonic piety expressed in stone. From it we can understand the main elements of temple architecture.

The approach to the temple from its riverside quay was by a dromos or processional way lined with ram-headed sphinxes symbolizing Amun-Re. The entrance, known as a pylon, is in fact from the later stages of building at Karnak during Ptolemaic times, but is the tradi-

above
Ramesses II changed the axis of the
court he added to Luxor, incorporating
a sacred way-station behind his pylon.

above left
Ram-headed sphinxes on the
processional way to Karnak protect
effigies of the pharaoh between their
paws.

above
The great hypostyle hall at Karnak: the
column capitals of the central aisle are
styled as open papyrus umbels, the
remainder as closed papyrus buds.

tional two massive towers flanking a
gateway. This is the last of six
pylons (the others constructed in
the New Kingdom) along the east-
west axis of the temple. A further
four stretch southwards at right
angles to the axis towards the
temple sacred to Amun-Re's wife,
the vulture-goddess Mut. Grooves
in the pylons were for cedar-wood
flagstaves. Beyond the second pylon
on the east-west axis is one of
the overwhelming architectural
achievements of the Ancient Egyptians – the great hypostyle hall.
Mainly the work of Sety I and
Ramesses II (both Dynasty XIX) it
is a forest of 134 columns originally
supporting a complete roof. The
only light filtered through small
grill windows. The central nave of
this hall is formed by twelve columns, 19.5 m (64 ft) high, with capitals in the open papyrus-umbel
style, the remaining columns, about
6 m (20 ft) shorter, have capitals
imitating the closed bud of the
papyrus. Towards the rear of the
temple is another hall whose purpose is to commemorate the jubilee
festival of the pharaoh Tuthmosis
III (Dynasty XVIII). Here the fertile mind of the Egyptian architect
has imitated in stone the wooden
poles supporting the pavilion in
which the pharaoh had celebrated
his festival.

On the western bank at Thebes
New Kingdom pharaohs con-
structed their funerary temples to
emphasize their privileged relationship with Amun-Re and keep the
royal name alive. During the Beautiful Feast of the Valley the cult
image of Amun-Re of Karnak was
ferried across the Nile to visit these
temples. Queen Hatshepsut
(Dynasty XVIII) built her temple
against an imposing bay in the
cliffs, today known as Deir el-Bahri.
Three terraces connected by ramps
exhibit uncluttered architecture like
the rectangular columns of the colonnades, which off set the detailed
reliefs commemorating for example
the queen's birth allegedly as the
child of Amun-Re or the maritime
expedition she dispatched to
Somalia for incense. Another chapel
sacred to Hathor the cow-goddess
surprises us with architectural ver-

satility because the capitals of its columns are carved as heads of the goddess shown as a woman except for her bovine ears. The whole column imitates the sistrum, a sacred rattle shaken by priestesses.

Cult temples of the Ptolemaic and Roman period built over the top of earlier sanctuaries are amongst the most perfectly preserved monuments from antiquity, especially the temple of the hawk-god Horus at Edfu. Above its gateway between the spectacular pylons is a narrow horizontal concave moulding, called a cavetto cornice, in which is carved the winged disk of the sun-god. The vertical grooves in this moulding represent the fronds projecting from palm bundles. The first courtyard has colonnades whose column-capitals are embellished with an abundance of palms and floral clusters in a far more ornate style than found earlier. Beyond the hypostyle halls is the sanctuary in which Horus's statue was kept, surrounded by an ambulatory off which were twelve chapels. The fear of pollution of this inner sanctum from the outside world is clear from the precaution of another ambulatory around the outer walls of the chapels, allowing in fact for the inclusion in the temple of a nilometer, by which priests could estimate the size of the annual inundation. A further protective device for the sanctuary were the water-spouts high up on the walls, carved in the shape of lions' heads magically to turn leonine ferocity against any threat.

Exhibiting extreme agility in bending natural phenomena to the dictates of government policy, the architects of Ramesses II (Dynasty XIX) carved two magnificent temples out of a mountain of sandstone on the banks of the Nile at Abu

above right
Obelisks were solar symbols whose pinnacles were often gilded with electrum. These are at Karnak.

right
Queen Hatshepsut's funerary temple, ascended by ramps, was built next to an earlier royal tomb and temple.

Simbel. The larger temple's facade shows four seated colossi of the pharaoh – a propaganda motif intended to impress the southerners. In the hypostyle hall the eight square pillars of the central aisle have been faced with statues of Ramesses II as the god of the underworld, Osiris. These osiride columns are a favourite architectural embellishment of the Ancient Egyptians. The sanctuary contains statues of the four gods worshipped here – Re-Horakhty, the sun-god Amun-Re, Ramesses II and Ptah creator god of Memphis. The axis of the temple is orientated so that twice a year at the equinoxes the rising sun penetrates the whole length, about 55 m (180 ft), to the sanctuary. In the 1960s the Abu Simbel temples were cut up and

above
Abu Simbel: the most impressive embodiment of pharaonic majesty, with four sandstone colossi of Ramesses II.

left
David Roberts's 19th-century view of the partially buried courtyard of Edfu Temple, sacred to Horus.

right
Kom-Ombo Temple: beyond several vestibules can be seen one of the two sanctuaries.

below
The hypostyle hall of Dendera Temple has screen-walls between its facade columns to conceal the rituals.

moved to prevent them being submerged by the newly formed Lake Nasser. Modern architects and engineers respected their Ancient Egyptian counterparts' intention by skilfully constructing a steel dome camouflaged as the original cliffs into which the temples were cut.

Ptolemaic temples developed a special building called a mammisi, where the mystery of the divine birth was celebrated. Architecturally they are interesting because they show a peripteral gallery around the cult room and annexes – a design derived from earlier Egyptian prototypes not classical models.

The peripteral gallery's columns with their capitals depicting the dwarf-god Bes, protector of the family, are indicative of the architect's desire to wed form to religious purpose.

Secular building

Lastly we can look at the legacy of the military architect. Egypt's need to defend itself against incursions from Palestine via the eastern delta and the desire to control the gold-mine routes of the south led it to develop sophisticated fortresses. The style of the now vanished northern forts is surprisingly recreated in southern Egypt at Thebes where Ramesses III (Dynasty XX) built a funerary temple-cum-palace complex now known as Medinet Habu. Within the eastern enclosure wall is a fortified gate (called the Migdol) whose towers are crowned with a crenellated cornice. The most impressive military architecture however was used in the Nile fortress of Buhen near the second cataract and now, after a thorough archaeological survey, below the waters of Lake Nasser. Behind the moat a buttressed mud-brick wall about a mile in perimeter was interspersed with towers from which archers could fire through loopholes orientated to cover any approach. This castle-like installation was impregnable as long as river supplies could reach it from the north.

above left
Dendera's 'mammisi' has columns crowned with carvings of the dwarf-god Bes, who assisted at the birth of Hathor's son.

left
Possibly the most exquisite monument of the Roman occupation was Trajan's Kiosk on the island of Philae (before relocation), sacred to Isis.

GREEK

Greek architecture was primarily religious, and the expression of religious beliefs through the architecture of the temple was the catalytic agent which consumed the intellectual and emotional energies of Greek artists. The resolution of architectural ideas, ideals and problems in the building of temples was reflected in the fields of lesser or secular architecture, producing synonymity of form and character and establishing functional and aesthetic links among buildings.

These developments reached their apogee in the latter half of the fifth century BC when the Acropolis of Athens was crowned with buildings which, individually and collectively, are by general consent regarded as the supreme achievement of Hellenic architecture. Yet little more than a century previously witnessed the beginning of temple building in stone throughout the Greek world. The stone temples of the sixth century were a fundamental statement of temple design; not an unheralded phenomenon, but the result of slow and clumsy development during the centuries which followed the collapse of the Bronze Age civilization about 1100 BC. That civilization of the Aegean, which is sometimes called Helladic, had produced characteristics in architecture which were transmuted and persisted in vernacular, impermanent building during the 'dark age' to influence in modified form

developing Hellenic architecture.

By the eighth century the city-state had emerged as the conceived basis of Greek society and political developments were making their mark. The Greeks adopted an alphabet from the Phoenicians which led to the rapid and unique development of language and literacy. Literacy diminished class barriers and through their language Greeks were able to express and rationalize thought, develop logical philosophy and attempt the difficult process of governing themselves. Geographically Greece is divided land, unconducive to national unity, and consequently settlements evolved as small, independent communities acknowledging no higher authority than their own. Helladic princely states had given way to self-governing cities; autocrats were superceded by varying degrees of oligarchy and popular dictatorship to what Greeks regarded as democracy. Architecturally, the palace in its citadel became the temple on its acropolis, and the fortress and palace were replaced by the market-place (agora) and assembly. Thus, the temple as the abode of the city deity was surrounded by the city and, in turn, the city was surrounded by its hinterland. However, the absence of political unity was, to some extent, countered by the federal unity derived from common language, religion and customs, hence the development of

Olympia, Delphi and Epidauros as common meeting-places and associated festivals.

The Hellenic period

The paramouncy of the temple in Hellenic architecture indicates the importance of religion. Pre-Hellenic architecture was essentially domestic; religious practices were restricted to small shrines or around open-air altars. Early religions invariably recognized the forces of Nature, and the Greeks, while adopting these attitudes, evolved anthropomorphic conceptions and their religion became polytheistic out of fetishism. The gods therefore became intimately connected with all aspects of Greek life and the result was a shift in the idea and arrangement of places of worship.

A shelter or protective dwelling for the deity became necessary. Once conceived, the idea of a formal enclosure became the generator of architecture closely related to the Olympian kind of religion. The Greeks peopled their heaven from earth, and the functions of Olympian religion and its attributes were parallel to, but higher than, the plane of the order which established the cosmos of the city-state. Gods created by imagination, particularly those minor deities in whom common people found a more immediate belief, were included in the family fold. Thus any association of families into larger groups produced common deities and ancestry and before a city became a political association of families it was, and remained, an association around the common worship. A city without a temple on its acropolis was inconceivable.

This essential element of the city was compounded by the requirements of places for government, assembly and market, recreation and culture. By its nature the acropolis was above, though of, the city. Civic architecture gathered near the agora, which from a loosely defined meeting-place became a framework of the city pattern, particularly when town-planning developed in later, Hellenistic times. The degree of organization was a response to civic function modified by commerce, places of assembly being required for business as well as administration.

The use of stoas irregularly, or later more systematically, placed developed out of the function of the agora, fulfilling not only their specific purpose but also defining the agora and acting as compositional features. Their form, an elongated portico, functioned as a covered extension of the agora onto which they faced. At the rear were shops, offices and stores. Increased demands on their use led to two-storey development – porticoed facades giving spacious, elegant galleries affording protection from heat or rain. The colonnaded front gave regularity to the building and to the open space of the agora by its rhythm of architectural elements. The stoa thus became a civic colonnade synonymous in form with that of the temple and established functional and aesthetic links among buildings around it. These included the house of assembly (ecclesiasterion), town hall (prytaneion), gymnasium, music hall (odeion) and theatre.

The theatre created problems. Its origin lay in the worship of Dionysos, in whose honour archaic frenzy provided the basis from which Greek drama was to flourish and, in a suitable topographical situation, the architecture of the formal classical theatre. Because of its size and the desirability of finding a natural setting which would alleviate construction problems and also provide harmony with the landscape, it became difficult to integrate the theatre with town plans. Eventually it was placed apart, a solution compatible with its religious associations and in many ways comparable with the acropolis.

The creation of a shelter for a god implied no space for worship; it provided space for ritual, but it was never a vessel for congregations. From the first temple design strove for a conscious external effect; the placing of a structure enclosing an effigy positioned the worshippers firmly outside and the building had no internal complexity. Early houses for gods would not differ much from those of man, and domestic architecture was simple, using traditional forms and methods descended from Helladic times. But the Helladic megaron, itself a monumentalized development of the primitive hut, afforded a link between the house of man and the house for the gods. Its columned

right
Temple of Demeter, Paestum (530 BC): a vigorous, monumental style typical of early western Doric.

below
Athens: Agora and Acropolis. The market place and sacred enclosure symbolized the city state's essential components.

A

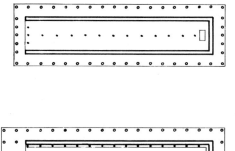

B

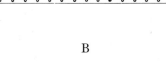

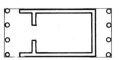

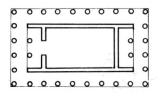

porch and anteroom provided a symbolism which motivated the idea of enhancing the shelter with architectural embellishment befitting the deity whose effigy was enshrined. There is a discernible link between the principal elements of the megaron and those of the later temple, and between the traditional house and the early temple, but a connection among all those elements is not apparent. The temple, as it came to be, was an Hellenic creation owing only its basic plan to Helladic prototypes; the rectangular hall surrounded by columns, free-standing and complete in itself, was to be purely Greek in invention and spirit.

This radical transformation occurred towards the end of the eighth century. There may have been practical reasons for it – perhaps in order to support the roof projecting beyond the walls for added protection. Alternatively, the idea may have been to enhance the shrine in a manner more fitting to the house of a god – a combination of religious inspiration and aesthetic appreciation. Development was tentative and uneven as the arrangement of columns in relation to the walls and the contained space was adjusted in response to functional and constructional needs, but once established the arrangements remained to become an architectural system.

The next impetus was the development of stone-building techniques and the replacement of brick walls, wood columns and superstructure by a stone architecture early in the sixth century throughout the Greek world. Dorian Greeks in Greece and Ionian Greeks along the coast of Asia Minor interpreted and expressed the solution of a common problem in their individual ways, the heritage of centuries of vernacular building. The new ways were to become the Doric and Ionic styles of architecture; Doric developed in Greece and the colonial settlements in Sicily and southern Italy, while Ionic pervaded the eastern Greek world.

The emergence of stone architecture coincided with a time of colonial expansion and the foundation of vigorous, progressive towns. Their early stone temples were astonishing examples, in size and surety of purpose. In Ionia, at Ephesus in particular, the first great Temple of Artemis was built *c.* 560 BC in a manner so imposing as to exceed most Greek building and seldom imitated except in a few of the wealthier cities in the west such as Acragas, Selinus and Syracuse. But the Doric architecture of the west had become a unifying and formalizing process that was to continue for two centuries of temple design. It was a process of gradual change in matters of degree rather than of kind, the modification of a basically accepted standard.

The inception of the colonnade and the substitution of stone for timber led to an architectural development destined enormously to influence the western world. Timber construction was the origin of the Doric and Ionic Orders. When translated into stone, however, some structural elements lost their validity and thereafter Doric architecture ceased to be concerned with structure as such but rather adapted the medium of structure as a means to an abstract composition of a building and its parts. Form and line became the ingredients of that composition and, be they major or minor statements, essential to the balance of verticality and horizontality in the form of the temple. Thus was ensured the completeness and static finality imperative in such a finite, unified composition.

Rising immediately from the stylobate, columns with clear-cut shallow fluting introduced a powerful vertical thrust, the fluting emphasizing the rotundity of the shafts and following a continuously

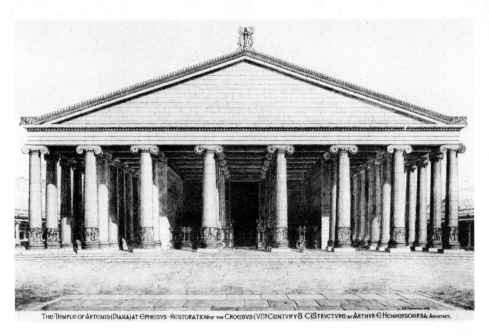

THE TEMPLE OF ARTEMIS (DIANA) AT EPHESUS · RESTORATION OF THE CROESUS (VIᵗʰ CENTURY B·C) STRUCTURE · BY ARTHUR E HENDERSON P.B.A. ARCHITECT.

above
Reconstruction of the vast archaic Temple of Artemis, Ephesus (560 BC): the most outstanding early Ionic temple.

below
Sectional view (reconstruction) of the Temple of Aphaia, Aegina (490 BC), showing the typical arrangement of the Doric temple.

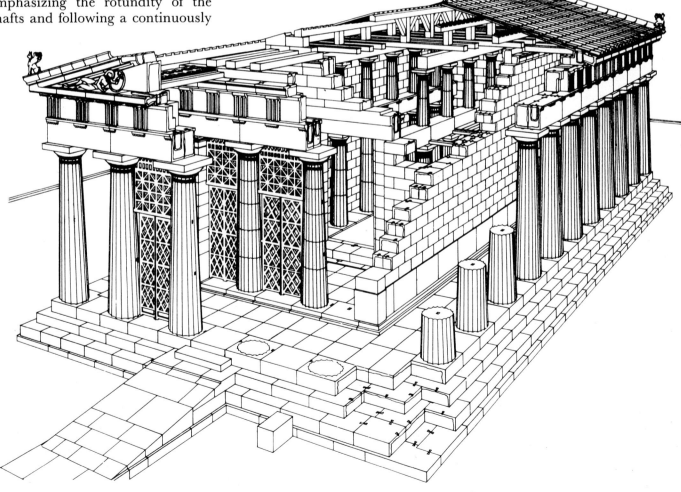

right
The sturdy virility of early Doric: one of
the first stone-built temples, the
Temple of Apollo, Corinth (540 BC).

below
The elements of the Doric Order: a
complex assembly of stone colonnade
and superstructure which screened the
shrine. (A) cornice, (B) frieze, (C)
architrave, (D) capital, (E) stylobate,
(F) flute, (G) metope, (H) triglyph.

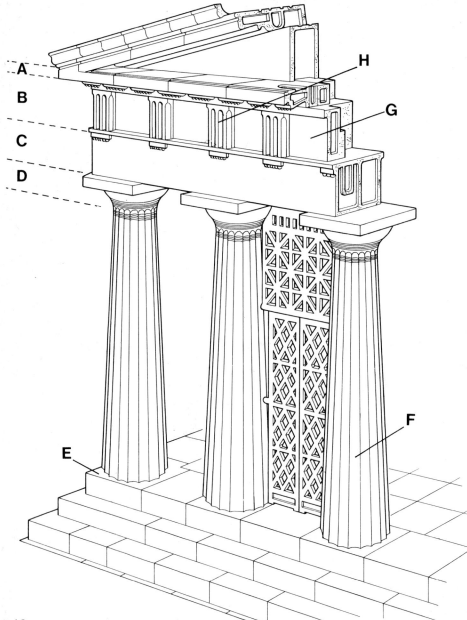

developed convexity (entasis) until
stopped at the necking by horizontal grooves which formed the transition to the capital. The entasis was
a device for correcting optical illusion, counteracting the hollow
appearance which is seen in
straight-sided columns as well as
imparting a sense of strength. The
capital was an obvious derivation
from the Helladic prototype subjected to remarkable refinement.
Above was the entablature, composed of three principal members –
architrave, frieze and cornice, all of
which had a structural origin
developed from a timber prototype.
The architrave was the beam spanning from column to column, a
strong horizontal member plain and
uncomplicated. The frieze was composed of triglyphs and metopes;
triglyphs represented in stone the
ends of crossbeams and were therefore structural in origin; metopes
were originally plaques closing the
gap between beams and were usually sculptured. Triglyphs ceased to
have structural purpose, but in the
aesthetic implications of the Doric
Order they expressed vertical support, restating in the frieze after the
interval of the horizontal architrave
the vertical emphasis of the columns
and, by their rhythm alternating
with metopes, provided stability in
the horizontal direction. Lastly the

overhanging cornice restated the horizontality of the stylobate and literally capped the sequence of contrasting vertical and horizontal elements between the two planes.

Horizontal and vertical lines, and repeated rhythms, were the themes of a composition at once simple and complex. The complete, unified balance of the effect produced by the colonnade depended on this subtle arrangement, demanding dimensional accuracy and mathematical exactitude in the assembly of such precision of line and moulding. And while mathematics provided the dimensional pattern and co-ordinates, the sensitivity to pro-

portion with which Greek architects and sculptors were concerned prevented a too-rigid adherence to number. Intellectual acuity was tempered and humanized by emotion.

The Ionic Order too was basically a structural form. The style varied locally and the development of an organized arrangement of components to form an Order was a slow process. The voluted capital is the remarkable feature; its derivation is uncertain and the development illustrates a structural member of which the form was modified by the decorative element. Here was introduced a delicate

above
Precision of organization and quality of design detail make the Temple of Aphaia, Aegina (490 BC), the most perfectly developed late archaic temple in Greece.

47

above
An example of the Corinthian Order used internally, for which its decorative characteristics were appropriate.

left
A classical interpretation of the Ionic Order, combining structural form with delicate and elaborated ornament.

balance between intellect and emotion. Designers working in Ionic were also sensitive to the relationship between plain construction and decoration, introducing decorative elements from other fields. Decoration became more functional and made its own contribution to the Ionic idea. The overall design was more slender than the Doric and its inherent freedom of interpretation and the increasing use of decorative motifs produced a style freer and less canonical. It was less austere and less epic and demanded less of the intellect, though the increasing use of decoration imposed its own discipline in restraint.

By the time of Periclean Athens Doric and Ionic styles had evolved

to their finest forms, exemplified in the buildings on the Athenian Acropolis. Significantly, perhaps fortuitously, there occurred at that time the tentative introduction of a third contribution to column design – the Corinthian Order. Its name is derived from its alleged source, the inspiration of a Corinthian worker in bronze in a conscious and original design and one not based on structural prototype. The distinctive element is the capital, in effect the swelling of the column in the form of an inverted bell-shape decorated with stylized acanthus leaves and other associated flower forms. Plant forms were conventionalized into shapes sympathetic to the structural 'bell' and tendrils were

stylized to form an ornamentation similar to an Ionic volute supporting the angles of the surmounting abacus.

By its nature the Corinthian capital was an invention capable of almost infinite variety, and in the hands of skilled designers it became remarkably beautiful. Its adaptability and freedom in design gave the Order a flexibility in use which was exploited in the changing conditions of the Greek world after the fifth century. Its introduction was tentative and experimental, being used for interiors or minor monuments in which its decorative characteristics were appropriate. Changes in taste and emphasis led to the supremacy of Corinthian,

right

Comparative elevations. (A) Olympia: Temple of Zeus (460 BC). Culmination of orthodox Doric; limestone, with marble sculptural decoration. (B) Paestum: Temple of Poseidon (450 BC). Severe Doric as practised in the west; limestone, without sculptural decoration. (C) Athens: Parthenon (440 BC). Apotheosis of Greek architecture, wrought in marble.

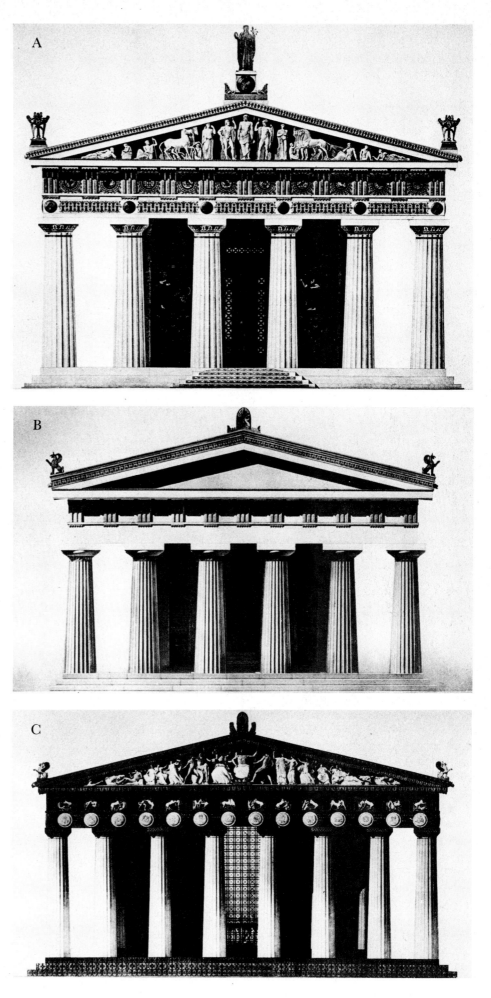

even eventually over Ionic, when Doric became old fashioned and went out of favour as the fourth century progressed.

By definition, the stone temple indicates mastery of layout, techniques of quarrying, cutting and assembly of the stones in a complex arrangement, and finishing the visible surfaces of work with exactitude. One of the reasons for this unique achievement was the availability and sensitive use of superb marbles, especially in Greece. But the use of marble was not widespread and was mainly introduced to temple building during the fifth century. Early temples were built of local stones, limestone being most common, and these temples, as well as important temples of the fifth century in Greece and elsewhere, achieved that precision of detail despite the use of a material of some coarseness. This paradox was overcome by the application of a coating of stucco which enabled the required perfection of surface and line to be obtained. Skill in limestone building generated a general masonry technique which was capable of meeting the meticulous demands of Doric architecture in a material which of itself did not in fact make that easily possible.

It is equally significant that building in marble did not entirely supercede limestone; the two materials were to continue in use contemporaneously.

The appearance and effect of the temple were not experienced in isolation. Its siting and the character of its surroundings were vital aspects of the paramount role of the temple in Greek life. The concept of the temple as a finite unity of composition, to be seen from all directions, determined the external

above
The temenos of Delphi from above: at successive levels the theatre and Temple of Apollo.

above left
At the tip of Attica is Cape Sounion, where the Doric Temple of Poseidon (425 BC) crowns a defiant headland.

left
Reconstruction of the temenos at Delphi: a remarkable relationship of structures and spatial development. (The Metropolitan Museum of Art, Dodge Fund, 1930.)

form of the building and considerations of siting. The temple was the shrine of a deity whose image looked out through the great door and the portico to the altar set in front. The altar was the focal point of ritual enacted against the magnificent screen provided by the temple front. Space around a temple was therefore essential to accommodate large and frequent gatherings. Thus the definition of the sacred site (temenos) was an essential ingredient of the architectural composition, delineated by a wall and entered through a portico (propylaeum). Within the temenos were arranged the temple and altar, a disposition of votive monuments, often a treasury, and a stoa for shelter.

The unity of the temple demanded the elimination of an irregular setting. The provision of

level platforms was not confined to temples but extended to include the altar, propylaeum and incidental structures. Thus paved terraces unified the buildings disposed about the temenos, in areas and changes of level. The evidence now is fragmentary, but the range of the solutions involved extended from the simple but taut, as at Aegina and Sounion, to the subtle complexity of the Athenian Acropolis.

The Acropolis dominates surrounding Athens, and the architectural composition was moulded to that end, reflecting willingness to subordinate the dictates and conventions of religion to the desire to create an arrangement surpassing all other sanctuaries in the Greek world. Two natural conditions imposed their discipline. Access to the uneven plateau was feasible at one point only; here the Propylaea

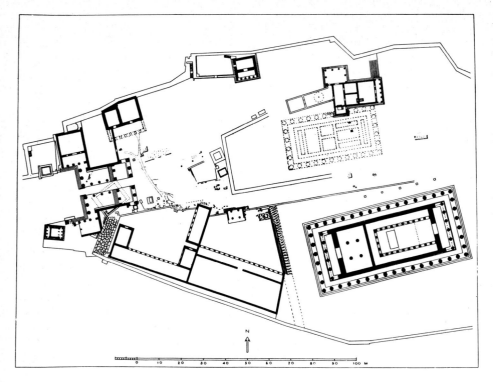

above
Plan of the Acropolis, Athens. Dictated by tradition, it is the finest sanctuary arrangement in the Greek world.

below
Reconstruction showing the architectural composition of the principal buildings of the Athenian Acropolis.

was placed. On the highest level: the temple of Athena – the Parthenon. Two more structures completed the arrangement: to the north of the Parthenon the shrine known as the Erechtheion, and the now-vanished colossal statue of Athena, which formed the visual pivot of the composition.

The Propylaea is arguably the most impressive entrance with which any building has been provided, a ceremonial gateway facing out to the city and in to the temenos. Its apparently orthodox form was complicated by the sloping site and its appropriately monumental size, problems brilliantly solved by the designer Mnesicles: the difference in level between the Doric porticos was effected within the depth of the building by the use of Ionic columns flanking the central passageway – an ingenious solution derived from the more slender proportions of the Ionic Order. Their introduction indicated willingness to experiment with and employ

FAÇADE OVEST
RESTAVRATION

different Orders in conjunction, as befitted the creative spirit of Athens. Superb in itself the Propylaea formed a unique frame through which to perceive the Parthenon and Erechtheion. Perspective alters at every move through a spacious complex of columns and changing levels in which the ordering of architecture was arranged with consummate mastery. Variety was achieved within order, lightness within mass; it was an enclosure and penetration of space unique in antiquity.

From the Propylaea the view of the Parthenon is of the rear. The entrance of a Greek temple faced east, so that the flank of the building has to be traversed before a right-about turn to face the east front and the entrance to the supreme creation of Hellenic Greece. Apart from its size what is immediately apparent is the front of eight columns, a departure from the conventional Doric six, the effect of which was to increase the width and broaden the proportion of width to length. The Doric Order was subjected to incredible refinement, which further added to the uniqueness of the design. Immense care, incredible precision and disregard of expense marked this apotheosis achieved through consummation of a tradition of building stimulated and controlled by mathematics and visual sensitivity and the exploitation of a superb building material which was in itself a challenge, discipline and aid – white Pentelic marble. The fine precision which it made possible demanded perfection in the sheer quality and sensitivity of detail, and the refinements to be expected in Doric architecture at the time were compounded by allowances for perspective and optical illusion. Thus there is scarcely a straight line on the building; apparently horizontal lines and planes curve with barely discernible convexity and apparently vertical columns and faces incline inward in intricate geometry.

Furthermore, within the outward form of the colonnaded temple a new attitude towards interior space was evolving. The naos was created to house a great statue of Athena and in this instance that congestion of space characteristic of Doric temples was avoided by increasing its width and narrowing that of the ambulatory within the surrounding

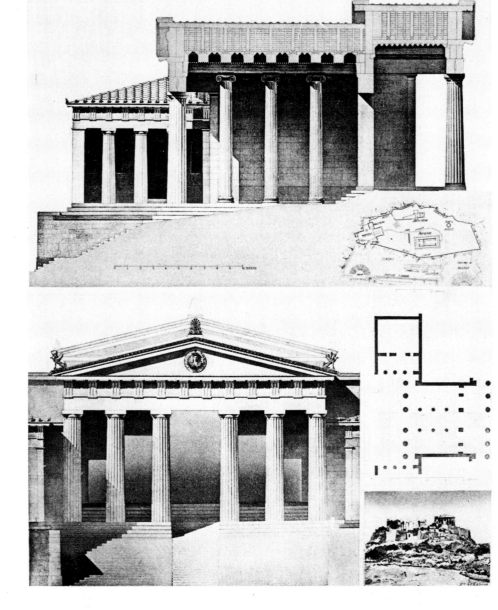

left
Section and elevation (reconstruction) of the Propylaea (437–432 BC): brilliant exploitation of the contrasting Doric and Ionic Orders.

below
South-west corner of the Parthenon: note the horizontal and vertical lines and repeated rhythms of Doric.

The Parthenon (447–432 BC): on it were lavished the wealth, genius and craftsmanship of Periclean Athens.

colonnade. Further experiment was indicated by the inclusion of a rear chamber, separated from the naos and entered from the rear portico, the purpose of which is unknown. Its architectural interest is in the use of four centrally disposed Ionic columns which supported the roof: a novel solution, as in the Propylaea, introducing the more slender and decorative Order, whereas in the larger naos the convention of superimposed Doric columns was maintained.

Classical sculpture also reached its climax in the Parthenon, based on myths closely connected with Athena and the Athenians. The metopes of the frieze and pedimental sculptures displayed a thematic invention, mastery of composition and technique and rhythmic subtlety. In addition, and uniquely, the top of the naos wall received a continuous sculptured frieze, in the Ionic manner, within which was depicted a procession of Athenians towards their shrine.

The Parthenon was in effect an embodiment of the synthesis of

Doric and Ionic cultures. Between them Ictinus and Callicrates the architects and Phidias the sculptor created an Athenian style in which they resolved the concepts of Hellenic civilization and produced a superb building, the astounding result of the coincidence of place, time and genius.

The Erechtheion was the last of the great new buildings on the Acropolis. Its siting was determined by religious and mythological associations rather than the requirements of architectural composition, and the uneven ground added problems to the complexity of designing a shrine dedicated to three deities. The architect was probably Mnesicles, whose success with the Propylaea fitted him well for the task. Though oddly asymmetrical the main body is a temple naos with porticos at the east end, on the north and south faces at different levels, and a false portico at the west end considerably above ground level. The small south porch is supported by caryatids (figures of

maidens) in columnar arrangement corresponding with the north portico. The Orders are Ionic and the columned porticos face away from the Parthenon; only the caryatid porch faces across the intervening space. It represented a different concept of things and, unlike the Propylaea and the Parthenon, posed questions of taste. The complications of the site and the complexity of the building were not easily resolved within the experience of classical architecture and as yet the Orders did not lend themselves to the unorthodox treatment demanded. The best was made of an intractable problem and if the composition as a whole remains uneasy it cannot be denied that the beauty and quality of Ionic detail were exploited in a wealth of ornament. The Erechtheion was a decorative feature of the Acropolis and a delicate, masterly foil to the epic Parthenon.

The buildings on the Acropolis were the supreme architectural achievements of the supreme city in

The Erechtheion from the south-east, showing the east Ionic portico and south caryatid porch facing the Parthenon.

Greece at the summit of its wealth and power. Its supremacy was short-lived and destroyed by the ultimate Greek tragedy of the Peloponnesian War, and with it the ideal symbolically monumentalized in the Parthenon. Fourth-century Greece was prey to a succession of attempts by city-states to replace Athenian dominance, a confused situation resolved by the supremacy of Macedonia and the unification and expansion of the Greek world by Alexander the Great. Alexander's vast territorial conquests enabled the extension of Greek civilization; Hellenic culture spread and, through dissemination and intermingling, became less narrow and more accommodating to change.

The Hellenistic period

The expansion of the Greek world, political and social prestige, and the growing or newly-founded cities of Hellenistic kingdoms generated the desire for increased building and afforded opportunity for the development of a civic architecture widely expanded in scope. Architecture developed a new monumentality, more variety and originality, and a more realistic attitude towards functional problems than Hellenic architecture admitted, though there was little change in techniques to accompany this grander scale of building. Buildings were large and ornate, as befitted the ostentatious display of wealth and prestige, and not infrequently, colossal. The new character was nowhere better displayed than in the great Hellenistic temples, outstanding among them being the rebuilt Temple of Artemis, Ephesus, and the Temple of Apollo, Didyma. They were vast structures, forests of columns surrounding with Ionic precision the naos, the size of which created problems of interior magnitude. Interior space became of more concern and development

had progressed considerably since the first indications in the buildings on the Athenian Acropolis. Attempts to integrate exterior and interior as an orderly expression of classical architecture produced novel effects of space and illusion. Nevertheless, indulgence of the taste for decoration and enrichment during the fourth century and later became symptomatic of the inherent limitations of an attitude to design of the temple form based on column and beam construction. Construction was unadventurous, even inept, and by the fourth century the possibility of development of the temple form had been largely exhausted.

Regular city-planning developed, leading to more formal composition of agoras and a philosophy of planning began to be expounded. Hippodamus of Miletus, the father-figure of town-planning was not so much responsible for the introduction of regular planning, which was neither new nor Greek in origin, as for advocating formality and the application of geometry to planning problems. Engineering works too were undertaken; aqueducts on

right
Hellenistic Temple of Artemis, Ephesus (reconstruction): a rebuilding of the archaic temple, in the contemporary Ionic Order.

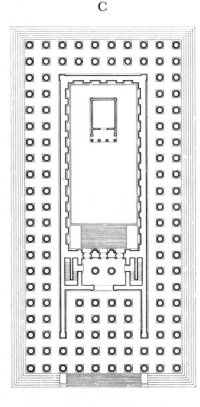

below
Comparative plans of Ionic temples showing prevalence of the colossal:
(A) Temple of Hera, Samos (525 BC); (B) Temple of Artemis, Ephesus (356–236 BC); (C) Temple of Apollo, Didyma (330 BC–AD 41).

A

B

C

THE·TEMPLE·OF·ARTEMIS·(DIANA)·AT·EPHESVS·RESTORATION of the HELLENISTIC·(IVᵀᴴ·CENTVRY·B·C)·STRVCTVRE·BY·ARTHVR·E·HENDERSON·FSA·ARCHITECT - SCVLPTVRE BY·GILBERT·BAYES·

arches probably carried water supplies to storage cisterns and arched drains were not unknown. Civic and monumental architecture turned not only to the big but also the strange, and varied from the classical idea of controlled perfection – splendid stone theatres, baths, elaborate houses, palaces, the great tomb of Mausolus at Halicarnassus which gave the name mausoleum to a whole class of later structures, colonnaded streets – expanding the architectural range of Hellenistic cities.

Much building in the largely eastern Hellenistic world had to be constructed according to the traditional methods of those regions. Brick arches and vaulted or domed structures were indigenous to the valley of the Nile and the Tigris–Euphrates plain from earliest times; in Mesopotamia they formed the practical solution to the problems of enclosing space. Hellenic Greeks virtually ignored the arch and it was only in Hellenistic times that its use in classical architecture was admitted, at first with reticence and then more generally, to the discipline and conventions of an architectural tradition based upon the Orders. To free design from these limitations a larger range of building types and construction techniques was needed and the recognition of the arch and vault as elements was the great new factor.

It was on these broadened achievements that the great engineering of Rome was raised, and the qualities of Hellenistic architecture were further extended and spread after the conquest of the Greek world by the Romans. In spite of the development of imperial architecture, the east maintained an Hellenistic tradition which confuses a distinction between Hellenistic (or Graeco-Roman) and Roman, but remained a vital influence, effecting a link between the classical spirit and Christian inspiration.

ROMAN

The Etruscans and early Rome
Roman origins are shrouded in myth and legend. At the time of its alleged foundation *c.* 753 BC Rome was an insignificant hill town in southern Etruria. The Etruscans had settled in central Italy, probably from Asia Minor, at the time of unrest and race migrations which accompanied the collapse of Bronze Age civilization. By the eighth century, contemporary with the evolution of the city-state in Greece, the Etruscans dominated the local inhabitants, their power increasing until it was the greatest in Italy and at sea to the west.

The expansion of Etruscan territory northward into the Plain of Lombardy and southward to the Bay of Naples created the need for some form of organized administration, and a kind of federation or league of cities and their lands was intermittently formed. The nature of this league, ruled by a series of elected kings, betrays an administrative character which pervaded life in general from the organization of the family to the organization of the collection of families that constituted the town. Etruscan life, secular and religious, was organized and institutionalized, with profound effect upon the nature of the state, its politics, government, religion and consequently its architecture. A sense of place, private and public, was introduced from the beginning.

The Etruscans were great build-

ers, surrounding their towns with walls of excellent masonry, displaying a mastery of stone construction which included skilled and architectonic use of true arched gateways. Drainage, irrigation and water supply exercised their engineering talents. They became skilled craftsmen in metalwork and pottery and attained an art of their own, vigorous, if coarse, until contact with the rich Greek cities in southern Italy, with their magnificent style of architecture and art, introduced an infusion of Greek refinement. Within their town walls a distinctive though limited range of buildings evolved from primitive huts into urban architecture, the highest expression of which was achieved in the design of temples and tombs.

Temples evolved from the simple house; early structures built of brick, roofed with timber and terracotta tiles. Development and elaboration of design introduced timber frames and columns to support wide-eaved, low-pitched roofs lavishly ornamented with painted terracotta plaques, the native tradition of design being modified by Greek influences. Later, walls and columns were of stone throughout as, at all times, were the high platforms or podiums on which temples stood. The temple raised on its podium, with the deep projecting porch, brought emphasis to the front of the shrine and the space before it. Tombs, which were built in great numbers, were located on special sites outside city walls, evidence of a concern for burial and belief in life after death. Consequently they evolved as monumentalized circular huts, taking the form of large conical tumuli: circular moulded bases of stone covered with a mound of earth concealing elaborate stone burial chambers simulating the interior of the contemporary house.

left
Model reconstruction of an *insula* or apartment block common in Rome and its port Ostia where space was precious.

far right
Segovia aqueduct (AD 10): well-preserved, magnificent Roman engineering in a procession of lofty double-tier arches.

below
The best preserved and one of the finest ancient structures in Italy: Bridge of Augustus, Rimini (AD 14).

Towards the end of the sixth century Etruscan supremacy in Italy began to decline. Rome had grown; a troublesome member of the league, it ultimately dominated and overthrew Etruscan control. The foundation of the independent city-republic of Rome *c.* 500 BC disrupted Etruria and through the fifth century Etruscan fortunes further declined as Roman influence increased among Etruscan towns. The declaration and development of a constitutional republic and civil service was indicative of distinctly Roman characteristics, albeit much

influenced by their Etruscan heritage. They were great organizers and lawyers – their constitution was complex and ingenious, full of niceties of balance but with inherent possibilities of deadlock – thrifty, patient farmer-soldiers narrow in outlook, dutiful to authority and law and concerned with justice and efficiency.

An expansionist outlook fostered opportunity and fame abroad and gradually, but with increasing rapidity, expansion fostered empire, the almost incidental conquest of the Italian peninsula being accomplished during the fourth century, including the Greek cities in the south. The conquest of Macedonia and Greece by the mid-second century stimulated the importation of Greek art and artists to Italy. In turn Greece formed a stepping stone to Asia Minor and the Hellenistic monarchies of the eastern Mediterranean, and by the first century the inclusion of Spain established the Roman Empire from the Euphrates in the east to the Atlantic in the west.

Later republican architecture

The prolonged and often desperate struggles had a deleterious effect on the Roman personality and on constitutional government. But, paradoxically, the political confusion of the collapsing republic and the excesses of military dictatorships coincided with a century of progress in the arts. For some time after the founding of the republic Roman building work retained its Etruscan character, though during the third century it derived much of its external complexion from Hellenistic sources and began to establish its own identity. This later republican architecture remained utilitarian in character, except for temples which were perhaps the first buildings to show the effects of Greek influence. The expansion of Rome into an empire made great demands on the builders – tenement housing, warehouses, barracks, arsenals, fortifications, aqueducts and bridges, works which tended to be regarded more as engineering than architecture. Amid such a plethora of secular architecture there was little time or

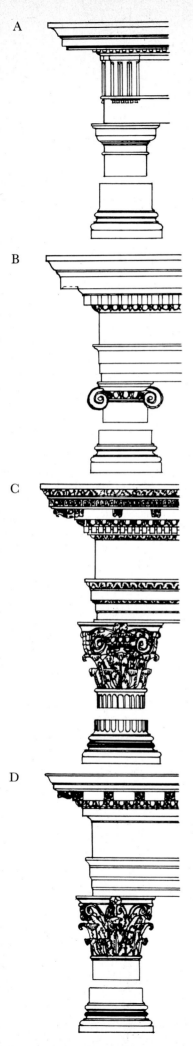

left
Roman orders: (A) Doric Order, (B) Ionic Order (both from Theatre of Marcellus), (C) Composite Order (Arch of Titus), (D) Corinthian Order (Pantheon). The Tuscan Order is a simplified version of Doric, the entablature being plain.

right
The aqueduct at Nîmes (AD 14) is part of a construction 40 km (25 miles) long: engineering raised to the level of art.

below
Model reconstruction of the Theatre of Marcellus (23–13 BC), the only ancient theatre now in Rome.

opportunity for the subtleties of artistic tradition and the practical problems were solved by the best means available.

However, after the conquest of Greece the rapid increase in Hellenistic influence, stimulated by wholesale acquisition of works of art, encouraged the desire for a veneer of culture not previously conspicuous in the Roman character. There was a shift of emphasis to the monumental, beautiful and essentially decorative. Roman architecture passed into a phase of quite remarkable transition as designers adapted the Etrusco-Roman tradition to the renewed impetus of Hellenistic art. Late republican regimes, of political patronage or dictatorship, with wealth and energy to spare for architectural luxury indulged civic embellishment of a new kind, building

theatres and stadiums, rebuilding
and enriching temples and developing the Orders and ornament to
satisfy Roman needs and taste.

The combined use of arch,
column and beam became the
devices and the keynote of the
Roman style, wherein structures of
piers faced by attached half-
columns supported arches which,
in turn, carried the entablature.
The best example displaying the
combination of these two features
throughout its structure is the Colosseum, Rome. The superimposi-
tion of Orders in a multi-storey
structure such as this called for
considerable inventiveness, and in
the search for appropriate variety
two Orders – Tuscan and Composite – were devised and added to the
original three Greek Orders. In
works of engineering character,
such as aqueducts, arches were supported on piers without facing columns. Thus the Orders which, in
Greek architecture, were essentially
constructive were employed by the
Romans as decorative features
which could be omitted, though
they remained in use constructively
in temple colonnades or buildings
where the arch was discarded.

Imperial architecture

The settlement of Rome's disorder
by Augustus was a watershed in
history. Central government was
reorganized to administer a world
empire and political and economic
stability were restored after a century of civil strife. The empire in its
true sense was formed and the
Augustan Age became one of the
great eras in the world's history, in
its way comparable to the Periclean
Age in Athens. Art, literature and
the springs of national life were
revitalized in the establishment of
the *pax Romana*.

Augustus is credited with the
aphorism that he found Rome a city
of brick and left it one of marble:
a colourful claim which held a
measure of truth as his principate
inaugurated a succession of vast
imperial building schemes overlay-
ing much republican architecture.
An imperial style, much affected by
Hellenistic influences, was created

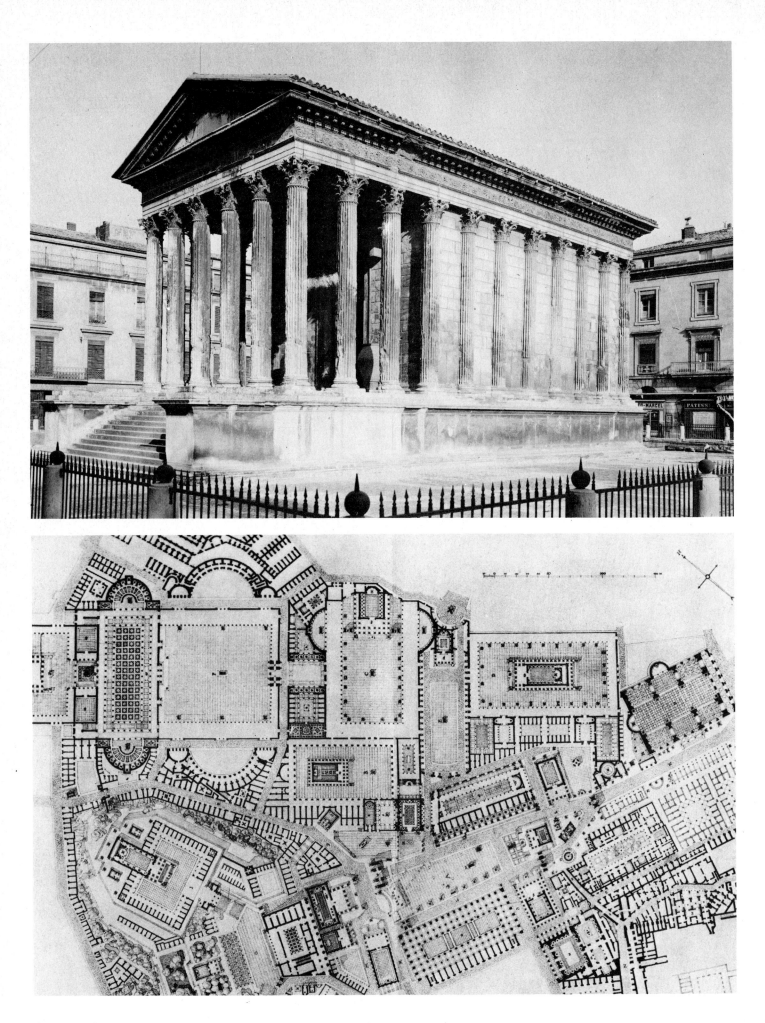

left
Maison Carrée, Nîmes (16 BC): the
Greek colonnade is reduced to a
columned porch with 'peripheral
columns' on a load-bearing wall.

to embellish the capital city, by then
the largest city in the ancient world.
The association of a ruler with
official works of art had Hellenistic
precedence and the Augustan
regime derived substantially from
that practice. A new forum built by
Augustus encapsulated in architecture the motivation, ideas and realization of the contemporary ethos.

The Roman forum was the equi-
valent of the Greek agora – a central
open space used as a meeting-place,
market, or gathering for political
demonstrations. In towns of organic
growth from small beginnings, such
as Rome, forums were often irregular in shape, but when towns were
newly founded or reconstruction
occurred forums were designed on
formal lines. The old, venerable
Forum Romanum in Rome was
originally a multi-purpose forum,
but as the city expanded its function
and character it changed to accommodate the increasingly required
public buildings – temples, basilicas, senate house, porticos, colonnades and monuments. By the
time of Julius Caesar it was a con-
gested, unorganized but imposing
assemblage of monumental architecture symbolizing the hub of the
Roman world. Caesar relieved the
congestion by the first of a series of
grand architectural projects which
collectively became the Imperial
Fora, a precedent followed by
Augustus.

The significance of Augustus's
forum lies in the amalgamation of
Roman planning and constructional
principles with architectural expression of Hellenistic inspiration. The
great rectangular space flanked by
stoas terminated in the large, magnificent Temple of Mars, all built of
white marble in a beautifully correct classical manner. Behind the

left
Forum Romanum and Imperial Fora:
the city centre expanded and a series of
imposing projects relieved congestion.

above
Forum of Augustus, Rome
(reconstruction): imperial style
combined Roman planning with
Hellenistic expression.

top
Forum of Julius Caesar, Rome
(reconstruction): the first of a series of
grand projects of formal splendour.

stoas, cross-axially related to the
temple, were two apsidal recesses.
Together with a profusion of statu-
ary, symmetrically arranged, the
complex was a definitive statement
of the Roman concept of architectural meaning, a synthesis of ideas
and functions which pervaded the
Augustan interpretation of the
Roman spirit with unequivocal concentration. The concept was facilitated – indeed only made possible –
and enhanced by the engineering of
the great retaining wall which
served as the back of the temple as
well as firmly controlling the effect
of enclosure.

The amalgamation of traditional
architectural and sculptural forms
facilitated by engineering techniques powerfully stimulated the
progress of imperial architecture.
Succeeding emperors – Vespasian,

Nerva and Trajan – during the first century AD elaborated the example of Augustus in the provision of new, imposing, symmetrical forums in an architectural display of magnificent complexity. Imperial architecture evolved a technique and style capable of dealing with the vast building schemes required or promoted by imperial administration to meet the demands of a large concentration of urban population in the imperial capital. New opportunities and tremendous demands were placed on Roman skills. The rate of change was such that the old stylistic devices could not be discarded before the rush of the new engineering spirit and they remained as modified adornments. A new architecture was evolving, the product of enormous requirements working on wealth of conquest, organizing ability, engineering skills, large supplies of cheap labour and tremendous drive of purpose – the architecture of power.

The combined use of arch, column and beam is the keynote of Roman architecture inherited from Etruscan and Hellenistic traditions and amalgamating into a new style during the last decades of the republic. Traditional techniques employed brick, timber and stone used in rubble work or as wrought masonry. These techniques could still apply and wrought masonry remained in use throughout Roman architecture, especially in great monuments, temples and theatres, but they could not keep pace with

above
Richly decorated porticoes, galleries
and niches surround the great court of
Baalbek's Forum (2nd century AD).

left
Forum Romanum: Temple of Saturn
(foreground), Temple of Castor and
Pollux (right) and Arch of Titus
(beyond).

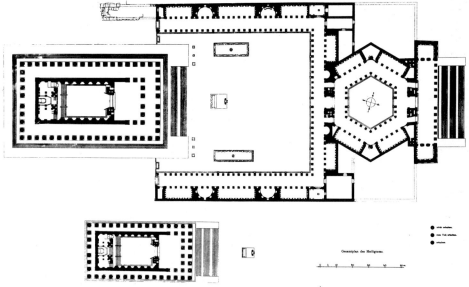

above
Baalbek's Forum was a gigantic formal
composition exploiting contrasting
hexagonal and rectangular courts.

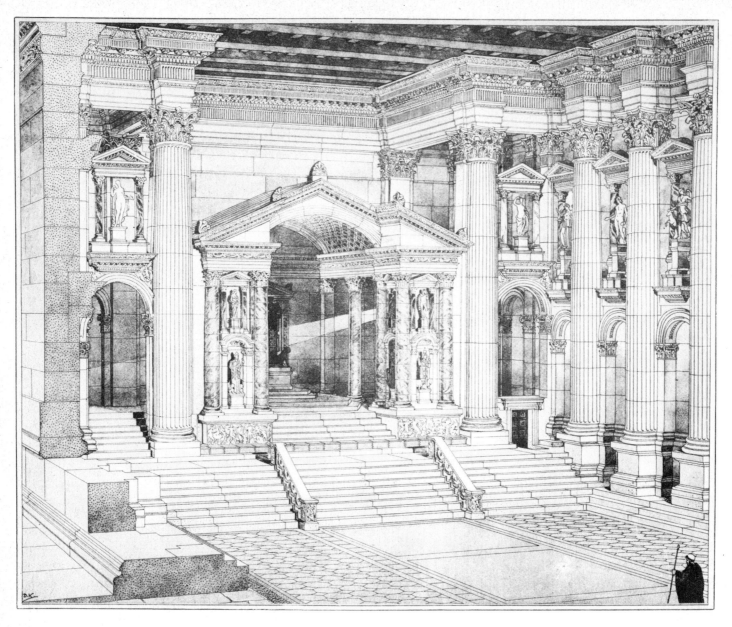

demands on the quantity and rapidity of construction. The practical Roman mind developed a sort of concrete, a hard composition consisting of small pieces of stone or broken bricks laid in an excellent mortar of lime and well-selected sand. The sand was pozzolana, a volcanic ash prevalent in Italy, which had high binding power and gave the concrete its strength.

The advantages of this new technique were that it economized in materials and skilled craftsmanship and speeded the building process. The important parts of the work were done by skilled craftsmen, who built the outer carcase of walls and the temporary timber centerings for arches and vaults. Under their direction unskilled labour performed the mechanical task of placing alternate layers of rubble and mortar which would solidify into concrete.

Concrete structures had therefore a special character, and a succession of techniques was developed to facilitate construction. Wall faces were built of specially cut stones or bricks, and bonding courses of large tiles were introduced to pass through the wall distributed at frequent intervals up the height. The faces and bonding courses thus contained the layers of rubble and mortar while in the fluid state, retaining the moisture in the concrete stage by stage and so controlling the setting. Once set the whole amalgam became a strong monolithic mass in which thrust was nullified. Concrete walls thus presented a succession of faces, depending on the type of bricks and bonding patterns, but never intended to be seen. Roman taste required a magnificent veneer of marble or stucco.

Similar techniques were used in the construction of vaults and domes; brick ribs connected at intervals by bonding tiles formed compartments for the concrete filling, supported on a temporary wooden framework. By means of these devices, arches were elaborated into the construction of barrel or tunnel vaults, cross-vaults formed by the intersection of two semicircular vaults of equal span,

hemispherical domes and semi-domes. The intersecting lines of cross-vaults are called groins and invention of the groin vault marked a portentous stage in the progress of architecture; the thrust and weight of the vault required support only at the four corners and this made possible greater freedom in the planning of buildings. Concrete as the important factor unifying walls and vaults made it possible to accommodate complicated plan forms without involving difficult and laborious stone cutting. It was upon this and the capacity to span enormous spaces that the character of mature Roman architecture

above
Arch of Septimius Severus, Rome (AD 203): the elaboration of the arch to monumental isolation was a symbol of imperial power.

right
Domes and semidomes, both based on the semicircular arch principle, were, in the Roman compound form of brick and concrete, structural systems used for roofing large spaces.

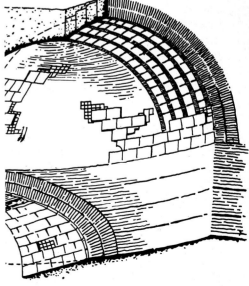

left
Colosseum (AD 70–82): a complex
structure of arches and vaults, Roman
Orders decorated and gave scale to the
exterior.

right
A monolithic arrangement achieved by
the use of concrete solved the structural
problems of the Colosseum: (A)
travertine, (B) tufa, (C) concrete.

below
Colosseum (arena and auditorium): the
Romans' greatest amphitheatre, it is a
unique concrete construction.

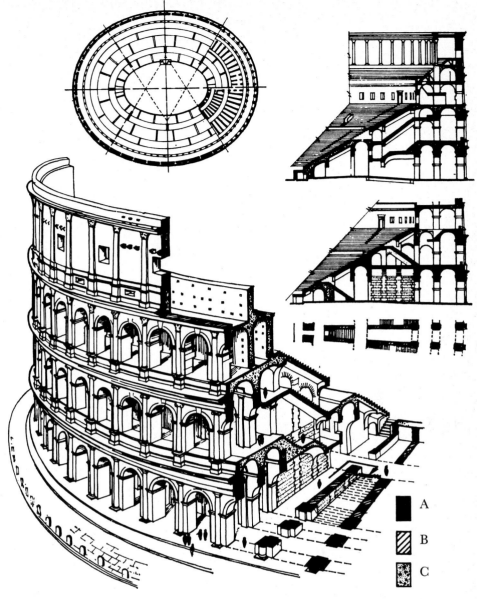

A

B

C

largely depended, making possible the construction of a vast range of public buildings and utilitarian structures quickly, anywhere and at much reduced cost and difficulty.

By AD 100 Roman architecture was approaching its prime. The daring exploitation of concrete structures stimulated the art of planning, which emancipated from precedent and inspired exploration of form and combination. Squares, oblongs, circles, hemicycles, ellipses, and polygons were explored singly or in complex arrangements controlled with masterly skill by co-ordinating axes which unified composition functionally and visually. An architecture of interiors was created, single cell or multi-cellular, with all kinds of devices being adopted to provide vistas, symmetry and formality, and nowhere better achieved than in the enormous complexes of the palatial public baths. These thermae fulfilled many functions of daily life, not only that of luxurious bathing, but as resorts for athletics, exercise, news, gossip, lectures and libraries – a general social rendezvous. Their provision invoked the complete range of Roman skills in architecture and engineering to solve the problems of planning, construction, servicing of water supply, drainage and heating, and decoration. The last ingredient splendidly exploited the availability of materials to the full, with polychromatic use of marbles for columns, wall casings and floors, ornamental plastering, wall paintings, mosaic, bronze for doors and screens, and sculpture.

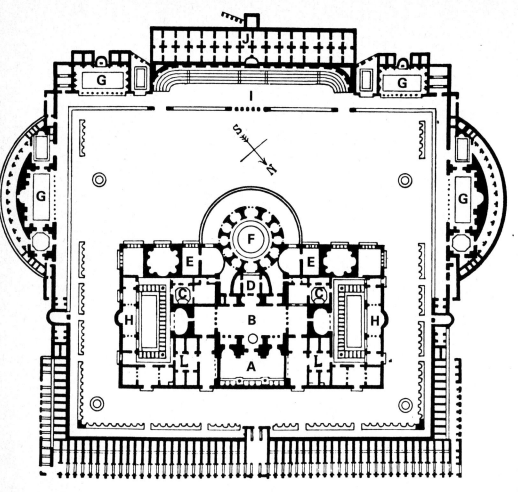

above

Thermae of Caracalla: (A) frigidarium, (B) central hall, (C) sudatorium, (D) tepidarium, (E) bathrooms, (F) calidarium, (G) lecture halls and libraries, (H) gymnasium, (I) stadium, (J) 2-storey reservoirs.

below

Reconstruction of the great central hall of the Thermae of Caracalla (AD 211–17).

But the ability to organize groups of complicated structures did not detract from the Roman capacity for achieving great simplicity and concepts of sheer genius. Two such, the Pantheon and the Basilica of Constantine, rank among the great buildings of all time, and perhaps the greatest single cells ever built.

Though late (built at the beginning of the fourth century AD) the Basilica of Constantine displayed in its fundamental clarity vaulted construction as applied to the multipurpose great hall which had long been a feature of large buildings such as the numerous thermae. The basilica combined the communal functions of a social and political meeting-place with those of a court of law, its traditional form being a central nave separated from flanking aisles by colonnades which supported a clerestory, somewhat resembling a classical temple turned inside-out. The vaulting techniques employed in the Basilica of Constantine had an astonishing impact on the expression of this simple arrangement. It became an enormous hall of three vaulted bays supported by huge piers, the spaces between which formed aisles opening to the central nave area. Barrel vaults over the aisle compartments were also supported by the piers, which were pierced by arches to give spatial continuity. In effect an enormous rectangular floor area was provided, interrupted by only four, though large, points of support.

The Pantheon was of a higher order of creation, symbolic of Rome at the peak of its supremacy during the principate of the extraordinary Emperor Hadrian. Of insatiable energy, he travelled all over the empire and, because his abilities included a sense of architecture, he instigated many buildings as benefactions and memorials. He was also a passionate lover of Greece. The combination of these attributes in conjunction with the spirit of the times, which Hadrian personified and encouraged, ensured an architectural synthesis which expressed the achievement and universality of the Roman mis-

right
The uncomfortable attachment of the Pantheon's conventional portico to its rotunda enhances the interior's inspiration.

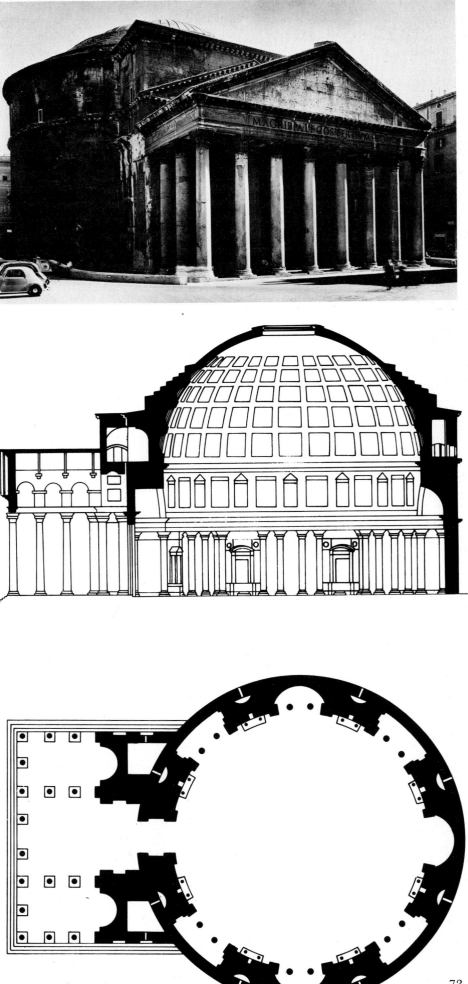

sion. His extensive villa at Tivoli was one statement; another, standing supreme among all the great works essayed under the patronage of that genius, was the Pantheon.

Conceived as a sanctuary to all the gods, the unique structure is deceptively simple. Externally the building is of no special account and the portico, though splendid, follows tradition. It enhances the originality of the building which it screens, for as an interior the Pantheon is unsurpassed – one of man's rare masterpieces. The encompassing wall and vault expressed the political cosmos of the Roman Empire, a superbly coffered dome of heaven united with the dome of heaven itself by the single unglazed circular opening in its crown. The rotunda, apparently a straightforward structure, is a complex system of arches carefully arranged to carry the enormous concrete dome. The lower half of the cylinder is enlivened by eight recesses; one which pierces to form the entrance and the apse opposite are arched, the remaining six screened by marble columns. These recesses effect a sense of depth within the structure, withdrawing the space but without breaking the continuity of the enclosure. Upon this cylinder, at a height equal to its radius, arches the dome, the whole being designed as perfect circles so that the diameter is exactly the same as the height. The simple geometric rotundities give the interior its sense of repose and grandeur, qualities enhanced by the light penetrating solely from the huge oculus by which there is neither shadow nor shade but overall illumination.

The Basilica of Constantine was almost the last great structure of Roman architecture. Within thirty

right
A monumental form of bold and simple geometry: the Pantheon in plan and section.

years of its completion the same emperor was responsible in succession for the acceptance of Christianity as a religion equal with other religions, the transfer of the capital from Rome to Constantinople and the building in Rome of the first great Christian church of St Peter. The Empire was in a state of change consequent upon the disorders and economic instability during the third century. Successive regimes had continued to build ambitious schemes in the imperial manner, but standards of taste and craftsmanship declined. Ostentatious art became increasingly coarse and not infrequently vulgar. The diminished resources of the empire and the consequences of Constantine's decisions determined the movement away from the imperial character of architecture to a new interpretation of old Roman traditions to meet the needs of a new culture and a new religion – Christianity. Nevertheless, the Roman absorption and reshaping of all the traditions of the ancient world ensured a manner which has had everlasting influence upon the development of the western world.

above
Basilica of Constantine (AD 310–13) exploits vaulted construction for a late Roman multi-purpose great hall.

right
An unsurpassed architectural symbol of Hadrian's philosophy of the coherent cosmos: the Pantheon (AD 120–24).

EARLY CHRISTIAN
and
BYZANTINE

By the Edict of Milan in AD 313 Constantine and his co-Emperor Licinius gave to Christians everywhere complete freedom of worship, finally ending the restrictions and recurrent persecutions that had hitherto limited, without ever really halting, the growth of the Church. To mark its new status, Constantine himself commissioned a number of magnificent new church buildings, both in Rome and at other major sites. These set the pattern for what we now know as Early Christian architecture – a pattern that was to endure with little change in the West through the uneasy centuries that followed the progressive breakdown of imperial authority.

But in the East a new pattern emerged in the first half of the sixth century. This we know as Byzantine since it had its roots in Constantine's New Rome, the old Greek colony of Byzantium subsequently called Constantinople and now Istanbul, and the capital from AD 330 up to its fall to the Turks in 1453 of the Eastern Roman or Byzantine Empire. It was the product of an intimate alliance of Church and State that found its supreme expression in one of the greatest buildings of all time – Justinian's Church of the Holy Wisdom, or Hagia Sophia. It lives on even today where the Eastern Orthodox Church still flourishes.

If we include the tentative beginnings of Christian architecture before AD 313, we shall therefore be concerned here with almost two thousand years of architectural history embracing, for a substantial part of that time, the whole civilized world except the Far East. It will be essential to concentrate largely on the highlights while ignoring most background diversity. The reader should also bear in mind that losses vastly outnumber what has survived from the earlier centuries, that these losses include virtually everything in major early centres like Antioch and Alexandria, and that surviving buildings dating back to the earlier centuries, and particularly to Constantine's time, have mostly been substantially altered if not – like St Peter's in Rome – completely rebuilt. We must therefore rely, to a greater extent than in tracing many other phases of architectural history, on the evidence of old descriptions and drawings or similar representations and on careful inferences from physical remains incorporated in buildings of a later date.

The beginnings of Christian architecture

Before Constantine, Christianity had been just one of several eastern cults concerned primarily with personal salvation. Throughout the Roman Empire they coexisted with an official imperial religion concerned more with ensuring the well-being of the state. On the whole it was, for the early Christians, a peaceful coexistence since conflict could usually be avoided by those who held no position of authority in the state until, by their very number, they were seen as a threat to its cohesion. The first Christians, however, had looked forward to an imminent Second Coming and had little need for buildings set aside for worship. And, when hopes of this Second Coming receded, most communities remained relatively poor and had no wish to attract official or other undesirable attention by building what might be described as 'great architecture'.

Their places of assembly and worship, even when purpose-built, seem therefore to have been simple and unobtrusive adaptations of contemporary forms of domestic building. In Rome itself they have been almost completely swept away in subsequent rebuildings and survive only in name – the *tituli* now assigned to cardinals of the Roman Church. But a chance survival in the eastern frontier town of Dura-Europos gives a clear picture of one such structure. It was a typical courtyard house of the region with adjoining rooms adapted for the performance of the Mass (with a dias for the presiding bishop against one wall), for baptisms, and for the instruction of those not yet admitted to full membership.

For burials and the commemoration of the dead normal contemporary practice was followed except in the details of the memorials and in a preference for burial alongside fellow Christians even when this separated families. Burial in open cemeteries was normal. But sometimes high land values and easy excavation in soft rock just below the surface made multi-tiered burials in catacombs an attractive alternative. To such catacombs outside the walls of Rome – or at least to some of the individual burial chambers within them – we largely owe our picture of the early development of Christian painted decoration. Above them, simple shelters might be erected for commemorative services and meals.

Constantine's churches

These modest beginnings hardly provided Constantine, or his architects, with adequate models for a new Christian architecture. Even the liturgy – the pattern of worship – underwent a subtle change, becoming more formalized and more akin to court ceremonial with a greater separation between officiating clergy and lay congregation. A permanent altar for the celebration of the Mass became the central feature and focus of the church proper, with seating for the clergy rising behind it.

Equally though, no pagan temple could serve as a model. Even if past associations had not ruled out this possibility, such temples were wholly unsuited to congregational worship. The only possible model was the basilica. This was essentially a place of assembly that had already served many purposes from market hall to hall of justice and imperial audience hall. Constantine, when still only co-emperor of the West, had himself built one alongside his palace at Trier to serve the last two purposes. It was a large rectangular hall terminated at one end by a semicircular apse. But the rectangular form, though commonest, was by no means the only one. In particular there were numerous audience halls of basically circular plan, like the so-called Temple of Minerva Medica in Rome and the large rotunda on the

An 18th-century view of the Temple of Minerva Medica, Rome, built as an imperial audience hall in the 3rd century. (Klengel, Gemaldegalerie Alte Meister, Dresden)

main axis of Diocletian's palace at Split.

Constantine's first act after he became sole Emperor of the West and formally recognized the Christian religion was to hand over to the Bishop of Rome the former imperial palace of the Lateran and have built alongside it a new cathedral, now St John Lateran. Though this is one of the churches that has been extensively rebuilt and remodelled, its original form is fairly well established. A long central nave terminating in an apse closely echoed the form of the basilica at Trier. At each side this central nave opened into pairs of lower aisles as in some other earlier basilicas. The outer aisles may well have been curtained off for those not yet admitted to full membership, serving the same purpose as one of the separate rooms at Dura-Europos. As yet there was no real transept: merely slight projections from the ends of the outer aisles to serve, perhaps, as sacristies. The apse held the seats for the bishop and clergy, with the altar a little further forward at the end of the nave.

In slightly later churches this basic form was varied in a number of ways, just as the earlier basilica

had varied in form from place to place and according to its precise use. In the Holy Land Constantine built two great churches to commemorate Christ's nativity and passion. In each case the church proper resembled the Lateran basilica, though there seem to have been galleries above the aisles in the church on the site of Calvary. But each church terminated not in a simple apse at the end of the nave but an octagonal or circular sanctuary – a sort of throne room of the Deity. That at Bethlehem rose over the Grotto of the Nativity. That in Jerusalem may have risen over the site of the finding of the True Cross by Constantine's mother, the Empress Helena. Beyond it, in a large courtyard to which it gave access, were the Rock of Calvary and the Holy Sepulchre.

In Rome the counterpart to these churches was the basilica erected over the tomb of St Peter. But here

above
A mid 4th-century burial chamber in a catacomb off the Via Latina, Rome.

there were two important differences. It does not seem to have been considered proper to accord a mere apostle quite the same honour as the Deity, so, in place of the octagonal or circular sanctuary, a large hall was placed across the main axis to house the shrine and visiting pilgrims. And the basilica was not intended primarily as a church. It had initially no permanent altar or clergy, and the main body of nave and aisles was more a covered cemetery for those who wished to be buried near the apostle than a shelter for a regular congregation.

Yet another variant was the original Church of the Holy Apostles

Mausoleum of Constantia, now Santa
Constanza, Rome, the size typically
exaggerated. Note the early mosaic
decoration of the ambulatory.
(Piranesi)

below
Constantine's Basilica of St Peter,
Rome, with the saint's shrine at the
front of the apse.

in Constantinople. Constantine regarded himself as the thirteenth
apostle and the church was built as
his mausoleum. His tomb was
placed in the centre surrounded by
twelve piers representing the other
apostles. And radiating from the
central enclosure were no less than
four naves forming a large cross. In
a sense this looked back to earlier
imperial mausolea – whose form
was taken over directly in the building of the mausoleum of his daugh-
ter Constantia.

Structurally and architecturally
these buildings conformed more to a
single pattern, as far as we can tell,
though there were local variations
just as there had been in the earlier
basilicas on account of such factors
as regional differences in the availability of materials. Apart from the
mausoleum of Constantia, they
were probably all roofed with
timber trusses with or without coffered ceilings below. Walls could
thus be relatively thin, whether

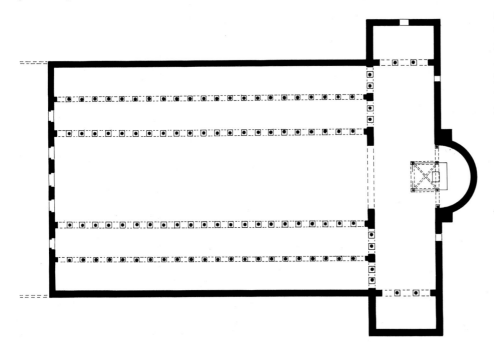

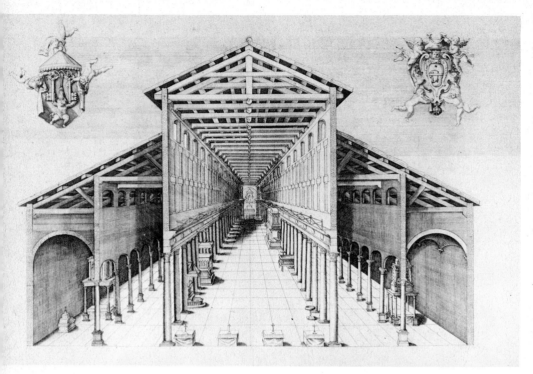

above
Old St Peter's, Rome, in the early 16th century. (Ferrabosco after Tasselli)

below
Plans: (A) San Lorenzo, Milan; (B) Saints Sergius and Bacchus, Constantinople; (C) San Vitale, Ravenna.

above
Roman colonnades carrying a continuous arcade (right foreground) and horizontal architraves (background) in Diocletian's palace in Split.

A
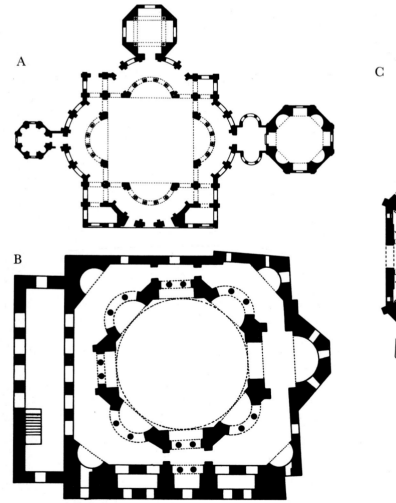

C
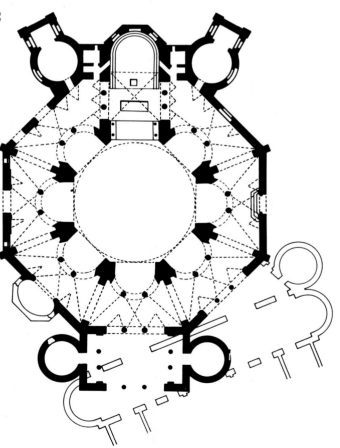

B

above
The central octagon of Charlemagne's palace chapel at Aachen looking towards the Gothic choir.

built of brick-faced concrete (as in Rome), of brick alone, or of cut stone. They could also be readily pierced by window openings and carried on rows of columns to give communication, at ground level, between nave and aisles. A horizontal architrave above the columns seems to have been preferred where columns of sufficient height and blocks of sufficient size for the architraves could be procured – usually as spoils from earlier buildings. But the alternative of a sequence of small arches, which had previously been less common, frequently took its place.

The structure of St Peter's was little altered before it was demolished to make way for the present church, so surviving drawings of it give a good impression of the total form. Particularly notable are the impressive colonnades at ground level, the broad expanses of plain wall above, the rows of windows high in the nave walls as the principal source of light, and the strongly directional character leading the eye forward – here to St Peter's shrine, elsewhere to the altar. The broad expanses of wall provided a perfect field for decorative revetments of rich marble to catch and reflect the light and for inset panels of fresco or mosaic to tell a story or proclaim the triumphant Christ and honour his apostles and martyrs. And the relative simplicity and economy of construction would have freed resources to pay for this embellishment and for correspondingly rich furnishings of bronze, silver, and gold, and other precious materials.

Later centralized structures and basilicas

Probably shortly after Constantine's death, a large rotunda was built in Jerusalem over the Holy Sepulchre behind the Constantinian basilica. It seems originally to have born some resemblance to the mausoleum of Constantia, but with two storeys of columns or piers ringing the tomb and a gallery above the ground-level outer ambulatory. Over the next two hundred years such free-standing centralized structures became increasingly common, especially for martyria and palace chapels, alongside derivatives of the related cross form of the Church of the Holy Apostles and of the rectangular basilica.

Most of the more compactly centralized structures that were related to earlier audience halls were built in the eastern part of the empire. But only one of the later examples is today well preserved – the sixth-century Church of Saints Sergius and Bacchus in Constantinople. In the West we still have the almost contemporary Church of San Vitale in Ravenna, Charlemagne's palace chapel at Aachen, and, beneath a sixteenth-century remodelling, the late fourth-century structure that is now the Church of San Lorenzo in Milan. Charlemagne's chapel is a deliberate revival built in the late eighth century and is a simple, rather tower-like, two-storeyed octagon. Inside it, one can almost sense a rather hostile world outside. The other three were more direct developments from earlier prototypes. In particular the central space, whether basically square or octagonal, was opened out in each by curved exedrae as in the Temple of

Minerva Medica. The original function of San Lorenzo is still uncertain, as is the manner in which the central space was roofed. But both Saints Sergius and Bacchus and San Vitale were also palace chapels, and both were domed. There is a much ampler space inside them, which expands, behind the columnar screens, into ambulatory and gallery.

The cross plan was adopted chiefly for martyria and similar commemorative structures. Its symbolism of the True Cross and the ability of barrel-vaulted arms to buttress a central dome may have been the chief reasons for choosing it for the small mausoleum of Galla Placidia in Ravenna, where the entire surface of the vaults and upper walls was covered in mosaic. For larger structures that were places of pilgrimage it would have had another practical advantage in allowing the maximum number of pilgrims to approach the shrine or object of pilgrimage in an orderly manner. This may well have been

below
Torcello Cathedral, near Venice, is a late Italian example of the early basilican church with Byzantine influence in furnishings and mosaics.

below
Saints Sergius and Bacchus today, as adapted for use as a mosque.

right
The 5th-century Mausoleum of Galla Placidia, Ravenna.

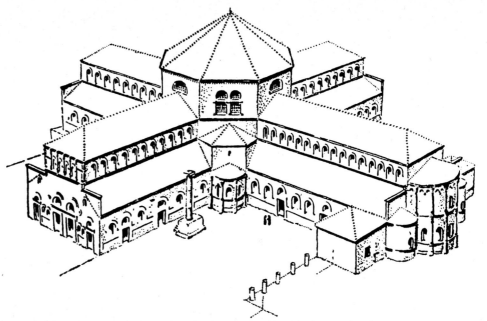

right
A bird's eye reconstruction drawing of the martyrium of Qalat Siman from the south east.

below
Santa Sabina, Rome.

the principal consideration at Qalat Siman in northern Syria, where the pillar of St Simeon Stylites was enclosed, about 470, in a large timber-roofed octagon. Radiating from this octagon were four large arms. Each was, in itself, a rectangular basilica complete with aisles. And the whole was constructed in the fine stone masonry typical of this area to create one of the most impressive monuments of its time.

For churches generally, the rectangular plan, with a single dominant axis leading towards the altar, was usually preferred. The scale and magnificence of Constantine's Lateran basilica and St Peter's were naturally reserved for a few of the most important structures like the later fourth-century church of St Paul and the early fifth-century church of Santa Maria Maggiore, both of which were also situated in Rome.

More typical of the fourth and fifth centuries in the West is the finely preserved church of Santa Sabina on Rome's Aventine Hill. Its closeness to the Constantinian model, despite its reduced scale and the absence of the outer aisles, will be seen. But the finely proportioned arcades of the nave gave it a lighter elegance than the powerful colonnades and horizontal architraves of St Peter's. In the corresponding churches of Ravenna (capital of the West during the hard-pressed fifth and early sixth centuries) the chief differences were that the aisles were now lit directly (and may have been partly curtained off during services) and that the nave walls were sometimes completely covered in mosaic. The persistence of the type, at least in Italy, is attested by numerous later churches of the eighth to the twelfth centuries.

The East largely escaped the troubles that beset the West after the effective partition of the empire by Theodosius in 395. It was thus freer to indulge in doctrinal controversy and liturgical experiment. The change that was to have the greatest architectural impact was a further development of the liturgy in the direction of court ceremonial. This called for the whole nave to be

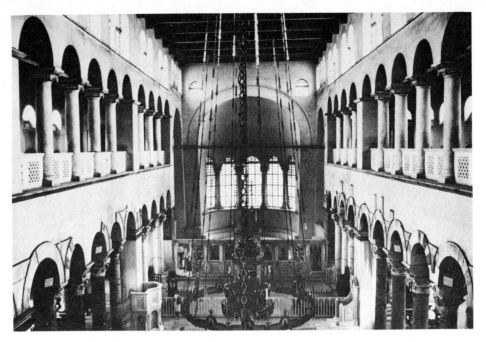

given over to the clergy for ceremonial entrances and the reading of the gospel and preaching of sermons, while the central part of the Mass was performed behind a screen towards the east end. The church became a sort of theatre-in-the-round, with the congregation relegated to the aisles.

The eastern counterparts to a western church like Santa Sabina tended, therefore, to be broader in relation to their lengths and, where they housed large congregations, to have galleries over the aisles which sometimes continued over the west end of the nave. The same structural pattern could still be followed to a large extent, and did continue to be followed up to the end of the fifth century, as may be seen in St Demetrius in Salonika. But the longitudinal axis was no longer so important, there was a definite centralizing tendency, and it could only be a matter of time before this tendency was openly expressed.

Justinian's churches

Tentative moves in this direction probably began towards the end of the fifth century with the raising of the roof over the central part of the nave, perhaps as a timber pyramid rising from a squat tower. But it was only under Justinian that the more radical step was taken of placing a large dome here and effectively fusing the rectangular basilica and the fully centralized form of the palace chapel or martyrium to give the first distinctively Byzantine architecture.

Justinian, as Emperor of the East from 527 to 565, did all he could to

below
Late 5th-century church at Alahan in Asia Minor, the centre of the nave emphasized by a squat tower.

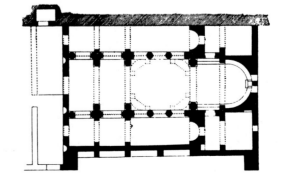

reunite the empire and restore it to its former power and glory. He attempted this partly by military reconquest of lost provinces, particularly in the West. But he also used all other available means, including the Church, of which, as emperor, he was secular head. His attempts at imposing doctrinal unity failed. But he was given a superb opportunity to proclaim, by a new church, the partnership of Church and State when the palace chapel and seat of the patriarch in Constantinople – the Church of Hagia Sophia – was burnt down in a riot in 532. He rebuilt it in the grandest possible manner, choosing as his architects two eminent geometers.

The church that was burnt down was already a Theodosian rebuilding of Constantine's church. It most likely resembled St Demetrius in Salonika, though about twice the size. If so, it retained, as rebuilt, the broad aisles and the gallery continued across the west end of the nave. But, in place of simple trussed timber roofs, it was vaulted in brick throughout, with a central dome 30 m (100 ft) in span. This dome was carried on four huge arches spanning between piers on each side of the nave and two of these arches were abutted by semidomes of equal span to east and west. Below these semidomes, semicircular exedrae covered by smaller semidomes further enlarged the space of the nave in much the same way as the four exedrae of the slightly earlier church of Saints Sergius and Bacchus. It was a masterly concept of interlocking part-cylindrical and part-spherical surfaces 'fitted together', in the words of the contemporary historian Procopius, 'with incredible skill in mid-air and floating off from each other and resting only on the parts next to them, producing a single and most extraordinary harmony in the work'. And it provided the perfect setting for the divine and imperial liturgy in the great elongated central space that was created beneath gilded vaults and between encircling colonnades of aisles and gallery and the marble-clad piers.

right
Cut-away isometric view of Justinian's
Church of Hagia Sophia,
Constantinople.

left
Hagia Sophia looking westward from
above the apse.

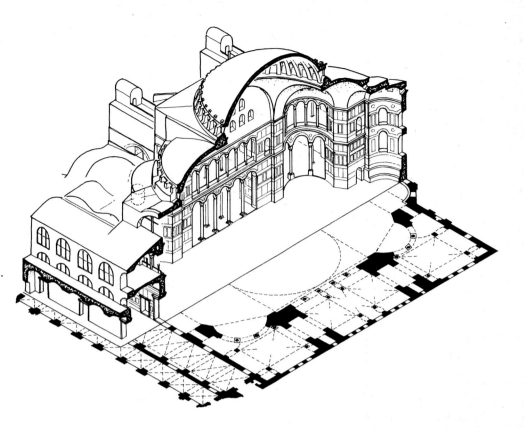

below left
The dome of Hagia Sophia: a mosaic
cross and later a figure of Christ
preceded the present Koranic
inscription.

below
Hagia Sophia looking towards the
dome from the gallery behind the
north-west exedra with parts of the
exedra semidome and main west
semidome (upper right).

above
The apse of Justinian's Hagia Irene,
Constantinople, showing typical
seating for clergy and a mosaic cross
dating from the 8th century, when
figurative icons were forbidden.

of the crown to fall forwards. The need for very substantial construction of the piers would also have been demonstrated, most recently, perhaps, in the building of Saints Sergius and Bacchus.

Only for the inwardly curving pendentives between the great arches that carried the dome was there no such direct precedent. And, for such a novel combination of elements on such a vast scale, it would have been impossible to be sure in advance just how much strength was called for at any point. The design had, therefore, to be modified more than once as construction proceeded and there have also been subsequent changes which have, in particular, altered the distribution of light. One must also bear in mind the loss of all the original rich furnishings and the substitution of comparatively modern Turkish ones appropriate to the subsequent use of the church as a mosque.

None of Justinian's other buildings, perhaps intentionally, was of this quality. The most important were all similarly rebuildings of earlier churches. Typically the earlier plan seems to have been largely retained. But colonnades and walls carrying timber roofs were replaced by widely spaced piers set at the corners of square bays and carrying a brick dome on pendentives over each bay. They included the nearby Church of the Holy Peace, or Hagia Irene, the Church of St John at Ephesus of cruciform plan with an elongated nave, and the Church of the Holy Apostles. Only part of this rebuilding survives in the present Hagia Irene, and only the bases of the piers, intermediate side colonnades, and outer walls of St John's. The Holy Apostles has gone completely. But we do still have several close copies of it. Of these, St Mark's in Venice probably gives the best impression of its character and quality.

Though the 'incredible skill' behind the novelty of the concept was primarily geometric, it also drew together past experience in a number of hitherto diverse fields as most great innovations do. The dome, though largely developed in concrete in the West, had already been taken up for simpler circular or near-circular structures in the East and transposed into brick. The semidome had been widely used over the apse or exedra and its buttressing capability must have been recognized from the tendency

Later Byzantine churches

Justinian's military campaigns and building activities drained the coffers of the state and an outbreak of bubonic plague further sapped its vitality. His grandiose plans came, in the end, to little; and Hagia Sophia remained an isolated *tour de force* until Ottoman sultans were stimulated to emulate it after Constantinople fell to them.

Subsequent Byzantine architecture was on a much more modest scale, a further reason being the fact that the more important churches were mostly monastic ones serving much smaller communities than became common in the West. It was also less adventurous, never again attempting the combination of dome and half domes or the spatial complexities achieved through the use of open exedrae in Hagia Sophia. It took the central dome as its basic element and subordinated all else to it, often emphasizing this primacy, and that of the liturgical action beneath it, by placing in it an image of Christ as Ruler of All.

In the principal surviving churches of the seventh to the ninth

above
The east end of the Church of Daphni, Greece.

below
Looking up to the dome, eastern (partly hidden) and southern cross-vaults, and the lower south-east corner vault (with mosaics) of the Church of the Blessed Virgin, Constantinople.

above
St Mark's, Venice: the west facade
viewed from the piazza.

centuries, such as Hagia Sophia in
Salonika, the basic form and structural system are those of the small
mausoleum of Galla Placidia. A
dome on pendentives is carried on
four main piers which are extended
outwards from the central square to
support also four barrel vaults forming, together, a buttressing cross.
Other small spaces might be fitted
within the angles of this cross or
wrapped around it, but they
remained isolated from the centre.

Between the late ninth and the

eleventh centuries a new form
developed in which the piers were
reduced to single columns or groups
of three much more slender piers,
and the subsidiary spaces within the
angles of the cross were thus
expanded to become parts of a
single square space at ground level.
This development can best be
understood by reference to the two
adjacent churches of the Monastery
of St Luke in Greece.

The smaller church is of the usual
simpler form with four single col-

above
Dome mosaic at Daphni, showing
Christ surrounded by standing
prophets between the windows.

umns carrying the dome and set
within the larger square of the outer
walls. It became so well established
as a norm that it was used even for
many rock-cut churches where it
was structurally quite inappropriate. The larger church has the more
complex form and comes as near as
any later Byzantine structure to
achieving something of the spatial
quality of Justinian's Hagia Sophia
– though lacking its amplitude and
more strongly focussed on the
central vertical axis. This church is
also outstanding for its decoration.
The rich marble revetments of the
walls and piers give way, in the
upper parts of the structure, to an
hierarchically organized scheme of
mosaic decoration perfectly adapted
to its spatial setting and the light
falling on it. Representations of the
saints give way first to representations (or icons) of the principal
feasts of the Church commemorative of Christ's earthly life and then
to representations of heaven and
Christ as Ruler in the high vaults.

above
Cut-away isometric view of the
churches of the Monastery of St Luke,
Greece.

After this, it is difficult not to regard all that followed as anti-climax. Innumerable variations were played on these forms, elaborating them, adding more domes, and raising these on high drums to give an exaggerated feeling of height. St Basil's Cathedral in Moscow is a late extreme example of this trend.

above
The base of the central dome and western barrel vault (background) of the Dark Church, Karanlik Kilise, Cappadocia. One supporting column has been broken away.

below
The 11th-century Hagia Sophia, Kiev: a basic cross-in-square plan elaborated by repetition of the outer bays.

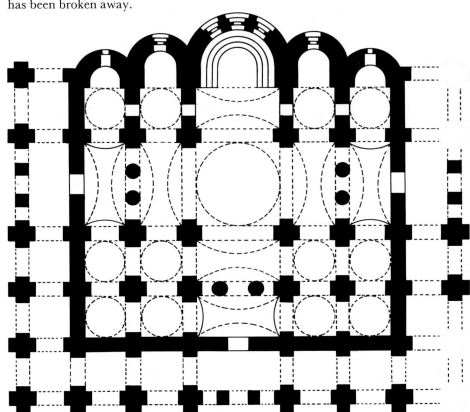

EARLY
ISLAMIC

With a history of nearly thirteen hundred years and an historical spread covering some half the world, inevitably there can be no one such thing as Islamic architecture. While its pattern is richly diverse, its remarkable feature is a coherence that allows some guidelines to be drawn and some rules to be given. The reason for this coherence lies deep. It springs from a similarity in behaviour between societies which have an established order stabilized round one fundamental philosophy. The same periods of fasting, the same demanding daily routines of prayer, similar structures of legislative authority, of schooling and of leadership, and perhaps above all the interaction derived from the annual pilgrimage to the focus-city of the religion brought to the whole Islamic world common characteristics, common fashions, and common aspirations.

The pattern of life in communities, disciplined by the routines of religion and the established traditions of a patriarchal society, shaped similar towns: idealization of gardens led to the creation of water-centred, geometrically patterned paradises contained within compound walls. The disciplines of thought, which accepted repetitive learning of the Koran, treated other aspects of learning, too, as dogma. An absence of questioning led to a repetitive and slowly

evolving architecture, remarkable for geometric pattern-making, avoidance of human representation and more concerned with conformity than originality.

Islam arose in an area where Christianity was rapidly supplanting the multiplicity of pagan religions. Concerned with the worship of the one god, Islam felt itself the successor to Judaism and Christianity, and it taught reverence for the Christian ethic. Politically the area was traditionally dominated by the two great powers of East and West. The Graeco-Persian Wars had been followed by the Roman trials of strength against the Parthians and then the Sassanian dynasty of Persia, whose forces early in the seventh century (immediately before the emergence of Islam) had swept down to the Palestinian coast and on into Egypt, establishing a province across Syria and Palestine. Hardly had they been dislodged by the Byzantine emperor, Heraclius, when there emerged from the southern deserts an apparently minor force of Arab tribesmen, seemingly propounding a sectarian version of Christianity. These Muslim armies spread along the northern shores of Africa, carrying their message westwards to the Atlantic and eastwards into Central Asia.

Leadership of the Muslim community had by AD 661 settled upon the house of Ummaya and this dynasty moved the leadership or

caliphate to Greater Syria, to Damascus and Jerusalem. There it built its power, using the administrative talents and commercial wealth of the region free from the internecine politics of Mecca and Medina. In these circumstances, the distinctive architecture of Islam began to evolve.

Building types
Muslim history is redolent with new cities. The streets of the city focused upon the mosque and upon the palace of the ruler. From the first, palace and mosque were closely related. The form of the mosque was early established on the example of the courtyard of the house of Mohammed at Medina. A strong axial emphasis derived from the requirement to focus prayer upon a specific place, initially Jerusalem but after the resolution of Mohammed's quarrel with the Meccans, towards al-Meccah. To establish the direction, a post or spear stuck in the ground proclaimed the kibla (direction of prayer). Early in the eighth century this mark was superseded by a semicircular niche, the mihrab, probably introduced by Coptic workmen employed to refurbish the Prophet's Mosque at Medina. Differentiating themselves from the Christians, Muslim communities made use neither of the clapper nor bell as a summons to prayer, but responded to the call of the muezzin, first given from the

93

walls of the Prophet's House. In building the Great Mosque of Damascus early in the eighth century, the community inherited square stone watch-towers which suited this purpose and so became the prototype minaret.

Islam enjoins upon its membership standards of cleanliness which not only require the provision of washing and sanitary facilities in the mosque but have led to traditions of community bathing. Public baths were a feature of the Roman Empire and, taken over in the eastern provinces, they were adapted and adopted by most Muslim communities; frequently they were closely related to the Friday Mosque.

The mosque served many functions. As a place of prayer, its use was primary and to disturb that use was ill-mannered: but equally, it was honourable to meditate there, to take refuge, even to sleep there on occasions or to meet and converse. Its use night and day by the faithful made it a safe storehouse for private treasures and from the beginning a special section of the building would be set aside for the safe-keeping of valuables. The administration of funds left to the community was centred upon officials of the mosque, who frequently lived there permanently, and so it became a point of administration where clerks and writers were available. The great mosque of a city was often directly connected with the residence of the ruler and, as community law was Muslim law, upon which theological guidance was necessary, the mosque became a place for the administration of justice and for many kinds of public pronouncements.

With such a multiplicity of functions, the evolution of small specialized sections of the building was inevitable, and one such evolution gave rise to a complete building type, the theological college known as a madrasa. Normally providing living cells grouped around a courtyard, the madrasa always possessed a series of covered spaces for teaching and discussion, and, of course, for prayer. Both madrasa and

mosque are sometimes associated with tombs. Funerary architecture plays a great part in the history of Muslim building, though it has little basis in doctrinal theology: indeed rather the converse.

Islam has a proud history of public buildings and works of engineering – canals, bridges, dams, aqueducts, fountains, reservoirs and fortifications. From this last, one special building type has emerged – the rabat, a fortified religious community poised on the frontier, an outpost of the faith.

Islam, with its specific requirements for travel and a great tradition of trade and communication across its extensive empires, developed buildings to service these functions. On the highways there were protected stopping places to shelter the traveller, the caravanserais, and in the cities there were hans, of similar function, which often became centres of marketing and manufacture. The protection given to shopping streets created labyrinthine bazaars of vaulted lanes fronted by booths and shops.

above
The gold-anodized aluminium dome
and tile-sheathed (originally
mosaic-faced) drum of the Dome of
the Rock in Jerusalem.

left
The central gable of the prayer
hall of the Great Mosque,
Damascus: from the north-eastern
corner of the courtyard.

The Ummayad period

At the outset Islam placed no
emphasis upon building but in AD
661 the Ummayad caliphs moved to
Syria, where they settled in a province of great architectural fertility,
whose stone masonry had reached
the highest levels of skill. Over the
principal Christian shrines of Syria
great domes were reared, and the
protected Christian population
practised its creed in buildings of
dazzling richness.

Islam is perhaps unique among
all great architectural movements in
possessing a building of complete
maturity surviving from the begin-

ning of its heritage. Between 689
and 691 the Caliph al-Malik caused
to be built on the Temple Mount or
citadel of Jerusalem a great dome to
serve as the focus for local pilgrimage. It was to compete both with
Mecca (the rival power base) and
with the Christian shrines of the
city. Its essential message was the
oneness of God and the truth of
Islam. Architecturally the Dome of
the Rock is a Byzantine building.
An octagonal arcade of Corinthian
columns and piers carries a mosaic-
sheathed drum from which rises a
dome sheltering the outcrop of the
summit of Mount Moria. A double

above
The central prayer space of the Aqsa Mosque, Jerusalem (late 7th century onwards), looking down the kibla axis.

left
The half-round towers of the wall of al-Anjar, rebuilt from the fragments of the ruined Ummayad city.

right
The central mosaic of the palace, al-Mafjar, Jordan. The central panel of the middle band suggests that the builder was al Walid ibn Yazid (743–44).

ambulatory surrounds the dome. An external sheathing of tilework has replaced the original mosaic and anodized aluminium has replaced the gilded lead which covered the dome (soon again to be replaced). What was distinctively Muslim about it was the avoidance of figurative decoration, the early pointed arches and the repetitive handling of the decoration. In this and in its rigid but vital geometry it contained the seeds of much that was to come.

The earliest city mosque to have survived is the Great Mosque at Damascus. Built within the compound of a pagan temple, later turned to Christian usage, it was taken over by the Caliph al-Walid and became the archetypal Ummayad mosque, combining a central aisle in the prayer hall with transverse double-height arcading. One side of the great courtyard was entirely roofed to give a prayer chamber some 122 m (400 ft) long by 37 m (120 ft) deep, and a central aisle terminating on the courtyard was faced in mosaic, the greatest field of this material ever laid, and unlike Byzantine mosaics free of human representation. Its subjects were gardens and cities. The Great Mosque became the prototype of many other city mosques in Syria.

The Ummayads built a complete new fortified city in the heart of the fertile Bequ'a Valley, at al Anjar, now in the Lebanon. The archaeological reconstruction shows it to have been contained within a giant rectangle of walls laced with half-round towers in the Roman manner and to have been divided into four quarters by two great colonnaded streets. Its richly decorated buildings were dominated by the influences of the Eastern Byzantine Empire but in the contemporary township standing beside an isolated caliphal palace in northern Syria at Qasr al-Hair-ash-Sharki eastern influences are much more apparent. Sassanian methods of vaulting are used in juxtaposition to Corinthian capitals, double arcading and a plan reflecting the Great Mosque at Damascus. In a palace of extraordinary luxury at al-Mafjar in the Jordan Valley the Syrian workmen who served the Ummayad princes so well went to extremes of exotic elaboration in the provision of bath-houses, halls and reception rooms; and here, too, are seen the

beginnings of eastern influence in the detailing of stucco decoration.

In two great vaulted palaces in Jordan, Qasr al-Mshatta and Qasr at-Tuba, eastern and local influences are compounded. Giant pointed-arched vaults in brick are matched with elaborately carved foliated friezes in stone. A new and special quality is derived from this admixture and with these buildings an integrated Islamic architecture begins to be discernible.

With two exceptions almost no building of importance survives from the Ummayad period outside Syria and Palestine. On the eastern highlands of Persia the provincial capital, Damghan, possesses a covered mosque originally roofed with high, pointed, semi-elliptical vaults and built upon brick piers radially constructed in the Sassanian tradition. The awkward subsequent insertion of mihrab and mimber, a

raised platform for ceremonial announcements, suggests that this building should be placed early in the eighth century. Further south in Cairo, in the city founded by the first Muslim conquerer of Egypt, 'Amr ibn al-'As, there is a mosque containing some fragments of the original construction and its ground plan faithfully reflects the original form. In this building the multi-pillared (hypostyle) prayer hall facing a great courtyard was roofed with a series of slightly pointed arches linked by carved timber tie-beams and carried on Corinthian columns to produce arcades supporting the traditional flat roof of the palm trunks.

Continuity of use obscures and modifies early structures, and some of the most significant evidence is lost in this way. At Mecca, the Ka'aba, and at Medina, the Prophet's Mosque, two of the most

revered Muslim buildings, have been many times remodelled and, being barred to non-Muslims, their vital part in the story of Muslim building has been obscured.

The courtyards of and adjoining the Prophet's House in Yathrib, now Medina, Saudi Arabia, were enlarged under the Ummayad Caliph al-Walid, from c. 707 to 710, to include the tomb of the Prophet. It may have been the teams of Syrian mosaicists who worked on the Dome of the Rock and the Great Mosque of Damascus that decorated the prayer hall and courtyard. A circular niche was introduced, possibly from Coptic sources, to act as a focus of prayer while emphasis on the central aisle and on the first transverse aisle is thought to have originated the T-plan subsequently taken up in the early mosques of North Africa. This plan survives within the enlarged mosque but

left
The reception rooms and bath-house in the Jordanian desert known as Quseir (Little Castle) 'Amr.

above
The 10th-century dome built in front of the mihrab in the extension of the Great Mosque at Cordoba.

Mamluk (fourteenth-century) and Ottoman (sixteenth-, eighteenth- and nineteenth-century) rebuildings have reshaped the structure with some obvious external influences, coming predominantly from Cairo.

The Ka'aba, the central shrine of Islam since 630, is a near cube which stands isolated in the irregular courtyard of the Mosque of the Haram, surrounded by modern multi-storey arcades. The original structure has been rebuilt and the surrounding pointed arcades are again being extended and reconstructed under the continual pressures of use. Nothing appears to remain of the early periods. Some Ottoman work of the sixteenth century survives, the majority of it in an overtly Islamic style peculiar to the Hejaz.

Western Islamic style

Further to the east in Mesopotamia and on the uplands of Persia, Islam ruled provinces peopled with able administrators, warriors and men power-hungry with memories of their own imperial past. The situation was ripe for conflict, feeding as it did on discontent over the Ummayad seizure of the caliphate. Leadership in the East focused upon the house of Abbas, whose military success in the year 750 was followed by a treacherous feast which eliminated every Ummayad prince of significance, with one exception, the young Abd-ar-Rahman. His flight westwards to the Magrib, the Muslim north-west coast of Africa, led to the later establishment of a rival caliphate based at Cordoba in Spain, whither a great many Syrians migrated. The Ummayads took with them the Arabic language, their administra-

tive system and their architectural style, and these they implanted upon the thinly populated provinces of Tunisia, Algeria, Morocco and southern Spain.

The Great Mosque of Cordoba, built initially in 784–6, with two further major periods of building in the late tenth century, was similar in form to the Great Mosque of Damascus. The great arcades of its prayer hall were lifted through two storeys and poised on antique columns, and its reflection of its Syrian origins even went so far as to give it a southward orientation which would have been correct in Damascus but was quite incorrect in Spain. Architectural originality flourished and in the subsequent additions the double ranges of arcades were intricately lobed and interlaced to produce a distinctive western variant of the original theme. The prayer chamber was extended in both directions until, by the eleventh century, it was the largest covered mosque in existence and its influence throughout western Islam was paramount.

It was in North Africa that some of the most typical and important rabats were built, at Bizerta, Tripoli, Sfax and Susa (Sousa) in the ninth and tenth centuries. Typically, they were square two-storey structures containing a central open courtyard with outer walls stoutly buttressed by half-round towers.

The great mosques of the cities of North Africa reflected the influences of Damascus and Cordoba but developed a distinctive plan in which, in the prayer hall, the aisles ran parallel with the kibla axis, the central aisle being heightened or otherwise emphasized, and against the kibla wall itself an equally emphasized aisle ran transversely. At their crossing, before the mihrab, there was placed a dome. The key mosque of this type is the Aghlabid Great Mosque at Qairouan, built in 836. Its massive square minaret stands dominant on the central axis.

Influences crossed and mingled as dynastic power flowed and ebbed across Iberia and North Africa. Under the Almohads a flowering of decorative styles lifted western Islam to a plane of achievement that was to be assimilated even in Christian Sicily and Spain and was to return to the east when the

left
The Great Mosque of Qairouan seen from the north-west.

right
The Hall of the Kings: a range of rooms terminating the Court of the Lions in the Alhambra Palace.

below
The 14th-century palace built into the citadel of Granada by the Nasrid dynasty and known, from its red walls, as the Alhambra: (1) Hall of Ambassadors, (2) Court of Alberea, (3) baths, (4) Hall of Two Sisters, (5) Court of the Lions, (6) Hall of Abencerrages.

left
The Palatine Chapel in Palermo. Muqarnas (stalactite) detailing of this quality is rare in non-Muslim building.

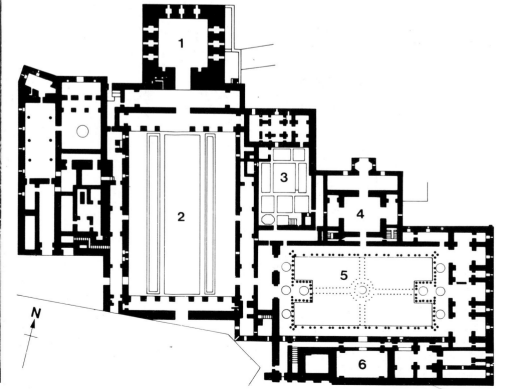

Fatimid dynasty came to Cairo.

Sicily was the first substantial territory taken by the Muslims to be recaptured by a Christian dynasty. Some three centuries of Islamic rule, however, left a heritage of architecture which continued into the Norman period in the twelfth century with the completion of buildings such as the Palace of al-Aziza, remarkable for its mosaic and muqarnas (stalactite) detailing, the cathedral at Cefalu, and the Palatine Chapel in the royal palace at Palermo.

In the twelfth, thirteenth and fourteenth centuries, among the high peaks of architectural creation were the Great Mosque at Seville and its Giralda Tower, uniquely fretted and patterned in its upper ranges. In the fourteenth century in Granada, under the Nasrid dynasty, the royal citadel was fortified and extended in a series of palatial courtyards to become the Qalat al-Hamra (the Palace of Alhambra). Construction continued even as late as 1391, by which time the palace contained all the elements of display, luxury and function that typified the fortresses of Islamic rulers. In the Alhambra stucco decoration, tiles, carved marble, plaster and paint were used with superbly controlled exuberance to reach a peak of artistry. The palace is made up of three major elements linked by two formal

courtyards. Each of its important reception rooms is in effect a pavilion supported by ancillary rooms and some of its most important spaces are outdoors – the Courts of the Lions and of the Myrtles.

The Abbasid period

With the annihilation of the Ummayads in Syria, Palestine and Egypt, that area was left a provincial vacuum, under Abbasid overlordship. Inevitably the architectural traditions of Sassanian Persia and Iraq played a dominant role in the architecture of the new caliphate. Nothing now remains of the great Round City on the Tigris which established Baghdad as the focus of Mesopotamia and of eastern

Islam. With this city surrounded by immense walls, the image of a military despot surrounded by a major static defence was first presented to the Muslim world.

Ukhaidir, the only building to survive from this period, lies in the deserts near Kerbala in southern Iraq. It too is a fortress but with a rectangular *enceinte*, buttressed with half-round towers. Within this great enclosure, which itself stood within a larger compound wall, there stands a palace complex on four floors, with reception courts, mosque and individual living quarters. It probably dates from the late eighth century and could well have been built by Isa ibn-Musa, dispossessed nephew of the caliph.

above
The Hall of the Ambassadors in the Alcahazar at Seville, datable to 1366, the Christian (Mudejar) period.

Early in the ninth century the caliphs established a new capital on the Tigris, well above Baghdad at Samarra. The city spread some 16 kilometres (10 miles) along the riverbank and reached a maximum width of 2·5 kilometres (1½ miles). Palaces, mosques and residential areas were built on a scale far greater than anything previously attempted in Islam and much of the work was in mud brick and rubble. The Great Mosque of Samarra (897) takes its name, al-Malwiya, from its distinctive minaret, a tall

tower wound about by a ramp up which the caliph could ride to a pavilion some 45 m (150 ft) above ground. The minaret was placed centrally on the axis outside the high burned-brick wall which enclosed arcades on three sides and an enormous hypostyle hall, nine aisles deep and 25 aisles wide. Its founder, the Caliph al-Mutawakkil, later built a further suburb to extend the city, and there he erected the mosque of Abu Dulaf, also boasting a spiral minaret on the central axis, with cusped pointed arches, engaged colonnettes and capitals which were bell-shaped.

The two greatest palaces, the Jawsaq al-Khaqani (*c.* 838) and the Bulkawara (*c.* 860), provide an important contrast and express a growing withdrawal and defensive outlook in the caliphate. The first is a veritable township, centred upon formal courts and imposing buildings which coalesce through lesser courts irregularly to merge with the adjacent streets in the town. The latter is a regular square *enceinte*, constructed on precise cross-axes, with courtyards on each and surrounded by a buttressed outer wall.

But amid all this grandeur it is one small and isolated building which left the most significant mark upon the architecture of Islam – the Qubbat as-Sulaibiyya (*c.* 880), a small, domed tomb. Its square chamber set in an octagonal body was surrounded by a single-storey octagonal ambulatory, originally tunnel-vaulted. Poorly conceived structurally and, until a recent reconstruction, in total ruin, the Qubbat as-Sulaibiyya has had as significant an effect upon Islamic architecture as the Dome of the Rock, which it appears to emulate on a smaller scale, for this building is the prototype Muslim tomb.

The Abbasid Empire was too extensive to be coherent, even though it embraced only eastern Islam. While the caliphs exerted power effectively over their central provinces, in the outer marches independent dynasties flourished. At Bokhara the Samanid dynasty left an extraordinary mausoleum

103

(c. 900). It is simply a cubic chamber, with slightly battered walls surmounted by a hemispherical dome carried on squinches. Inside and out the entire surface is patterned and fretted with a complex mesh of decorative brickwork, elaborated with carved stucco. The corners of the cube are treated as great colonnettes. Unique as it now is, the composure and perfection of every aspect of its detailing testifies to the existence of a series of buildings of this calibre and quality in the ninth and tenth centuries.

In the ninth century also, the influences of Samarra spread south-westwards into Egypt, carried directly by the governor, Ahmed Ibn Tulun, who in his turn built a new city outside Fostat, the first Muslim capital of Egypt and now part of Cairo. Of this city, al-Qatai, the significant survivor is the Mosque of Ahmed Ibn Tulun, whose spiral minaret proclaims its ancestry in Iraq. Within the mosque, the handling of the stucco decorations, the shape of the windows and the general form are immediately recognized as Iraqi rather than Egyptian, but the influence was assimilated as Ahmed shook off the Abbasid yoke to become independent. The new style was in turn absorbed, to leave its mark upon Egyptian architecture.

From Samarra the caliphs returned to Baghdad. There the second phase was remarkable for a series of great brick buildings, among them the madrasa of an-Nasir (c. 1230) and another madrasa built only a few years later, the Mustansiriyya. Of a similar period are the great brick fortifications, whose finest surviving part, the Talisman Gate, was blown up in 1915. From the late thirteenth century (the Il-Khanid period) there survives the Mosque of the Suk al-Ghazl. All these buildings depend for effect upon carved and patterned brick decoration, and the same is true of provincial examples in Mesopotamia, such as the Mosque of Nur ad-Din at Mosul (1170–72). This taste for rich and elaborate brick patterning, always divided into zones and disciplined by the

above
The north-western arcade of the Mosque of Ibn Tulun, behind which rises the helical minaret set on a square base.

top
Abbasid nilometer, Roda Island, Cairo (9th century): note the pointed arches on niches facing the measuring shaft – centuries before used in Europe.

architectural features, emerged in the Abbasid period. The most important of the early surviving examples is the famous fragment of a vaulted city entrance, the Baghdad Gate at Raqqa, probably of the tenth century.

By the end of the thirteenth century, Abbasid influence can be seen to have contracted to an area centred on Baghdad and to have stabilized its architecture with many of the features that were to become fundamental to the later Muslim styles, using muqarnas vaulting, richly carved and decorated brickwork, two-centred and four-centred pointed arches, cusping, colonnettes, bas-relief calligraphic friezes, crestings and blind-arched arcades. Two late structures at Samarra epitomize this work – the tomb of Imam Dur (late eleventh century), a cubic chamber topped by a muqarnas dome, and the Jisr Harb, a bridge over the great canal, employing four-centred arches and decorated on the parapet with a fine calligraphic frieze in moulded brick.

The Seljuk period
Towards the end of the Abbasid period, in the eleventh and twelfth centuries, the effective power of the caliphs waned over northern Islam, giving way to the overlordship of the Seljuk dynasty. The Seljuks inherited rich techniques of decoration, still to be seen in the stucco arabesques of the mosques on the Iranian plateau, notably at Nain in a very elaborate mihrab bay added to an existing mosque in the tenth century. More than is now apparent, they took over a rich technique of ceramic decoration used to give brilliant points of relief on a decorated surface. They also inherited one very original building form, the multi-faceted tomb-tower with a conical cap, of which there survives the staggering Gunbad-i-Qabus (1007) in northern Iran. From the eleventh to the thirteenth centuries the Seljuks enriched central and southern Asia and the highlands of Turkey with palatial caravanserais, domed mosques, tomb-towers and a new generation of tall, circular, fret-ted minarets. During this period the four-iwan plan assumed fundamental importance. In this plan, each face of the courtyard centres on a major open-fronted recess or iwan.

A prototype that survives is the Friday Mosque at Zavareh (1135–36). In this example, unequal iwans front the courtyard and behind the largest rises serenely a high pointed brick dome. At Ribat-i-Sharaf there survives an early twelfth-century caravanserai whose inner courtyard is similarly based on the four-iwan plan. The patterned brick facade employs another standard element of later Persian architecture – the pishtaq – an arch set within a rectangular panel. Such arches were frequently surrounded by a great calligraphic frieze. They dominated

right
The tomb tower (or gunbad) of Sultan Qabus in north-east Iran. Built in 1007, it is 51 m (167 ft) high.

below
The courtyard of the Great Mosque at Aleppo in Syria. The lower stages of the minaret are of the Seljuk period.

the rhythmically repetitive arcading in which they were embedded.

It was in Iran that the greatest Seljuk domes arose and none greater than those of the rebuilding of the Friday Mosque at Ispahan. There a great brick-domed chamber was set in front of the main mihrab of the mosque behind a deep iwan, and at the extreme opposite end of the axis a royal entrance pavilion was built, originally separate from the mosque, covered also by a high brick dome somewhat smaller than the first. The mosque is famous for the poetic proportions of these twelfth-century chambers.

right
The minaret of Jam in Afghanistan is an outstanding, richly decorated example of 12th-century brick building.

below
The great minaret of the contemporary Qutb Mosque, Delhi, stands isolated outside the enclosure, built in 1197.

India

The cultural impact of Islam upon northern India was less sudden than elsewhere, but by the twelfth century Persian influence was significant and in one building in Delhi, extended several times over a period of two hundred years, the

below
The tomb of Iltutmish, who in 1230 extended the Qutb Mosque, building his sepulchre hard by.

absorption of the Muslim architecture of southern Asia can be traced to the royal courts of India. The complex of the al-Islam Mosque, Delhi, begun in 1197, started with a simple courtyard mosque at its core. Immediately outside this, two years later, was begun an enormous minaret now known as the Qutb Minar. The minaret was symbolic of the emergent dominance of Islam. Rising in five great stages to a height of approximately 76 m (250 ft) and standing on a base 15 m (50 ft) in diameter, it was banded with calligraphic and geometric bas-relief inscriptions.

The body of the minaret is fluted and faceted in the tradition of Persia and Afghanistan. By 1230 a second series of arcades had been thrown around the original mosque and the lateral multi-domed prayer chamber extended. In 1235 an exquisitely-detailed, domed cubical tomb chamber was added, the sepulchre of Iltutmish. Before the century was out, the whole complex was more than doubled in size again. In the early part of the fourteenth century there was begun a colossal minaret which, if finished, would have been three times the size of the Qutb Minar itself.

Egypt

Egypt, meanwhile, existed in something of a separate world. Ibn Tulun had established the independence of the province and founded his own garrison city, al-Qatai. His enfeebled successors were conquered in 969 by a Shia dynasty of Ifriqa (Tunisia), the Fatimids, who rode in from the west to find the first Muslim city, Fustat, smouldering at their feet. They too built a new capital, calling it al-Qahira, which became the medieval Cairo. The great Fatimid Mosque of al Hakim (990–1013) is of the courtyard type with the hypostyle prayer hall carried on lateral arcades, pierced by a central aisle terminating in a minor dome before the mihrab. Emphasis upon the first transverse aisle and the central aisle, marked by a dome at their crossing, is to be traced to the mosques of Tunisia.

The new city was girdled with heavy bastioned walls, built in mag-

nificent stone masonry by architects from northern Syria in the eleventh and twelfth centuries. Under the succeeding Ayyubid dynasty, with its northern connections, Seljuk influence brought the Persian form of the madrasa to Cairo.

above
The citadel of Aleppo, its entrance guarded by a massive gate tower and barbican built in the early 13th century by the Ayyubid dynasty.

top
The prayer hall of the Mosque of al-Ahzar in Cairo. The mihrab is on the left.

ISLAMIC
after the Mongols

The whole of northern Islam was disrupted by the explosive emergence, in the thirteenth and fourteenth centuries, of Mongol and Turkish tribesmen from Central Asia under leaders such as Ghenghis Khan. Initially pagan, they were converted to Islam, but their destructive instincts were not assuaged until the whole intricate system of irrigation in Mesopotamia had been destroyed and the cities and centres of Abbasid government had been razed. In the wake of this catastrophe there grew up in southern central Asia a series of independent khanates, centred on cities such as Balkh, Bokhara, Merv, Samarkand, Khiva, Tashkent and Herat. For the new rulers, predominant among whom was Tamurlane, builders and craftsmen were drawn from the conquered cities and peoples. The emergent Timurid style had all the elements of Persian architecture but nevertheless grew to have a special quality of its own. This, in turn, was transmitted to India and influenced Afghanistan, Iran and Iraq. In Anatolia the rising power of the Ottoman Turks was defeated but within a couple of generations they were again established, creating the foundations of their own remarkable style. Further south the Mamluks of Egypt, who had checked the Mongol advance in Syria, produced a distinctive architecture in Cairo until subjugated by the Ottomans in 1517.

The Central Asian khanates

The greatest of fourteenth-century tombs was built to the south-west of the Caspian Sea by Oljeitu, an independent khan. This high-pointed, double-shelled dome (*c.* 1300), which towers 48.8 m (160 ft) above the plain, stands on an elaborate arcaded octagonal base and was intended originally as an important shrine. To make his capital a focal point of pilgrimage, Oljeitu intended to move here the body of Ali, one of the early followers and successors of the Prophet. Frustrated in this, the building became his own tomb. The exceedingly high quality of its decoration must be seen as a reflection of its intended importance in Islam, while its structural elegance, with its double dome and extensive lower vaulting, demonstrates an impressive mastery of technique by both Timurid and by Mongol builders.

An extraordinary unity pervaded Central Asia in the late fourteenth and early fifteenth centuries. With the discovery of the potential of ceramics, huge buildings were coated largely or entirely in this seductive and glittering material. One of the first of these great buildings was the tomb of Tughtabeg Khatun at Urgench (*c.* 1370), still complete, with its dome and high facade externally sheathed in turquoise glazed briquettes and internally with an intricate tile mosaic. Its

above
The complex ribbed construction of the Tomb of Oljeitu (*c.* 1305) in north-west Iran, now partially restored.

below
The Mosque of Bibi Khanum, Samarkand: the great gateway flanked by minarets was echoed by the iwan before the great dome.

above
The high, bulbous dome of the tomb of
Tamurlane, Samarkand, dominates a
complex which originally included a
monastery and a college.

right
The two nearest tombs, erected for
members of the Timur family, mark one
end of the street of funerary
architecture in Samarkand known as
the Shah-i-Zinda.

high pishtaq fronts an unusual octagonal tomb chamber.

On the Iranian plateau, tile mosaic makes its appearance in the Friday Mosque of Kerman (1350) and in Yazd, in the main chamber of the Friday Mosque (1375). By 1400, Tamurlane's capital, Samarkand, saw rising too fast for its safety a colossal new mosque known by the name of the ruler's wife, Bibi Khanum. In this grandiose building a great entrance portal on a scale never before attempted fronts the four-iwan courtyard, which is surrounded by ranges of domed cross-arcading, four bays deep on the lesser faces, and nine bays deep in the prayer hall.

An urge towards monumentality and self-glorification was apparent in the works of Timurid and Mongol rulers. Tombs abound and many of the large madrasas were built specifically to honour a triumphant ruler. The greatest such complex is that of the Gur-i-Emir, the tomb of Tamurlane at Samarkand. The complex is dominated by Tamurlane's tomb itself, whose high drum now stands unintentionally gaunt above the decayed lower structures. Though much of the decoration has disappeared, the great fluted glazed dome of curious profile survives almost perfectly. The long-repeated legend that Timur was dissatisfied with the dome when he first saw it and ordered it to be made higher may give a clue to the extraordinary high-shouldered contour which set a local fashion.

At Samarkand there also survives an important street of tombs built in the fourteenth and fifteenth centuries, associated with an earlier mosque and madrasa. After the Mongol destructions in the early thirteenth century the Shrine of the Living King (Shah-i-Zinda) was itself rebuilt and in the succeeding hundred years a series of richly decorated domed tombs was built in the vicinity and along the lane leading to the shrine. The tombs are sumptuous, with moulded carved glazed brick and tile mosaic rich with stucco, gold leaf and carved alabaster. Though damaged, the

Shah-i-Zinda remains a rich testimony to the artistry of the era.

The Mamluk period

The period of great Egyptian achievement was from the late thirteenth to the beginning of the sixteenth century under the Slave or Mamluk dynasties. Almost the whole of their architectural endeavour was concentrated upon Cairo, and there the first Friday Mosque, built by Az-Zahir Baybars, was completed by 1270. The prayer chamber in this building is dominated by a greatly enlarged domed pavilion, indicating the growing significance of the dome before the mihrab.

However, in the combined madrasa, maristan (hospital) and tomb of Qala'un (finished about 1286) a much more intricate and condensed building type was evolved. This, and similar madrasas such as that of Sultan Barquq (1386) and Amir Mithqal (c. 1370), enjoy an ebullient display of marble inlay on pavements and on marble wall surfaces enriched with fine muqarnas detailing and fretted skylines.

The sepulchral tendencies of Ancient Egypt reasserted themselves and Mamluk sultans built a series of noble high-domed tombs whose outer surfaces were deeply carved with fretted patterns that lent to their high-shouldered contours an extraordinary richness. Counterpoised beside them, multi-balconied slender minarets took on a distinctive Egyptian profile, terminating in an open pavilion peculiar to Cairo. The architect who built the mausoleum of Sultan Qaitbey (finished 1474) modelled his high iwan-faced courtyards on an already rich tradition, and on a round-shouldered stone cube he contrived a typically high Mamluk dome where ribbing has given way to complex arabesque bas-reliefs. Self-glorification became almost obligatory among Mamluk sultans and emirs from the time of Salar and al-Jawli. To the east of Cairo an immense necropolis grew up at the foot of the Muqattam hills, but in 1517 the Ottoman sultan Selim I conquered the city and the loss of revenues effectively extinguished monumental building in Egypt.

The Ottoman period

The first stages of Ottoman architecture can barely be differentiated from other Anatolian styles heavily dependent on Seljuk precedent but with the establishment of their capital to the west of Constantinople, at Edirne, a distinctive architecture emerged. It is best seen in the Beyazit II Mosque and Hospital (c. 1490). A single great dome, 19.8 m (65 ft) in diameter, roofs the prayer hall and dominates the multi-domed courtyard complex. Built a decade or two earlier on the main hill of Edirne stands the first great mosque with a truly Ottoman quality to it, the Uch Sherefeli. Its prayer hall was dominated by a giant hemispherical dome approximately 24 m (80 ft) in diameter, carried on a hexagonal system of arches. The forecourt, arcaded on

below
The mihrab and mimber in the main prayer hall of the madrasa of Sultan Hasan, Cairo. The tomb can be seen through a grill beyond the mimber.

below
The complex built for Sultan Qala'un in Cairo in the late 13th century is remarkable for its advanced design.

all sides, boasted minarets at each
corner. These features were virtually archetypal, though the
geometry of the plan, in which a
square enclosed both forecourt and
prayer chamber, produced a con-
stricted proportion which Ottoman
architects were later to avoid.

Ottoman sultans trod the heights
of autocratic power. Their
architects and builders were totally
their servants and the standards of
skill demanded were the highest.
The period of greatest achievement
was the sixteenth century, when the
architect Sinan served in succession
Suleyman the Great, Selim II and
Murat III. The fundamental Ottoman concept of a hemisphere set
upon a cube buttressed by half
domes was notably established in
Istanbul by the end of the fifteenth
century in the Mosque of Fatih
(now destroyed), which itself refined the Edirne prototype. The
Fatih Mosque had a single half
dome before the mihrab. It was
followed by the Beyazit Mosque,
where two opposed half domes buttressed the main dome. In Sinan's
great metropolitan mosques – the
Shezade (1545) and Suleymaniye
(1550–57) – the dome buttressed by
two or four half domes achieved a
new and extraordinary perfection in
geometry and size. These great
imperial mosques covered space in
great single vaults, achieving spans
and volumes never before attempted by the architects of Islam. Every
mosque was the centre of an entire
group of buildings of social purpose
– schools, bazaars, hostels, baths,
poor-kitchens, hospitals, oratories
and tombs. The greatest such complex surrounds Sultan Suleyman's
own mosque in Istanbul, the Suleymaniye.

In an ultimate triumph at Edirne, Sinan built for Selim II, between 1569 and 1575, the great perfectly-domed Selimiye, whose shell leaps out across a space 30.5 m (100 ft) in diameter. The dome stands upon a great octagon of columns contained within an outer cube whose galleries effectively form a double wall. At each corner of the cube rise three-balconied slender ribbed minarets, some 73 m (240 ft) high, pencil-slim in proportion and the perfect counterpoint to the great leaden dome. This ultimate peak of Ottoman architecture was never to be exceeded but other domed mosques of Istanbul in the late sixteenth and early seventeenth centuries, the Yeni Valide and Sultan Ahmet, show that little was lost in level of achievement, and even into the eighteenth century that extraordinarily vital and long-lived dynasty continued to produce highly original buildings on the same theme.

A great and peculiar glory of Ottoman architecture in this period is the quality of its decoration. Limestone walls, leaden roofs, cool marbles, gleaming and sumptuous Iznik faience, lustrous windows of carved plaster and brilliantly coloured glass provide a visual quality quite unlike other forms of Muslim building.

Later Persian architecture
The great courts of Persia actively and purposefully rivalled Ottoman achievements. At Ispahan the architects of Shah Abbas produced an extension to the city whose complex geometry of gardens, palaces, canals, bridges and roads culmi-

above left
The perfect proportions of the Mosque of Sokullu Mehmet Pasha built on a sloping site in Istanbul in 1571.

left
Set on a hilltop, the Selimiye Mosque is the crowning point of the city of Edirne. Sinan completed it in 1574.

right
Immensely rich tiled interiors distinguish the Royal Mosque of Shah Abbas, the Masjid-i-Shah, in Ispahan.

nated in a royal square flanked by two mosques and the Ali Kapu, an almost unique royal pavilion combined with a formal entrance to the palace. The square or maydan is an elongated polo ground which terminates in the royal mosque, the Masjid-i-Shah. The entrance portal, flanked by the traditional twin minarets, terminates the maydan like an iwan, and, on an axis swung through 45 degrees to give the correct orientation for the mosque, four iwans front the

below
The 17th-century Sultan Ahmet (or Blue) Mosque in Istanbul is a work of the mature Ottoman style.

below
The Tekkiye, a pilgrimage mosque built in Damascus in the mid 16th century by Sinan, the great Ottoman architect.

below
Provincial Ottoman architecture represented by the mosque of Mohammed-Ali, built on the citadel of Cairo (1830–48).

bottom
The 17th-century mosque built at Ispahan by Shah Abbas required a change of axis to align Mecca and the maydan – the royal polo ground.

mosque courtyard itself, each backed by high tile-covered domes. The whole building is overlaid with an intricate pattern-work of ceramics. Later ages continued the traditions and attempted to emulate them, notably at Mahan, but never with equal success.

The Moghul period

Moghul India continued to be influenced by Timurid Central Asia and subsequently by Iran. Many of its greatest works were of funerary architecture, culminating in the best known of all, the Taj Mahal. In the fourteenth century India had produced a number of notable tombs with a dome set upon a square base or, in the rarer cases, on an octagon surrounded by an octagonal ambulatory. In the fifteenth century a higher and squarer profile is seen, reaching perfect proportions under the Moghuls, in the tomb of Humayun (1565). This, one of the first marble domes in India, stands on a cubic base set in a reticulate network of gardens. At Lahore, by contrast, the Emperor Jehangir was buried in a single-storey, widespreading pavilion, similar in plan form but entirely without a dome, boasting a minaret at each corner. The tomb of the Emperor Akbar (1613) at Sikandra, near Angra, is a

above
The Taj Mahal, Agra, built in memory of his wife by the Moghul emperor, Shah Jehan, viewed from the gardens.

above right
The tomb of Humayun, Delhi: built in red sandstone and trimmed with white marble.

right
Built in 1325, the massive battered red sandstone tomb of Ghiyath ad-Din Tughluq reflects the character of the great city walls built at the same period.

multi-stage variant of the same theme, three recessed storeys rising to 30.5 m (100 ft) above the base to form a truncated pyramid. The theme was abandoned by later generations for the simpler and more effective dome-on-cube principle of the tomb of Humayun. The Taj, Shah Jehan's great creation for his wife, which was finished in 1654, was the focal point of a series of gardens by the riverside, in which the centralized tomb, sheathed in near-white marbles, confronts red sandstone pavilions. Deep iwans indent its cubic base and lead to the central chamber over which rises the double-shelled, slightly bulging dome. Minarets stand on the corners of a plinth, respectfully detached. Paths, borders, canals and banks of trees complete the formal seclusion within the walls of the compound. A similar tomb faced in black marble was to have been built on the opposite bank of the river, and the two were to have been linked by a bridge.

The mosques of the subcontinent vary considerably. Some are small and jewel-like adjuncts to great palaces, such as the pearl mosques at Agra and Delhi. A particularly perfect example was built as a private oratory for the Emperor Aurangzeb. The six-domed prayer hall of this highly finished white marble building reflects, in its curves and wide eaves, the downward sweeping shapes of the architecture of Bengal.

Mosques destined for the use of large congregations rather than the private and secluded prayers of emperors include the Royal or Friday Mosque at Delhi (finished 1658) and the Badshai Mosque at Lahore (finished 1673). In each a powerful entrance portal dominating great flights of steps leads to a wide courtyard whose prayer chamber carries three bulbous domes, the central dome before the mihrab being substantially larger than its fellows. At Fatehpur Sikri the Emperor Akbar built after 1570 a royal mosque to serve his new capital. A triumphal gate was added to its south face in 1596. Here too a triple-domed widespreading prayer hall dominates a courtyard of enormous proportions. Within the courtyard stands the exquisite tomb of Shaik Salim Chisti, marble-domed and surrounded by pierced marble screens of great intricacy, with elaborately bracketed marble eaves.

The city of Fatehpur Sikri was built as an extended palace complex in the second half of the sixteenth century, in the deep red sandstone of the Agra region. It is an interlacing system of courtyards, providing for all the ceremonial and working functions of the sultan's court and entourage. A curious central building is the throne room, the Diwan-i-Khass. The throne stands isolated in space, both vertically and horizontally, being carried in the central void of the chamber on the top of a pier reached by four bridges. Other palaces are concentrated in the great citadels occupied by the emperors.

The architecture of the great Moghul emperors is distinguished by sumptuous detailing on a scale beyond the contemplation of other Muslim rulers, even the Ottomans.

Distinctive techniques include the extensive use of very delicate inlays of precious stones in marble with complementary carving in bas relief and jali work – pierced carved stone or marble screens of extraordinary perfection. Much of the quality of Moghul architecture derives from the handling of external spaces, which are manipulated and controlled as though they were rooms. The integration of inner and outer spaces in Moghul palace architecture is both remarkable in itself and a reflection of a way of life befitting the climate.

Of the many less than royal buildings aimed at service to the community, the mosque of the Wazir Khan at Lahore (1634) is outstanding. Faced in an intricate and vivid display of mosaic tilework and dominated by tall but chunky minarets at each corner of its courtyard, the building has something of the power if not the detailing of Timurid Central Asia.

Like many Islamic gardens, those of Moghul India depend greatly upon their buildings. The enclosed paradise of water, greenery and pavilions, arranged on formal axes, reaches perfection in the Shalimar Gardens of Lahore (1633–43). Built on three levels, linked by cascades, the architect placed greater emphasis than usual upon water and fountains. Causeways cross the pools and the centrepiece is an island of carved marble, a throne room on water, linked by four bridges to the surrounding walkways. Even the cascades are surmounted by marble pavilions.

above
The horizontality of much Moghul architecture is nowhere better expressed than in the Palace of Akbar, Fatehpur Sikri.

below
The Badshai Mosque, Lahore (late 17th century), was an imperial foundation attached to the ruler's residence.

HINDU

For more than two thousand years Hinduism has dominated much of Asian civilization. Extending beyond India to mainland South East Asia and the Indonesian archipelago, Hinduism has had a profound influence upon the architectural traditions of these countries. Many different beliefs and practices are embraced by it, from the most abstract philosophical speculations to the simplest rituals of protection and fertility; they are bound together by a cultural cohesion that is ultimately Indian in origin.

The characteristic artistic expression of Hinduism is the temple. Providing a focal point for both the social and spiritual life of the community, the Hindu temple operates as an essential link between the world of man and the world of the gods. It is a setting for rituals of worship, an expression of the power of its patron and an embodiment of the greatest artistic and technical resources of its time. The temple is adorned with images of cult divinities as well as incorporating into its layout and forms a symbolism which is profoundly and fundamentally cosmic.

Within the temple religious activities are undertaken on behalf of an individual, a family, a community or even an entire population. Education, celebrations of birth, marriage and death, and performances of sacred drama, dance and music also take place within the temple, which therefore functions as the centre of religious, intellectual and artistic life. However, the temple is also the product of a desire to transcend the world of man: the principles of its construction, the images on its walls and the rituals it shelters are all aimed at spiritual liberation.

Symbolism

The Hindu temple is the temporary residence of the gods among men. As such, it is intended to resemble the sacred mountains and caves favoured by divinities. Temple towers are known as 'peaks' and are sometimes named after mythological mountains – the Kailasa mountain of Shiva, for example. It is no accident that rock-cut architecture with its cave-like environment represents the earliest phase of Indian temple architecture. Throughout Hindu temples both mountain and cave images are present. The interior room housing the image of the god to whom the temple is dedicated is the 'womb chamber'; it is confined and unlit, like a cave. The summit of the tower generally coincides with the centre of the sanctuary beneath and is tiered, clustered or curved, according to the regional stylistic interpretations of the mountain image. Linking these cave and mountain images is an invisible axis of great significance, identified with the great cosmic mountain or

above
Imitating a free-standing construction, the 8th-century Kailasa Temple, Ellora, recreates Shiva's cosmic mountain.

central axis of the universe. Sometimes this axis appears above the tower as a small finial, the climax of the building and an emblem of perfection and enlightenment.

The temple plan has a particular importance; it is regulated by a geometrical configuration, the mandala, symbolizing the pattern of the cosmos and the process of its creation. The temple mandala usually consists of a central square around which are positioned other squares in a variety of concentric arrangements. The mathematical nature of the mandala indicates a subtle geometry which permeates both the elevation and interior space of the temple, providing an important symbolic connection with the mathematical nature of the universe itself. Thus the temple is considered to be an image of the cosmos. Even the time of its construction is fixed by astrological calculations.

Sometimes specific cosmic myths are incorporated into temples. Angkor Vat in Cambodia is surrounded by a gigantic moat spanned by a bridge with serpents as balustrades. These represent the serpent Shesha wrapped around Mount Meru, which rises out of the cosmic ocean at the beginning of creation.

Ritual

Worship within the temple consists of treating the image of the god or goddess as a royal person. The image is awakened, dressed, fed, entertained and venerated at particular times of day; once a year it may be publicly displayed in temple festivals. Only Brahmin priests can approach the god and thus temples have confined sanctuaries; congregational space, where provided at all, is generally a columned hall or open porch. It is here that performances of sacred music and dance take place. An essential rite of worship is the act of walking around the image in a clockwise direction. This circumambulation takes place within the temple in an enclosed passageway, or outside the building in a courtyard. Appropriate divine images are positioned along the route. Before circumambulation, the priest or devotee has to approach the sanctuary – from well-lit, open and large spaces there is a progression towards dark, confined and small spaces. In festivals, when mobile temples or chariots are utilized, rituals of circumambulation and progression are performed outdoors. Royal ceremonies are also

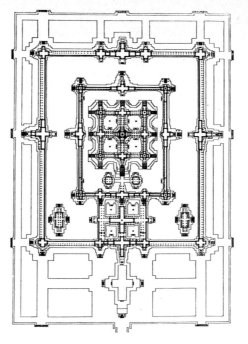

above
Moats, gateways, colonnaded corridors, staircases and sanctuaries: the complex symmetry of Angkor Vat (12th century).

an important part of temple ritual with a particular emphasis on procession through corridors, colonnades and doorways.

Patrons and craftsmen

Royal patrons play a significant role in the construction of large-scale temple projects, generally in stone. Building temples enhances the prestige of the ruler and is even sometimes a method of legitimizing claims to power. Temple inscriptions often record the name of the founder, and certain temples and rulers even share the same name, suggesting an identification of the temple god with the temple patron. This is particularly explicit in South East Asia, where temples often function as royal commemorative monuments. Angkor Vat is actually a mortuary temple; the circumambulation carried out within its corridors always proceeded in an anticlockwise motion, indicating a ritual 'descent' into the underworld.

Techniques

The earliest stone temples in India preserve many details which indicate a vanished timber architecture (with curved and vaulted roofs, cir-

cular windows and carved door frames), but it is in stone that Hindu architecture developed its most characteristic expression. The technique is that of dry masonry with flat or sloping roof slabs supported on columns, capitals and beams. Corbelling is also utilized, especially for the hollow towers rising above temple sanctuaries. Brick construction is rare and here arches and even domes are sometimes found. In Nepal, Kerala and Bali, all areas with heavy rainfall, timber roofs with sloping and diminishing tiers appear. Wooden beams and brackets are skilfully concealed behind sloping thatched or tiled roofs.

Carving lies at the very root of Hindu architecture and temples are usually elaborately ornamented with mouldings and images. Temples are often conceived as solid monoliths which require sculpturing and there even exist true monolithic temples, the most celebrated being the Kailasa Temple at Ellora. Massiveness is a general feature of Hindu temples and is essentially linked to the twin symbolic images of mountain and cave. Considerable virtuosity is found in the manipulation of carved mouldings and in the play of light and shade on building surfaces.

Stylistic development in Hindu temple architecture is often at variance with a distinct technical and conceptual conservatism, though evolution within well-defined architectural formulae does occur – such as repetition of the same architectural element on different scales and increasing elaboration of surface decoration. These tendencies are especially evident in large temples constructed between the ninth and sixteenth centuries, the period of greatest economic and political power for many Hindu kingdoms.

North India

From the fifth and sixth centuries AD up to the thirteenth and fourteenth centuries, the period of Islamic invasions, the northern part of India fostered a distinct temple type. Characteristic is the small

square sanctuary, usually with an ambulatory passageway, adjoining an open porch with balcony seating. The elevation of the temple is divided into three parts – an elaborately moulded base, numerous sculpture niches on wall projections and a towering superstructure. The tower has a curved profile and is surmounted by a finial in the shape of a ribbed fruit and pot. Inside the temple, columns with inclined brackets are finely carved and ceilings are often corbelled in rich designs; doorways are decorated with a host of protective and magical motifs.

Continuing the rock-cut traditions of the Buddhists, Hindu cave-temple architecture first appeared in the sixth century, as at Elephanta and Badami, both in the Deccan. Though the interiors of these cave-temples are massive, delicate ornamentation is richly applied to columns, brackets and ceilings; of great importance are the deeply carved sculpture panels. The shrine is set into the back wall (Badami) or is detached (Elephanta).

The earliest free-standing Hindu temples, as at Deogarh (sixth century) in central India, are now mostly ruined: their small chambers probably had curved superstructures and ambulatory passageways. But it is not until the seventh- and eighth-century temples at Aihole, in the Deccan, that these schemes became clear. Here, in the Hucchappayya Temple, the division between towered sanctuary, enclosed hall and open porch with bal-

above
By the 17th century, as at Madurai, south Indian temple towers are massive and crowded with heavenly beings.

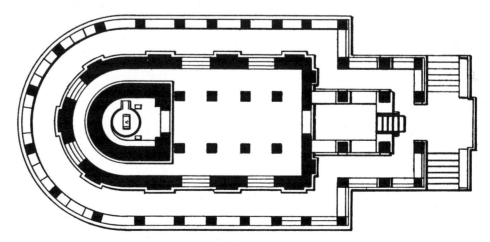

right
Unusually apsidal-ended, the Durga Temple, Aihole (8th century), derives from rock-cut Buddhist architecture.

cony is evident. In the Durga Temple, at the same site, this formula is adapted to an unusual apsidal-ended design, imitating earlier Buddhist sanctuaries. An open passageway surrounds the Durga Temple, in which richly carved wall panels are located, and the temple is raised on a high plinth.

In Orissa a particularly spectacular evolution in temple style took place between the ninth and fourteenth centuries. The hall of the Mukteshvara Temple, one of the earliest monuments at Bhubaneshwar, has pierced stone windows and a tiered roof; the sanctuary has a curved superstructure with intricately carved window-like motifs and an enlarged ribbed finial. In the nearby eleventh-century Rajarani Temple the walls have multiple projections with carved deities, while the slightly later Lingaraja Temple

right
The temple superstructure as the mountain of the gods: the Kandariya Mahadeo Temple at Khajuraho (11th century).

left
Curved and clustered towers are typical
of north Indian temples, as at
Khajuraho (Lakshmana Temple, 10th
century).

above
Every surface of the open columned hall
of the Surya Temple at Modhera (11th
century) is richly carved.

has its superstructure decorated with miniature repetitions of the principal tower. The climax of the series occurs at Konarak, where the ruins of the thirteenth-century Surya Temple are found. Here the myth of the sun-god, to whom the temple is dedicated, is given visible expression and the base of the temple is carved with wheels and erotic subjects. In front of the sanctuary is an open dancing pavilion, the base of which is ornamented with innumerable dancers and musicians.

At Khajuraho in central India another large group of northern-styled temples were built in the tenth and eleventh centuries. The Vishvanatha and Kandariya-Mahadeo temples position the sanctuary and ambulatory passageway at the end of a columned hall and porch; the interior is lit by open balconies. Over the hall and porch rise tiered roofs culminating in the great curved tower above the sanctuary. The typical mountain-like silhouette of these temples is created by the cluster of miniature towers around the central mass. The deep hollows of the balconies, the overhanging eaves and the richly moulded high bases are features of this style. The eleventh-century Surya Temple at Modhera represents the greatest achievement of the northern-type temple in west India.

South India

Temple architecture in south India is continuous in its development and the Deccan and Tamil Nadu preserve countless examples from all periods. The earliest temples date from the seventh century, as at Mahabalipuram, where a remarkable group of monolithic temples is found. These display well the typical south Indian style – walls are divided by pilasters and sheltered by curved eaves; superstructures rise in diminishing tiers, copying the wall systems beneath, and there are square or octagonal roofs above. Barrel-vaulted roofs are also found. This style is exemplified in the delicate towers of the twin sanctuaries of the eighth-century Shore Temple at Mahabalipuram.

The next stage in the development of the south Indian temple is seen in the Virupaksha Temple at Pattadakal and in the monolithic Kailasa Temple at Ellora, both in the Deccan. In these eighth-century Shiva temples the sanctury is enclosed in a rectangular courtyard with a detached pavilion for the bull mount of Shiva, various minor shrines and gateways. The walls are greatly elaborated with numerous sculpture niches, and animal reliefs adorn the bases.

By the eleventh century the south Indian temple had reached gigantic proportions, as in the pyramidal tower of the Brihadeshvara Temple at Tanjore. Pilasters in two tiers frame numerous panels on the walls beneath. The temple is surrounded by a complex of structures including a brass column, stone altars and a towered gateway with carved door guardians. In fact, it was the gate-ways of the temple that now evolved independently. In the sixteenth-century Pampati Temple at Vijayanagara, for example, the gateway tower is larger than the tower above the sanctuary. At Srirangam, the fourteenth- to sixteenth-century Vishnu Temple consists of a number of concentric rectangular enclosures with gateways in the centre of each side. The gateways are surmounted by towers with curved profiles and barrel-vaulted roofs. Countless images of divinities crowd the ascending storeys, suggesting a heavenly pantheon. The seventeenth-century Minakshi Temple at Madurai is one of the largest of the south Indian walled temple complexes. It has four towered gateways leading into a labyrinth of columned halls, colonnaded corridors, and sanctuaries.

left
The tower of the Brihadeshvara Temple, Tanjore (11th century), is conceived as a massive pyramid.

right
Triple-shrined Keshava Temple, Somnathpur (13th century), is a regional variation of the south Indian style.

below
Minakshi Temple, Madurai: the typical south Indian temple plan with sanctuaries, columned halls, corridors and tanks in a walled enclosure with towered gateways.

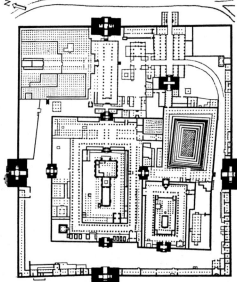

Himalayan valleys, Kerala and Bengal

These high-rainfall regions developed unique building styles, and inclined roofs arranged in ascending tiers are typical of temples in Nepal and Kerala. The Dattatreya Temple at Bhadgaon in Kathmandu Valley, for example, probably dating from the seventeenth or eighteenth century, has inclined carved brackets supporting overhanging roofs. The brick core is inset with carved timber doorways and windows. The stone temples of Kashmir, dating back to the ninth century, have sloping gables in imitation of timber roofs, as in the small Shiva Temple at Pandrethan. The additional influence of Hellenistic architecture can be seen in the use of Corinthian pilasters. Also of interest are the brick temples of Bengal, mostly dating from the seventeenth and eighteenth centuries. Often imitating mud and thatch huts with curved roofs, Bengal brick temples are adorned with terracotta sculpture which sometimes covers the entire wall surface.

Java and Bali

As early as the eighth century stone temples were built in central Java. On the Dieng Plateau several of these early examples are clearly of Indian origin. Typical is Chandi Bhima with its square sanctuary, sculpture niches on the outer walls and tiered tapering tower. The largest Javanese Hindu temple is the great complex known as Larajonggrang at Prambanan, possibly built in the ninth century. Here, three sanctuaries dedicated to the triad of Hindu divinities – Shiva, Vishnu and Brahma – are set in a vast enclosure, together with accessory shrines for the animal mounts of the gods. The principal Shiva sanctuary is surrounded by an open ambulatory passageway with epic myths carved on the walls. Above

right
The central Shiva Temple, Prambanan (Java, 9th century), incorporates stupalike finials in its tapering superstructure.

left
The roofs of pagoda-style temples in the
Kathmandu Valley are supported on
wooden brackets (Patan, 17th century).

below
South Indian temple towers are
pyramids of masonry capped by
octagonal roof forms: an early example,
the Shore Temple, Mahabalipuram
(8th century).

rises the tower in a complex of storeys, finials and cornices arranged in a tall pyramidal mass. Base mouldings, doorways and walls are all richly carved with ornamental motifs and above the doorways are protective monster masks.

Bali preserves to the present day an unique Hindu culture, and temples are still being erected. A typical Balinese Hindu temple consists of several towers with thatched sloping roofs above small wooden sanctuaries. In important temples the number of roof tiers is increased so that the towers become exceedingly slender, as in the 'mother temple' at Besakih on the slopes of the volcano Gunung Agung. Enclosure walls surround Balinese temples, often arranged in a number of courtyards on different levels and connected by narrow gateways. These gateways are mostly of brick and stone with carved decoration, especially monster masks; sometimes there is no lintel, the gateway being open to the sky.

Cambodia

Between the ninth and twelfth centuries the ancient kings of Cambodia constructed a number of large-scale Hindu temples. Typical of these great complexes is the uni-

left
Balinese temples with thatched roofs and carved stone guardian-figures are decked out at festival times.

right
Triangular pediments and turned window bars clearly betray timber origins (Banteay Srei Temple, Angkor, 10th century).

below
Five shrines crown the elevated terraces of the Pre Rup Temple at Angkor (10th century).

132

fication of small structures by axial planning and the use of tiered platforms and moats of water. At Roluos, the Bakong Temple was erected in the ninth century as the king's own private shrine. The sanctuary is located at the summit of five square ascending terraces, reached by staircases in the centre of each side, and has a pyramidal superstructure with flame-like motifs at the corners. Above the doorways are carved lintels and mythological panels. Pre Rup, one of the first mature temple projects at Angkor and dating from the tenth century, essentially preserves the same scheme but adds small shrines at the corners of the upper terrace and flanking the staircases. This is probably the first temple at Angkor used as a ruler's permanent shrine.

The temple of Banteay Srei, not far from Angkor and also belonging to the tenth century, represents one of the finest achievements of the Cambodian temple tradition. Three small shrines are arranged in a row, elevated on a terrace and surrounded by concentric enclosure walls with gateways. Above the doorways are triangular pediments intricately carved with narrative myths. Windows have stone bars and corbelling is freely employed to vault interior spaces.

Undoubtedly the masterpiece of the whole series, and indeed one of the most remarkable of all Hindu structures, is the twelfth-century Temple of Angkor Vat. Not only a sanctuary for the god Vishnu, it also served as a mortuary monument for its royal founder. The central part of the temple consists of an elevated complex of five shrines, reached by steep flights of steps and linked together by colonnades. The towers surmounting these shrines are combined into a dramatic external elevation focused upon the central and highest shrine. The temple is approached by an extended platform and road flanked by a balustrade fashioned into the body of a serpent. The extensive sculpture carried along the walls of the inner colonnades depicts episodes from Hindu epics, various gods, goddesses and guardian figures, as well as the life of the founder king. Hindu symbolism, mythology and ritual are here given an unique architectural expression.

The sanctuary of the god Vishnu and the mortuary chamber of the temple's royal founder (Angkor Vat, 12th century).

BUDDHIST

The pervasive power of Indian Buddhism has had an enormous impact upon the religion and way of life of people throughout Asia. Particular architectural forms were developed in which the Buddha was at first commemorated and then worshipped, his teachings studied and the order of Buddhist monks housed.

Preaching in north India at the beginning of the sixth century BC, the Buddha revealed a new doctrine in which he analyzed the source of all unhappiness and proposed the Noble Eightfold Path to ultimate liberation – nirvana. By the third century BC, during the reign of Emperor Ashoka, Buddhism had become a distinct religion and, associated with kingship and imperial rule, came to be exported to other parts of Asia. During the following centuries the Buddha was transformed into a divine being; the notion of a saviour, or Bodhisattva, also became extremely popular, especially in Mahayana Buddhism, which flourished in north India, the Himalayas and, eventually, the Far East.

But Buddhism was not to survive in India and by the ninth and tenth centuries AD there was a definite decline; however, Buddhism was still alive on the peripheries of the subcontinent – the Himalayas, Burma and Sri Lanka – as well as in Thailand and Cambodia in the mid-twentieth century.

Commemoration and worship

At the sites in north India associated with the life of the Buddha a funerary architecture rapidly developed as it was believed that the ashes and relics of the master required a monumental setting. Buddhist architecture drew upon the earlier practice of creating hemispherical mounds. Later, these mounds, or stupas, were erected at sites not directly connected with the life of the Buddha or his followers, but the association survived and stupas functioned symbolically as a commemoration of the life and teachings of the master. Sculpture and painting depicted significant events from Buddha's life, and particular emblems such as the lotus, the wheel, the trident and the tree served as reminders of the fundamental principles of his teachings.

Buddhism is essentially devotional in character and makes prominent use of the dynamic ritual of circumambulating a sacred object in a clockwise direction. This explains the preference for circular and apsidal-ended buildings. There is also the need to house a congregation in which no movement is necessary but for which a sacred object or image provides a focus.

Architecture was used to promote the spread of Buddhism and there is often a striving for monumentality, particularly in the use of permanent building materials. Under Ashoka, stupa worship was encouraged as part of a policy of using Buddhism as an instrument of imperial unity. Architecture also provides a setting for an art which is fundamentally didactic in character, aimed at both the devotee and the newly converted. Considerable building activity is sometimes concentrated at sites suitable only for retreat and meditation. There is also significant emphasis on centres of learning where Buddhist doctrines are taught, and some north Indian universities were celebrated throughout Asia.

Mounds, temples and monasteries

Beyond their original funerary function, stupa mounds were invested with an elaborate symbolism as they developed into objects of veneration and sanctity. The stupa symbolizes the death and ultimate enlightenment of the Buddha at a time when the Buddha himself was not yet worshipped or depicted in sacred art. The ceremonies determining the orientation of the stupa and the system of proportions fixing its dimensions indicate a definite cosmic symbolism, possibly pre-Buddhist in origin. The solid hemispherical mound or dome is identified with the dome of heaven enclosing the cosmic axis, revealed by the mast with umbrellas protruding from the summit of the mound; the tier of umbrellas indicates the ascending layers of heaven. Circumambulation is performed around the stupa, the devotee tracing the course of the sun through the heavens. The route is defined by a path and also by a railing, sometimes with gateways positioned at the four points of the compass, as at Sanchi in central India.

The architectural evolution of the stupa concentrates on the development of the drum and moulded base (sometimes with flights of steps leading to open terraces), the subtle alteration of the curvilinear profile of the mound, the introduction of niches on four sides housing Buddha images and the extension of the finial above. Stupas often become the focal point in a complex of structures or, in miniature form, crowd around a central mound or shrine.

Buddhist temples function as sanctuaries where rituals of worship take place, generally concentrated upon a stupa model or Buddha image, sometimes both. Circumambulation is frequently combined with congregational worship and temples are also associated with commemorative and residential structures in a complex of buildings. An important architectural element is the free-standing column. First used by Ashoka for royal edicts and religious proclamations, the column is also identified with the cosmic pillar, the support of the heavens.

Monasteries generally consist of rows of small cells around a hall or courtyard used for teaching purposes. In more elaborate examples a shrine is introduced for congregational worship. Kitchens, cisterns and storage spaces are also sometimes incorporated.

Indian stupas

One of the oldest stupas still standing is that at Sanchi, originally founded by Ashoka but enlarged many times, particularly in the first century AD. It is a simple stone hemisphere at the summit of which is a small square railing enclosing a mast with umbrellas. Two circumambulatory pathways around the stupa have similar railings, stone imitations of wooden posts and rails; the upper pathway is reached by a double flight of steps whereas the lower one is entered through four gateways. Each gateway has

right
A stupa forms the focus of the Karli Temple; timber ribbing and carved columns rhythmically articulate the interior.

bottom
Railings in stone, imitating timber forms, surround the two pathways of the hemispherical stupa at Sanchi.

below
The Great Stupa, Sanchi (1st century BC to 1st century AD): its plan is actually a cosmic diagram.

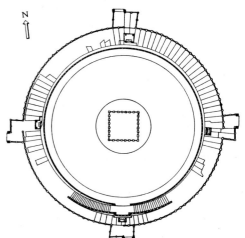

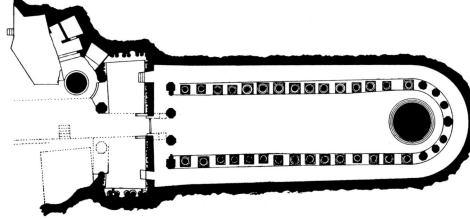

above

The columns of the apsidal-ended
excavated Karli Temple (1st century
BC to 1st century AD) create a 'nave'
and side aisles.

tive divinities and auspicious emblems. Outside the south gateway
once stood a column with an Ashokan inscription and the characteristic inverted lotus and lion capital
(the finest example is at Sarnath in
north India, where Buddha had
preached his first sermon).

Other early stupas introduce a
cylindrical drum on which the
hemisphere is raised, as in the stupa
models within the rock-cut halls at
Bhaja and Karli in the Deccan (first
century BC to first century AD). At
Karli the stupa drum is provided
with a carved band imitating posts
and rails, and the mouldings at the
summit of the hemisphere proceed
outwards in an inverted pyramid.
The original timber parasol on a
mast is still preserved.

two posts, with inverted lotus and
animal capitals, supporting three
successive lintels interlocking with
the posts as if fashioned in timber.
The gateways are richly carved with
Buddhist legends, including scenes
from the life of the Buddha, protec-

above
The gateways of the Great Stupa,
Sanchi, are richly carved with motifs
including the wheel, trident and lotus –
important Buddhist symbols.

Over the following centuries the stupa in India underwent a variety of transformations. In the north-west and in the valleys of the Hindu Kush, as at Taxila and Swat, numerous stupas were erected between the second and fifth centuries. The stepped square bases of these stone stupas are decorated with plaster niches often housing Buddha images: Corinthian-styled pilasters and classical base mouldings are freely utilized, testifying to a distinct Hellenistic influence. However, only stone models give an idea of the slender pyramids of ascending umbrellas that once surmounted these stupas.

During the same period in south India, at Amaravati and Nagarjunakonda, brick stupas are provided with elaborately carved limestone railings. Some of the carved panels on these railings depict the stupas as they must have once appeared – hung with lotus garlands, approached by impressive gateways and accompanied by tall columns supporting sun discs. An unusual feature of these stupas is their construction, utilizing concentric rings of brickwork with connecting 'spokes'.

In north India stupas were also erected, especially from the fifth century onwards, at such sites as Sarnath. Contemporary with that example are the monolithic stupa models inside rock-cut shrines at Ajanta in the Deccan. Cave 19, for example, has a stupa with a large sculpture niche at the front; the drum is divided into moulded base and cylindrical shaft with pilasters. Rising above the hemisphere, now considerably diminished in proportion, are ascending umbrellas.

Nalanda, in east India, is one of the most important sites of the last phase of Indian Buddhism. The great stupa (eighth to ninth century) consists of a central brick mass elevated on a platform, now unfortunately ruined. Better preserved, however, are the four miniature stupas decorated with plaster positioned at each corner. These are divided into storeys by horizontal mouldings and have sculpture niches flanked by pilasters.

Indian temples and monasteries

The earliest Buddhist temples were timber structures with barrel-vaulted roofs and apsidal plans, but only rock-cut copies have survived. The excavated halls, known as chaityas, at Bhaja and Karli in west India have stupa models at the ends of their apsidal plans. Columns distinguish a central 'nave' from side 'aisles' and ribbing on the barrel vault indicates the original curved timbers. At Bhaja there is no outer facade, but at Karli three doorways are surmounted by a large horseshoe-shaped window. The outer porch at Karli has carved images and there is a monolithic column of the Ashokan type but with a pot base: the interior columns are of the same type. Examples of later rock-cut shrines occur at Ajanta in the fifth century. Apsidal-ended shrines

139

are also known, built in brick, as at Ter in the Deccan, or with stone columns, as at Sanchi.

Without doubt, the most important Indian Buddhist sanctuary is the Mahabodhi Temple at Bodh Gaya, the site where Buddha gained enlightenment. The present temple probably dates from the fifth or sixth century and consists of a central chamber surmounted by a tall pyramidal tower with straight sides. The tower is divided into storeys by miniature window-like motifs and has a finial consisting of a ribbed fruit motif with umbrellas above. It is elevated on a high platform with four smaller towers at the corners. The brick structure provides one of the rare instances of the use of pointed arches in India. The fame of this temple spread well beyond India and thirteenth-century copies are known at Pagan in Burma and Chiengmai in north Thailand.

below right
The monastery at Takht-i-Bahi (2nd and 3rd centuries) groups open cells around a rectangular courtyard.

below
Bodh Gaya, site of Buddha's enlightenment, is dominated by the tapering tower of the Mahabodhi Temple (5th or 6th century).

Indian monasteries, or viharas, follow a standard pattern – small accommodation cells are arranged around an open square or rectangular courtyard at the centre of which may be a stupa or other votive object; the entrance is generally in the centre of one side. Numerous Buddhist monasteries dating from the second and third centuries are found in north-west India – Taxila and Takht-i-Bahi, for example – as well as throughout Afghanistan and Central Asia, along the silk route to China. In later centuries, when some of these regions came under Muslim rule, Buddhist viharas influenced the forms of Islamic madrasas or theological colleges.

Rock-cut monasteries are also to be found, as at Ajanta, where central halls with columns lead to small cells on three sides. The Ajanta viharas are celebrated for their wall paintings, depicting scenes from the past lives of the Buddha. The most famous monastic site in India is the great university at Nalanda, where a series of brick viharas are built close together. Here were taught the different schools of Buddhist philosophy and theology.

The Himalayas

Tradition ascribes the spread of Buddhism into Nepal and the other Himalayan valleys to Ashoka, and it may be that some of the stupas in the Kathmandu Valley were originally founded by him. The stupa at Bodhnath, however, has typical late Nepalese features – a square box-like compartment painted with pairs of eyes rises above a massive hemisphere on a stepped and indented base. These eyes are interpreted as the all-seeing eyes of the supreme Buddha. Above is a slender pyramid with a gold umbrella. The whole is decked with flags and surrounded by a railing on which hundreds of brass prayer-wheels are fixed. Tibetan stupas, or chortens, are simpler in form than Nepalese examples – a bulbous dome set on one or more square bases has a

below
Above the Swayambhunath Stupa in the Kathmandu Valley, a tier of umbrellas: below, the all-seeing eyes of Buddha.

series of umbrellas compressed into a narrow finial tapering to the top.

Buddhist temples in Nepal are often indistinguishable from Hindu temples. Mostly dating from the seventeenth and eighteenth centuries they have brick cores from which project sloping roofs in ascending and diminishing tiers, supported by inclined timber brackets. In Tibet, temples and monastic establishments are massive constructions with tapering whitewashed walls. Only the upper storeys are timber, often with cantilevered balconies. Characteristic are the great wooden posts, the complex system of brackets and beams supporting the inclined roofs and the painted decoration, indicating close connections with Far Eastern architectural traditions.

Sri Lanka

Buddhist architecture here also goes back to the time of Ashoka. The most important examples are found at two royal sites, Anuradhapura and Polonnaruwa, where sacred structures and Buddha images are combined with palace complexes. Stupas, or dagobas, preserve an early form: the massive brick Ruvanveli Dagoba at Anuradhapura has a circular moulded base, a hemispherical mound surmounted by a square box and a narrow mast with umbrella-like ridges.

The tendency to incorporate stupas into temple-like structures is well illustrated in the Wat-da-ge at Polonnaruwa, probably dating from the tenth or eleventh century. Here the dagoba is surrounded by a circular brick wall with a carved stone plinth and entrances on four sides. Each entrance has a flight of stone steps, the first of which is known as a 'moon stone', being semicircular in shape and delicately carved with rows of animals and lotus flowers. The dagoba is raised on a circular platform with an entrance to the north and surrounded by stone columns that once supported the roof.

Temples sometimes take unusual forms in Sri Lanka. The Sat Mahal at Polonnaruwa is built as a solid square brick pyramid with seven diminishing storeys and may be

compared to a similar temple at Lampun in north Thailand. Other temples at Polonnaruwa incorporate gigantic brick and plaster Buddha images, as in the twelfth-century Lankatilaka Temple.

Burma

The most inventive phase of Buddhist architecture in Burma dates from the tenth to thirteenth centuries when Pagan, the capital, was adorned with numerous brick constructions. The Pagan stupa, or pagoda, is distinctive, as is well illustrated by the thirteenth-century Mingalazedi Pagoda. This is elevated on a series of ascending terraces with open walkways, reached

above
The Ruvanveli Dagoba, Anuradhapura (3rd to 11th centuries), shows the traditional stupa form preserved in Sri Lanka.

right
Some Buddhist temples are unusually stepped, as the Sat Mahal at Polonnaruwa in Sri Lanka (12th century).

below
Burmese stupas with tapering finials
are elevated on stepped terraces:
Mingalazedi Stupa, Pagan (13th
century).

bottom
A central north Indian styled tower and
smaller pinnacles crown Ananda
Temple, Pagan (11th century).

founder king of temple and city.

It is not until the fourteenth century, with the establishment of Ayudhya as the capital, that Thailand developed a distinctive Buddhist architecture. The many brick stupas, or prachedis, erected at Ayudhya function as shrines for the ashes of Buddhist holy men as well as for kings and other members of the royal household. The typical prachedi has a circular moulded base, an inverted bell-like dome and a tall tapering finial.

by flights of steps in the centre of each side. The stupa has an inverted bell profile and out of the hemisphere rises the tapering pyramidal mass of the finial, miniature replicas of which appear at the corners of each terrace. It was once covered with plaster decoration.

Temples at Pagan generally utilize towers derived from north Indian Hindu structures as surmounting finials and miniature pinnacles above a number of ascending and diminishing storeys. Open passageways are sometimes also incorporated, as in the twelfth-century Thatbinyu Temple. Here vertically arranged chambers are reached by connecting interior stairways and spaces are covered with pointed vaults. The eleventh-century Ananda Temple has sloping roofs covering a double passageway around a solid brick core with niches housing Buddha images.

Cambodia and Thailand
Only at the end of the Cambodian temple-building tradition was Buddhism adopted by the rulers of Angkor. The Bayon is one of the most complex of the Angkor temples – sanctuaries, connecting colonnades and galleries are here crowded together in an elevated pyramid. Unique is the carving of gigantic masks of the Bodhisattva Lokeshvara on the four sides of each sanctuary tower. Similar heads are repeated on the towers above the entrance gateways of the city, Angkor Thom, at the centre of which the Bayon Temple is located. These are probably portraits of the

above
Chandi Mendut (9th century): the simple sanctuary on a carved basement adopted for Buddhist temples in central Java.

left
18th-century Buddhist temples in Bangkok combine typical spired stupa forms with traditional tiled roofs.

After the eighteenth century important architectural developments took place at Bangkok. Wat Arun illustrates well the new towered-temple concept, the praprang. Here a slender tower, some 74 m (243 ft) high, rises in a gentle curve out of an elaborately moulded base; a walkway surrounds the square shaft, in which small sanctuaries are placed. The finial has a curved top. Also typical of Bangkok Buddhist temples is the imitation of timber architecture. The eighteenth-century Wat Pra Keo Temple has steep gabled roofs, in the vernacular manner, supported on columns and brick walls. The roofs ascend in tiers, the triangular gables being richly carved with royal emblems, and above the crossing rises a high brick tower of the praprang type.

Java
Several remarkable Buddhist temples were erected in central Java in the eighth and ninth centuries and it is here, at the periphery of the Buddhist world, that perhaps the greatest of all Buddhist architec-

left
From the outside Borobudur is a solid mass of masonry: niches contain seated Buddhas.

below
Seventy-two miniature stupas crowd the upper open terraces at Borobudur.

below
Borobudur (9th century) is one of the greatest stupas: three circular terraces and five square galleries combine in an ascending and concentric scheme.

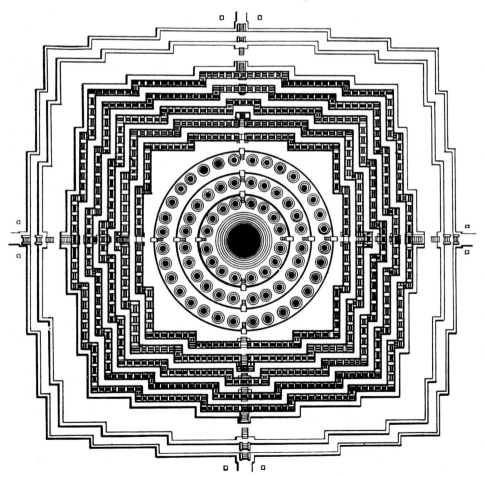

tural concepts, Borobudur, was realized.

Almost nothing is known of the circumstances under which Borobudur came to be erected. This gigantic stupa-temple consists of four enclosed square galleries, with indentations, and three open circular terraces, arranged concentrically in an ascending sequence. Staircases centred on each side ascend to the central stupa, which is the highest part of the temple and the focal point of the whole design.

Ritual movement through Borobudur leads the devotee from enclosed galleries, with carved scenes of the lives of the Buddha and various Bodhisattvas, to the austere forms of the 72 hollow stupas of the open circular terraces. This progression from lower to upper levels, from closed to open spaces, from square to circular forms and from narrative art to simple emblems is invested with great symbolic significance, for Borobudur is actually a sacred mandala, a geometric pattern of the universe given architectural form. The incompletely carved Buddha statue found inside a chamber deep within the central stupa may even be a portrait of a divinized king, the founder of the temple. Borobudur, then, is the ultimate architectural representation of the Buddhist concept of the universe, a definition for the worshipper of his spiritual path towards nirvana, as symbolized by the great central stupa.

CHINESE

The most salient feature of Chinese architecture lies in its continuity, the strength of the tradition. This conservatism is most apparent in the reliance on wood as a building material (with the concomitant structural methods and decoration) and in the plan which is, and has been for centuries, consistent whether the building is a small house, a temple or a palace.

The reliance on wood

The use of wood produced various results, one of which was gradual deforestation, especially of north China. This was particularly acute by the nineteenth century, but by then the Chinese were quite capable of building large, brick-vaulted buildings; the Wu liang dian, of 1381, was a fine example. A move away from timber structures would therefore have been feasible. It did not however take place.

One factor that influenced the use of wooden structures was the earthquake and its effect on building. Much of China is subject to earthquakes and all of China has relatively earthquake-proof wooden buildings. Since their history goes back beyond even Chinese seismological knowledge, the use of wood cannot be ascribed to earthquakes; it is however quite feasible that continuing reliance on timber was reinforced by its relative efficacy in earthquake zones.

Structural reliance on wood has

led to the dominance of trabeate construction, load-bearing walls being almost entirely unknown. In all parts of China this construction method has been used certainly since the Han dynasty (206 BC– AD 220) and probably long before. In the north where the winters are long and cold, the screen walls may be up to 1 m (39 ins) thick; in the south they may indeed be little more than wooden screens, but in all cases they do not support the load of the roof. In construction, after the floor has been prepared,

above
The Garden of Harmonious Interest, Summer Palace, Peking: a lotus pond viewed from lattice verandahs.

the wooden frame of the building is erected, the roof timbers put in place, and then the walls are built.

Aside from structure, the use of wood has given rise to the characteristic decorative features of Chinese architecture, such as lattice windows and the use of colour. Lattice dates back certainly to the second century BC, perhaps earlier, but reaches a peak of perfection in the house-garden complexes of the Song dynasty (AD 960–1276). There, the garden with its rocks and bamboo is seen through delicate wooden tracery in a multitude of designs from sinuous floral patterns to the angular and irregular 'cracked-ice' lattice.

Colour is used in all sorts of Chinese buildings, although the greatest variety of painted decoration appears on palace buildings: red pillars are surmounted by beams painted with landscapes or scenes from literature, which are in turn topped by brightly painted eaves-bracketing. In non-imperial southern garden houses, the use of colour is restrained, restricted to

151

left
Covered walk, Summer Palace. Along
the lake, a mile of brightly painted
verandahs link tiny garden pavilions.

whitewashed walls as a background
to greenery framed in dark red
wooden doors and windows.

The use of colour must have
developed from the practice of coating exposed wooden parts with lacquer to protect them against damp
and insects. Later buildings were
protected in a different way, with oil
washes, lime washes, a coating of
'hemp stuff, brick dust and raw
Tong oil' and then painted, usually
with vermilion. The difference in
the use of colour on imperial and
non-imperial buildings was partly a
matter of expense but was also laid
down in the sumptuary regulations
of each dynasty. These rules explain
the roof colours of Peking, where
low houses with unglazed grey-tiled
roofs surround the yellow-tiled
Imperial Palace (only the emperor
could use imperial yellow) and
green-tiled temple buildings.

Principles of planning

The roof colours of Peking clarify,
too, the layout of the city with the
imperial complex at its centre, surrounded by ordinary dwellings and
shops. Though the existing city was
laid out quite late, in the early
fifteenth century, it represents the
ideal in Chinese town-planning.
The main street runs north to south,
the secondary avenue passing west
to east across the southern gate of
the Imperial City, and all the minor
streets are arranged on a grid
system.

This rigid north–south axiality is
one of the fundamentals of Chinese
planning, together with balance on
either side of the axis and enclosure.
These principles apply to towns
and cities but also to all types of
building. Southwards orientation
appears consistently from as far
back as 6000 BC. At this early
stage, turning buildings towards the

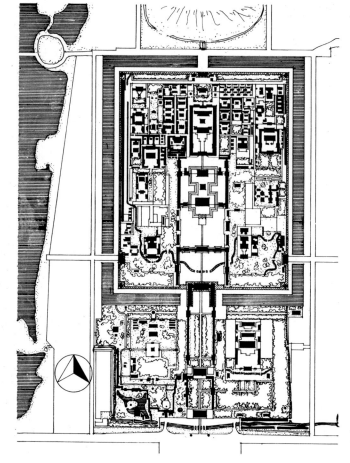

left
Plan of the Forbidden City, Peking: on
a north–south axis, rigidly symmetrical,
the perfect Chinese city plan.

south must have been primarily
practical – to make the most of the
sun's warmth and to protect the
inhabitants against cold winds from
the north. As it was not uncommon
for burials to be similarly oriented,
the south must have achieved a
magical significance, probably for
the same practical reasons.

By the end of the Han period
(second century AD), the system of
feng shui had developed and this
maintained the south-facing orientation and other practical aspects of
building and city planning but overlaid them with mystical significance. The term means 'wind and
water', and the geomancers who
practised feng shui sited buildings
in places where they would harmonize with nature and not upset
the magic forces of a locality. By
consulting special texts and using
the geomantic compass, they could

above
Courtyard in the Summer Palace,
showing regular balance on either side
of the axis of the complex.

below
Ming tombs, Peking. The feng shui
system dictated the site, within
protective, encircling hills.

determine sites of houses, temples, and graveyards. Most of the features of Chinese planning had, however, emerged well before the geomancers took over: the remains of the cities of Shang (*c.* 1500–1027 BC) and Zhou (*c.* 1027–221 BC) reveal axiality, central location of buildings of religious and royal significance and enclosure of the whole.

One of the most striking things about Chinese building is the consistency of the principles underlying the whole range of architecture. A small, private courtyard house represents the city in microcosm: temples, houses and palaces were all built on a north–south axis with openings to the south (not to the north, the source of evil) and with balance to left and right of the axis. As the city wall enclosed Peking, so each small house was enclosed within a wall.

Walking down the narrow side streets of a Chinese city, it is almost impossible to see into courtyards because they are concealed behind walls and even the gate has a 'spirit wall' inside, blocking the view. Spirit walls, free-standing barriers of brick sometimes decorated with coloured tiling, cut-brick work or an auspicious character painted in black on white were originally intended to stop evil spirits from entering. It was believed that they could travel only in straight lines and thus could not get round such an obstruction.

Inside the courtyard (whether it is on the grand scale or that of a single family) the main building (the most sacred part of a temple, the residence of the patriarch in a family house) invariably faces south. On either side are the east and west wings, where less important religious functions are carried out or where less important family members live. As the courtyard is the core of a home or an institution, expansion was carried out by

right
Garden of the Hanshan Temple, Suzhou: the pavilion's upturned eaves, through the moon gate, are typically southern.

adding further courtyards. The rich might have up to 20 linked courts and perhaps devote some space to a garden.

The Chinese garden

The garden was an important part of the Chinese aesthetic. The Chinese have had a very special view of nature for centuries, an ideal developed from Taoism, which held that man should try to become one with nature instead of establishing a rival, human order (the Confucian system). The dream of the educated man came to be that of a retreat into the mountains, to write poetry and paint pictures which represented, for example, the spirit of a bamboo or plum branch. But retreat was clearly an impractical ideal so the scholar-official would content himself with writing nature poetry in his spare time and, perhaps, creating his own landscape in a garden. The Chinese garden is essentially one of concealment and illusion. The aim is to remake nature in miniature, to have little rocks that seem like mountains, pools like lakes: the illusion of size in a tiny space. The garden becomes an urban retreat. The best-known are those in the city of Suzhou, many of which were first laid out in the Song.

It might seem difficult to connect the light and intricate house-and-garden complex of Suzhou with the square grey courtyard of northern Peking, but rocks and plants were important to northerners even if the climate enforced restrictions. It is too cold in Peking for the open lattice, mingling house and garden, but the courtyard was used as much as possible. Almost every one has a tree to provide shade in summer. Even a Peking garden would have its Lake Tai rocks, winding pools and pavilions for looking at the moon or listening to orioles.

Chronological survey

From the Neolithic period onwards, the use of timber as the primary building material has presented problems for the architectural historian. Wood does not survive well and this, together with the fact that archaeology is a relatively new science in China, means that there are gaps in the record which can only be filled by reference to indirect evidence.

The Neolithic period is, however, well represented since the discovery of the village at Banpo (near Xi'an). The remains include 45 house floors with the foundations in sufficiently good condition for the excavators to reconstruct three different house types. The houses were set in a cluster, protected by a ditch (the precursor of the city wall which was to appear by the end of the Neolithic era).

The houses at Banpo were either circular or rectangular in plan, the rectangular plan (the precursor of most later building) being slightly more recent in date. Some of the houses were semi-subterranean, which meant that the roof structure was largely supported on the walls – not as in the other houses by upright timbers. In the ground-level houses, posts were sunk into the ground round the floor area and a post was placed in the centre. The posts supported the roof, which was probably thatched and then covered with mud as a further protection. All the houses were entered from the south and had a fireplace set quite near the entrance.

This pattern was continued in the Shang and Zhou dynasties when, whilst the houses of artisans were built on the same lines as the later houses at Banpo, the greatest development seems to have taken place in grand construction and city planning. At Zhengzhou, one of the Shang capitals, there was a political and ceremonial centre where the royal family lived (as in the central Imperial City of Peking) surrounded by the dwellings of artisans, with the whole city encircled by a high tamped-earth wall. The

houses of the royal family and those of the bronze casters (apparently the aristocrats amongst the artisans) had well-prepared *pisé* or limed floors and stone pillar bases, often carved into animal forms. These stone bases represent an improvement over Neolithic construction as they help to prevent damp damaging the pillars. It is clear that the use of timber posts to support the roof was the primary structural method but we do not know what the roof itself looked like though we begin to find ceramic tiles, in two forms, semi-cylindrical roof tiles and decorated circular end-tiles dating from the middle to late Zhou period, when tiling must have begun to replace thatch in grand building.

As with the preceding period, little remains of Han building apart from floors. It is, however, a period rich in secondary references, and the most useful indicators of architectural development are ceramic. These fall into two categories, both associated with burial. The most dramatic are the models of buildings which were placed in graves to accompany the spirit on its journey to the other world. Small houses, raised granaries, farmhouses with chickens on the roof and dogs in the yard and many storeyed pavilions have been found. Their detail reveals that the Han builders were still using wood and had developed a system of support for projecting eaves by setting brackets on the columns, with the eaves carried on corbels. This may have become necessary because of the greater weight of the now tiled roofs but it is an important step towards what was to become the characteristic Chinese structural system. Roof tiles are clearly indicated on many of the models: semi-cylindrical tiles laid with circular end-tiles at the eaves and decorated with impressed animal designs or auspicious characters, probably designed to protect as well as embellish. The roof ridge was often built up, sometimes with 'owl-tail' raised points at either end, and gabled and hipped roofs are found. Some of the tall

above
Reconstructed Neolithic house, Banpo: wooden columns support the roof as in all later Chinese building.

below
Han tomb model. A terracotta house showing roof tiles, a verandah and bracketing at the top of the columns.

155

right
Stone pailou were set up to
commemorate virtuous widows or at
the entrance to temples and palaces.

pavilions have lattice windows
though this is usually only indicated
as a squared or diamond pattern,
not the lavish and varied designs
later to be found.

The other group of ceramics
relevant to architectural history are
the impressed tomb tiles, used to
line tomb chambers. These sometimes bear designs of buildings. One
brick from Sichuan province shows
a fortified house with a tall gate and
a series of courtyards with wells and
chickens and finally, at the back, in
the deepest part of the complex, a
hall with an open verandah on
which two men sit. The gable end of
the hall reveals clearly the characteristic roof structure of a series of
beams (of diminishing length) set
one above the next, supported on
queen posts with, at the top, a king
post. This stepped structure, seen
here in its simplest form, has been
used as the primary roof system
until the present day. It could be
varied by increasing the number of
beams and posts to heighten the
roof, shortening the posts if a gentle
profile was required and so on.

The columns supporting the roof
formed bays which could be made
into separate rooms by building
wooden screen walls from the front
to back column. The Chinese do not
use the word for room when refer-
ring to building size, employing
instead the word 'jian', which
means the space between two roof
beams. As buildings were not necessarily internally divided, a three-
jian building is not automatically
three-roomed. The most common
constructions were three or five jian
units.

Thus, by the end of the Han, the
basic structure was already established and the earliest projecting
eaves could also be seen. If Chinese
architecture may be viewed as a
linear tradition, unaffected (almost
untouched) by external events or
influences, it was towards the end of
the Han, also, that the only foreign

influence to have any effect on Chinese building was first felt. This was the introduction of Indian Buddhism. As a religion, it was to be most influential in China in the seventh to tenth centuries but it added more permanently to architecture by introducing a concept of permanence and monumentality, particularly in the form of two building types that the Chinese were to make their own, the pagoda and the pailou (memorial arch). Pagodas and pailou were often constructed in durable materials like brick and stone and have consequently survived where contemporary wooden structures have perished.

It is ironic that Tang (AD 618–907) building is better illustrated by survivors outside China than in. The concept of permanence in building introduced with Buddhism from India took better root in Japan, where the temples of Nara were constructed on Chinese models during the Tang. They have since been reconstructed with great

157

reverence for the original so that they give a good idea of what Tang building was like. (See page 169)

In China itself, the earliest surviving wooden building is the main hall of the Fo guang Temple in Shansi province, built during the Tang in AD 857. It was part of an important temple though not a major Tang building. It shows, however, the lightness of line and appreciation of structural parts which were a feature of Tang and Song building. The roof is hipped with a low pitch and the line of the ridge is slightly curved between the ridge end-ornaments and at the eaves. The building has seven bays; the central five in the south wall open with wooden doors so that the

above
The interior of the Temple of Heaven (1420), decorated with the dragon and the phoenix, symbols of the emperor and empress.

right
An Indian form, the pagoda was sinicized: windbells hang from the eaves of a typically Chinese wooden structure.

158

A

B

C

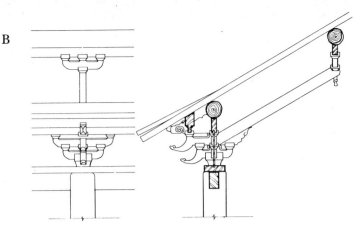

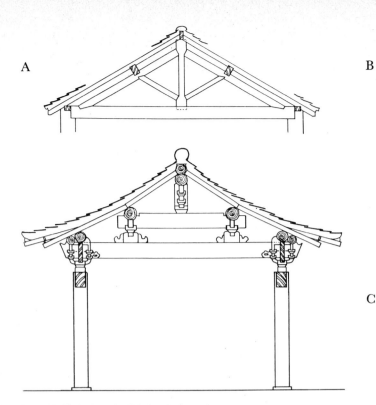

above

Eaves bracketing system:
(A) comparison of the western
triangulated truss and the Chinese
beam frame system which is capable of
extension in all directions; (B) the high
raked bracket, developed to support the
considerable eaves overhang; (C) a
bracket cluster carrying the weight of
the eaves out over the columns.

Buddhist figures inside may be seen from without.

It is the eaves bracketing, the four-tier clusters of cantilever brackets set directly over the columns, that is most characteristically Tang. The brackets are called *ang dou geng*, high or raked brackets. The outermost eaves purlin is carried on a rafter-like member which crosses through the centre of the bracket cluster and is tied back into the interior structure. It is characteristic of Tang and Song design that the bracket tiers set above the columns are not reinforced by a great deal of intermediate bracketing; the points of support are emphatic and decorative. In the later buildings of the Ming (1368–1644) and Qing (1644–1911) dynasties, the eaves overhang was much reduced (as the curve of the eaves line disappeared) and the bracketing system was reduced to an even size running continuously over the beam, creating a horizontal rather than a vertical emphasis.

Two important points of change in the Song were the concentration (especially in the south) on the garden as part of the house and the publication of the *Ying zao fa shi*, a master-builder's manual, in 1103.

159

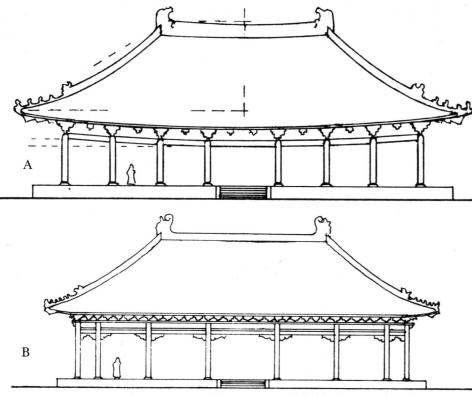

A

B

right
The Temple of Heaven, Peking. Built for imperial sacrifices, it is unusual in plan but typical in constructional methods.

left
Comparison of roof types: (A) Song dynasty hall with lightly upturned eaves, (B) heavier Ming or Qing hall.

below
A mandarin and his son in the courtyard of a Peking house. Lattice windows open onto the private garden.

One of its most important revelations is that the Song builder determined the proportion of internal dimensions on the basis of a part of the bracket system, a modular type of construction.

If Tang and Song building is characterized by an emphasis on structural members and a lightly curving eaves line, the monumental buildings of the Ming and Qing may be said to have gained in majesty by their size whilst they lost that lightness. Bracketing was reduced to a balanced line under the eaves and the roof curve disappeared. All columns were increased in height and girth. Decoration was also increased. False ceilings and external beams were painted brightly with patterns, lotuses, dragons and phoenix or landscapes. Decoration also increased on the

roof. The two owl-tail points of the Han and Tang grew into dragon heads and a line of lion dogs and magic beasts sat on the hip, all intended to frighten evil spirits.

The magnificence of the Forbidden City complex in Peking is an overwhelming compensation for loss of individual lightness of line. The palace is about 1.6 km (1 m) long and designed to overawe. Massive halls, with red columns supporting yellow-tiled roofs, stand on white marble platforms set in huge bare courtyards. From one courtyard you enter a huge hall, then another vast courtyard, another hall, another expanse of courtyard until you reach the smaller, more intimate buildings where the imperial family and retinue lived with their rock and fountain-filled garden.

Though enclosure is a feature of all Chinese buildings and of the city in which they stand, and the original reason for enclosure was presumably defensive, the house within the city wall was enclosed both to

protect personal property and the women of the family. In traditional China, city women were not supposed to be seen outside or by outsiders. If they went out, it was in curtained sedan chairs. All they knew was the world within the courtyard. Today the courtyard houses are inhabited by several families. New apartment blocks are being constructed on the outskirts of the cities, but the older buildings which served the social structure and ideals of the past are still in use, reflecting the continuity of community and of building that has been part of China for centuries.

JAPANESE

The Prehistoric Age

Architecture is the most conservative of the arts. Nowhere more than in Japan. There, as in many other places, its roots can be traced back to one of the prehistoric shelters found by man in the cave or made by him in a lean-to of branches and upright poles.

In Japan the prehistoric age began very early with a hunting and gathering culture from about 8000 BC. This first prehistoric period is called Jomon, a name derived from the cord marks made by impressions on its pottery. The earliest shelter whose remains survive has a roof lashed onto posts and beams which are sunk into a prepared hole. There is more significance in this than appears at first sight. For reconstruction suggests that in the small gable over the hipped flanks of the roof may be found the antecedents for generations of later farmhouses.

The fireplace was originally outside but from about 4000 BC it moved inside – first in the middle of the floor or between the main posts on the short side. Figurines of a fertility goddess type with a red-ochre colouring found by some fires suggest that the house may also have served as a shrine. We do not know if the deity was thought to come down the main post, bringing fertility to the edge of the fire, but such folk beliefs have a long antiquity in Japan.

The Jomon era was succeeded by another called Yayoi, which brought with it a wet-rice culture via several routes from the continent in about 500 BC. This is the period of the first villages larger than 300 or so inhabitants. The pit dwelling was surrounded by a ridged ditch, a useful improvement in a humid summer climate with

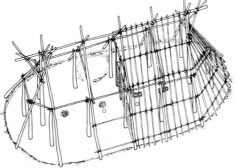

high rainfall. A major structural innovation was the sinking of posts with a board attached to their foot, thus improving the lateral stability of the building in earthquakes. A stable platform could also now be raised with the roof resting on the board walls rather than supporting part of its weight directly on the ground. Where Jomon man had

left
Reconstruction of Jomon dwelling (*c.* 4000 BC): the roof rests on the ground; the fire is on the long side.

below
Reconstruction of Yayoi dwelling: the roof is over a wattle screen wall surrounded by a damp-excluding ditch.

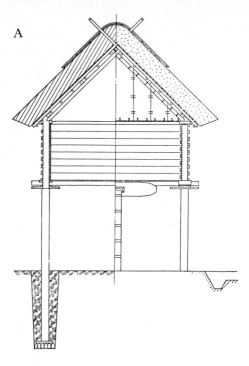

A

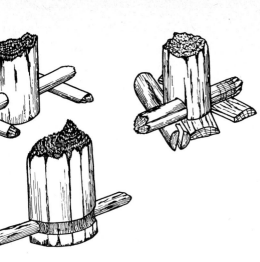

B

C

above and right
Yayoi dwellings: (A) post with foot-
board, on top a board wall;
(B) varieties of post foot-boards;
(C) buildings on a 3rd or 4th century
mirror: (top to bottom, left to right)
storehouse, priest's house(?),
farmhouse, ruler's house(?).

relied on building with ropes or vine, the Yayoi people seem to have passed directly to the Iron Age. Their timbers were finished with tenon joints and iron tools.

There seems also to have been a division of wealth in that society between the ritual priests or shamanesses and the farmers. By the early years AD petty kingdoms had arisen which are mentioned in the Chinese chronicles. Mirrors and other relics show buildings which correspond to such social stratification. But it is significant that pit dwellings continued in recorded use alongside the raised-floor buildings. Indeed some farmers slept on straw palliases on an earth floor in the late nineteenth century.

In the third or fourth century AD the petty kingdoms were forced to accept the great king of Yamato as their suzerain. The emperors of the now unified country raised great burial tumuli, after which the period is called Kofun. These had regional variations in their shape but gradually assumed the distinctive key hole and surrounding moat form which is different from the rectilinear shape of their probable antecedents in Korea.

Their monumental shape is not haphazard. It was constructed in accordance with the unit of a pace, which is six feet of 23.1 cm (9 ins) each in the Chinese Han and Jin standard. Nintoku's tomb has been shown to be laid out with the length of the tumulus at 350 paces (480 m/525 yd), the length of the whole including the moat at 450 paces (630 m/689 yd) and the diameter of the round tumulus at the end 180 paces (247 m/270 yd). Monuments on such a massive scale testify to a major increase in the wealth of the rulers. Such social power may be connected with the association of the Imperial Family with the presumably antecedent cult of the sun-goddess.

At Ise there survives a Shinto shrine which is dedicated to the sun deity and is rebuilt on the same plan on adjoining sites every 20 years. It remains as a direct link with the fourth century. Beneath the shrine is the vestige of a tree called the 'heart post' (of the god), which is covered every time the site is alternated. There is a similar emphasis on a tree at the shrine of Izumo, where the two-bay interior has as its centre a much larger post than those in the wall plane.

The Izumo building survives from 1744, but its metal decorations, lattice windows, stone base and monumental layout are more obviously continental in origin than those of Ise. The building preserves a sense of grandeur; it was built for a god and is so mentioned in the early eighth-century histories. But the god was intended as a symbol of the emperor's power and the building is described as made like the emperor's palace and under his order by the side of the sea.

right
Tomb of Emperor Nintoku, Osaka Prefecture (*c.* 399). Imperial tomb is unexcavated, but is probably in the circular end.

below
Shrine to sun-goddess, Ise (originally 4th century). Here the posts are continuous from ground to roof.

The Ancient Age

The Ancient Age coincides with the introduction into Japan of Buddhism. A statue of Buddha was presented to the Japanese court by a Korean king in 538; by 604 Prince Shotoku had introduced his Seventeen Laws, which promulgated the Confucian ideal of social harmony and reverence for the Buddha, the Law (Dharma) and the Priesthood (Sangha). The Ancient Age encompasses the wholesale introduction of Chinese learning and a Chinese script by the burgeoning aristocracy, who did not overthrow the emperor, but used him against other families and the hereditary Shinto priests. The Chinese architecture of a non-Chinese religion popular in China was also introduced. And so the seventh century marks the accession of Japan not merely to the history of East Asia but to the world beyond it.

In the course of the three periods of Asuka (552–646), Nara (646–794) and Heian (794–1185), each of which is named after a different capital, that contact with China loosened and in 894 the last ambassador was exchanged with the Tang court. A native syllabic script derived from Chinese ideographs was devised and the aristocracy made its own synthesis of native and imported forms in both architecture and literature. Shotoku originally intended that land be allocated under the theoretical Chinese model from the centre, but the traditional clans asserted themselves and wealth was inherited by heads of families who owned estates.

The Asuka period saw a new kind of architecture, profoundly influenced by the new religion. The Buddhist architecture which reached Japan first via Korea and then directly from China was far removed from the simple grave-mounds or stupas around which the second-century BC Indian believers had perambulated. Not merely had the grave-mound been absorbed into the pagoda under the influence of the Han Chinese pleasure pavilions, but behind it had been located a golden hall full of gold-encrusted images provided by the faithful. Their worship was still circumambulation, although now this was via the roofed corridors around the main buildings which were usually closed except to the priests and their doors opened only for special festivals.

Most of these buildings have lost their original colouring but their impressiveness remains. They were huge edifices rising up on stone platforms with elaborate roof brackets under heavy tiles. With painted red columns, green shutters, white boards under the eaves, yellow ochre on the tips of bracketing accented with gold decorative nails and bells hanging down from the eaves, the contrast with the bare wood and thatch of Shinto shrines and domestic housing must have been spectacular. The aristocrats who had such temples built can only have demonstrated their access to both profane and sacred power.

Shitenno-ji is a modern reconstruction of a temple built in 588. It displays the prominence given to the pagoda on an axially symmetrical plan. Golden halls gradually gained more importance and displaced what became two pagodas, one on each side of the main axis. These consequently became little more than architectural decorations, if extravagant and imposing ones. At Horyu-ji after 670 a unique plan was devised with the Golden Hall and Pagoda alongside each other. This rebuilding, made necessary after a fire to reconcile an existing mortuary chapel (which became the Golden Hall) with the new pagoda complex, illustrates a remarkably flexible attitude to the formation of plans. In aristocratic houses there was also a later tendency to rebuild as need arose, by attaching buildings with hole-inserted posts which had a lifetime of about 30 years around the longer lived core where the posts were mounted on stone.

This raised base of stone and tamped earth may be seen in the Golden Hall of Horyu-ji. There the columns also have a deliberate taper that may have come in via Central Asia and have been of Greek derivation. The area of a post and beam building was not increased with arches, which in China were used mainly for bridges, but by adding more bays or inter-post spans outward from the central

A

B

above
Corner of Horyu-ji Golden Hall:
decorated post added later to support
inadequate bracketing. Lowest roof is a
lean-to.

right
Additional bays from the centre
increased the area of Horyu-ji's Golden
Hall. The lean-to is an ambulatory.

left
Reconstructions of temples.
(A) Shitenno-ji, Osaka (after 588):
ambulatory symmetrical around axis of
gate, pagoda, golden hall, lecture hall;
(B) Horyu-ji, Nara (after 670): pagoda
alongside golden hall.

core, or by the addition of lean-to galleries on the lowest floor. The gallery can be an independent area forming a cloister for circumambulation. Within the different structural constraints of stone, this solution was also adopted in south Indian and south-east Asian temples.

Here at Horyu-ji there was an important structural innovation. Where posts are not inserted in holes, lateral stability must be provided by adequate bracing, at least at the post head where the weight of the overhang of the eaves is borne. The arm parallel to the rafters was intended in Chinese buildings to function as a lever in support of the eaves. It required adequate bracing where it left the post head as well as at its extremity. This bracing strength was inadequate at Horyu-ji

and later rebuilding added a dragon-encircled post so that the upper eaves could be supported at the corners.

A mature construction in the Tang style from the Nara period is the Golden Hall of Toshodai-ji, erected after 759 by the Chinese monk Jian-zhen, called Ganjin in Japanese. Its brackets are firmly anchored laterally in the wall plane as well as at the eaves. With a long parallel rafter used as a lever, there was clearly subsequent rebuilding. The roof line was raised by adding a further parallel rafter to cantilever up the section of the roof span between the main posts in a perhaps oversophisticated substitution for the naive but logical directness of the Chinese system.

The capital was moved eventually to Heian, the present Kyoto,

after 794 and so began the Heian period. One reason for the move may have been a desire to escape the malevolent influence of the Buddhist clergy in politics. There was less land for temples available in the new capital and after the introduction of new sects with a Tantric theology some located their head temples in mountain areas away from the capital, such as those founded at Hiei-zan and Daigo near Kyoto.

A temple on the mountain at Daigo was founded in 874 and a subsequent pagoda has been lost. But at the foot of the mountain a five-storey pagoda survives which was begun in 931 and completed in 952. The new Shingon sect believed in the two Diamond and Womb worlds, and the inside of the pagoda is decorated as mandalas of these

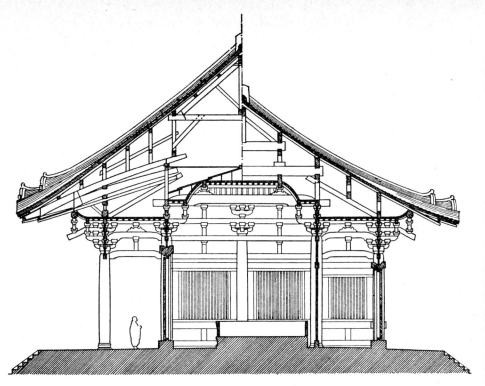

above
The original Chinese roof-truss system of Toshodai-ji's Golden Hall (right) produced a very different effect.

left
Golden Hall, Toshodai-ji Temple, Nara (after 759). Bay size increases towards the centre, giving a sense of progression.

right
Five-Storey Pagoda, Daigo-ji, Kyoto (931–52): a three-bay square, one column rises as an inner spire in the central square.

right
Eaves bracket detail, Daigo-ji Pagoda: three-tiered brackets lift out from the post head to support the overhang.

worlds; that the original also had Bodhisattvas on the four main pillars was discovered in repairs in 1960. The sturdy logical strength of the brackets had not yet blossomed into decoration and is in complete sympathy with the mandala-prescribed worlds the building embodies.

In the late Heian period Buddhism became more accessible to the believer through the rise of the Amidist sects who called on Amida, the Buddha of the West, before or at the moment of death in order to enter his paradise. The necessity was a pressing one, because a millennial cosmology marked the year 1053 as the moment when the era of the End of Buddha's Law would commence; however diligent, beneficial karma would be progressively more difficult for a believer to

obtain thereafter. Aristocrats had
pictures of this paradise or statues
of Amida brought to the houses
where they were dying (houses of
parturition), and these small buildings gradually became shrines
which embodied a vision of that
future. Since the religious vision
was closer to humanity, the vision of
paradise was also more earthly, as
seen in the Amida Hall at Chuson-ji
in north Japan, which was gilded
and decorated with lacquer inlays of
mother-of-pearl.

The Phoenix Hall of the Byodo-in
near Uji points to the populariza-
tion of Buddhism which now dif-
fused beyond the aristocracy and
the monks. A window has been
opened in the front of the Amida
room to allow believers and the
dying to glimpse Amida's paradise
from the opposite side of the lake.
The inside is decorated with flying
sensuous, if not sensual, angels that
might well have satisfied the court-
ier Fujiwara no Yorimichi (990–
1072) for whom it was consecrated
in 1053. The bracketing is of three
steps out from a wall as had become
standard for great temples since the
Nara period, and is similar to that

used on the neighbouring Daigo-ji
Pagoda.

Little survives to indicate accurately the ordinary domestic housing of the Heian period. But the
living quarters of aristocrats and
monks can be adjudged from some
picture scrolls. The evidence of the
Phoenix Hall itself also points to a
main building with parallel sub-
buildings joined to it at either end
facing a lake, so retaining a flavour

above
Rice mats were originally placed on the
floor of the Seiryo-den, not laid into it.
Screens divide a space without
structural walls.

top
Reconstruction of the Seiryo-den,
Imperial Palace, Kyoto, after 11th-
century original: has extra bay under
eaves.

170

Phoenix Hall, Byodo-in Temple, Uji, near Kyoto (1053). Through an aperture under the centre secondary roof is the Amida.

of the symmetrical alignment so typical of Chinese architecture.

The nineteenth-century reconstruction of the emperor's residential quarters called Seiryo-den or Clear and Tranquil Hall has eaves extended by one bay at the front to provide shade from the eastern sun, which can also be shut out by a variety of grilles and shutters. The Heian courtiers sat on individual mats moved over a board floor as appropriate, not yet on mats laid into the floor. The large corridors could be shut off, as could different sections of the interior space, by hanging silks or folding screens, decorated with Chinese flowers or Japanese landscapes according to the formality of the occasion. It was these screens which from the late twelfth century came to be fixed to runners laid between the vertical posts. Since the wall did not support the roof, it could be removed where necessary and the room opened to the corridor, the verandah and the world.

The Middle Age
The Japanese Middle Age refers to that period between the fall of the aristocracy and the establishment of a stable feudalism in the late sixteenth century. The size of the great estates and temple lands had gradually increased during the Heian period but many landowners managed to exempt themselves from central taxation and so drew peasants in from the taxed lands. With the practice of absentee provincial governors central authority declined. It was the regional lords or the bailiffs of those remaining in the capital who, by fighting to preserve their own rights or the regional authority of the court, gradually usurped civil authority and founded the distinct military caste. By 1185 a military dictatorship was established at a new capital of Kamakura in the east.

The Kamakura period of 1185–1333 is marked by the introduction of new architectural styles from the continent and the reassertion and development of existing and now naturalized practices. The first Song style came from south China and was called the Great Buddha or Indian style because it was used by

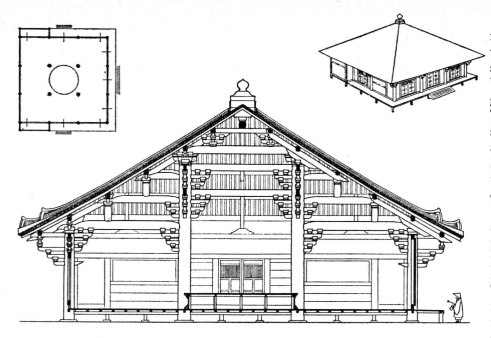

right angles to it, in accordance with the Chinese belief that evil spirits can only fly in straight lines. Within the outer gate is the main gate, called the Third Gate after the Three Liberations. Then on either side are the bath and toilets that assume some importance because of Zen emphasis on religious practice through even the most menial tasks of daily life.

The sites were often at the edge of a city in a small blind valley. The pagoda was relegated to an unimportant site at the back behind the Buddha Hall and Dharma Hall. These main buildings are surrounded by many smaller subtemples for various abbots – necessary in Zen temples, where the period of tenure for high office was short.

In Kamakura itself the Engaku-ji relic hall shows how massive bracket systems were increasingly redundant because of the extended long-lever rafter above. Methods of increasing an unsupported span were devised with the use of thicker columns and beams and inter-post studs at the centre. Its present high-pitched shingled roof shows where native aesthetic ideals were imposed during a subsequent rebuilding.

above
Pure Land Hall, Jodo-ji Temple, Hyogo Prefecture (1194): built 'Indian' style with great bays and massive posts directly supporting the roof.

below
A 15th-century view of Tofuku-ji Temple, Kyoto (from 1236): main and outer gates offset, pagoda to the rear. (Attributed to Sesshu)

the monk Chugen to rebuild the Todai-ji Temple at Nara with its Great Buddha in 1195, burnt down in 1180.

But the main Chinese influence showed itself in the building of temples for the new Zen sect which was associated with the rulers at Kamakura. A major feature of Zen temples is their selfconsciously haphazard plan. For although the main buildings may be in line, the main outer gate is off this line or at

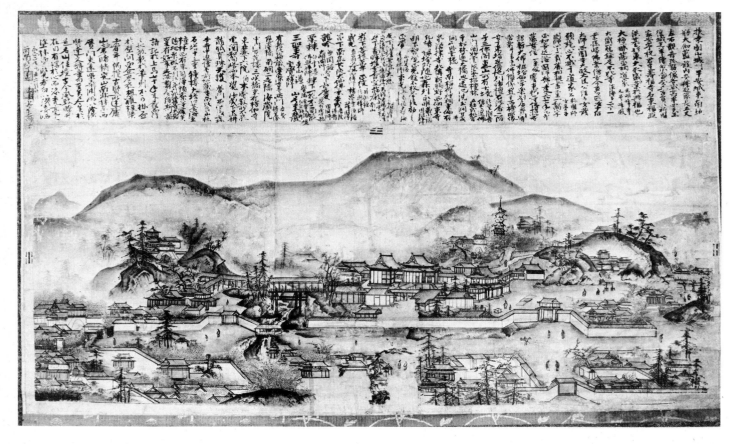

The warrior dictatorship degenerated into a system of regents, and the government became ever more shaky when it was returned to the old capital of Kyoto in 1336. In this era, named Muromachi (1392–1573), the regional lords who had once owed their lands in personal fief now attempted to remove themselves from central control in a virtual repeat of the situation which had led to the Heian decline. It may not be strange that the warriors should now have been imbued with

right
Relic Hall, Engaku-ji Temple, Kamakura (after 1285): cantilever inserted on rebuilding (left) indicates bracketing is now purely decorative.

below
Togu-do, garden of Ginkaku-ji, Kyoto (1486). The tea room is behind the white screens with a modular unit of one bay.

the aristocratic ideal of retreat from the meddlesome business of controlling distant and barbarous regions, when their own income could be comfortably guaranteed by licensing the extremely profitable foreign trade with China.

Despite the establishment of metropolitan Zen temples in a strict hierarchy, Chinese influence was not over-present and the Golden Pavilion built at Kinkaku-ji in 1397 has a Heian-style fishing pavilion attached to a lower floor of Japanese lattices and plank doors. The uppermost storey has the then fashionable cusped windows of Zen temple study-rooms, but the use of unpainted wood and white plaster for the first floor, in contrast to gold for the upper two, suggests an epicurean eclecticism in which taste rather than purposive symmetry dominates.

In the garden of the Silver Pavilion of Ginkaku-ji on the opposite and eastern side of Kyoto there is a small house, Togu-do, which was built in 1486 as the private Buddha Hall of the retired military dictator Yoshimasa and is where he founded the inward-looking Eastern Mountain culture. In this hall is a room

for his tea-master, Shuko, which has offset shelves and a study-room window together with sliding paper-screens on to the garden. These were to be the elements from which a certain type of domestic architecture would be composed down to the present day. Furthermore, four and a half mats were built to the standard inter-post span and are an early example of the module, a standard unit of measurement which can be subdivided or multiplied to provide all the other sizes from timbers to screens.

The Feudal Age

From 1500 to 1590 Japan was in continuous civil war. There was then a short intervening period

right
Golden Pavilion, Kinkaku-ji (after 1397). An eclectic effect is produced by the different surfaces of each storey.

below
Himeji Castle, Hyogo Prefecture (from 1570s). Trees mask massive stone walls on which these splendid keeps rise.

above
'Great' Shoin, Nijo Palace, Kyoto
(1614–25). Military dictators sat on the
higher level, bodyguards behind
screens at right.

right
Tai-an tearoom, Myoki-an Temple,
Kyoto Prefecture (*c.* 1582). The hearth
was originally set in the left corner.

before the establishment of the new eastern capital at Edo in 1615. That began an era which lasted until 1868. As a result of the wars all fiefs were vested by the military dictator, who was the head of the family of the last of the great generals, Tokugawa Ieyasu.

The countryside had been rapidly occupied by high castles whose lower walls were of stone and whose upper keeps were of compacted and flame-resistant plaster to defy the new firearms technology introduced via the Portuguese after 1543. In famous castles such as Azuchi, soon destroyed by a more successful general's family, the upper interiors were decorated with fabulous gold screen-paintings. But with the strengthening of central authority in Edo, now Tokyo, only those castles which were the principal seat of clans loyal to the dictatorship were allowed to survive. At the feet of these cluster the castle towns with a distinctive provincial urban landscape to be found all over Japan.

The feudal dictatorship was stable only on the surface, for beneath it lay a frantic and perpetual balancing of clans against each other. The direct consequence was the system of alternate residence of feudal lords and their families in their fief and in the capital. Vast districts had therefore to be laid out to contain them in Edo. But each residence kept its secrets, and even in the domestic residence within the Nijo castle at Kyoto the flowered screens to the right of the raised dais conceal a room for armed retainers of the bodyguard. Ceilings were normally board overlays hung from rafters, but in this case the ceiling was decorated in a splendid and ostentatious style in deliberate contrast to the plain mats; the lords of lesser status sat on the level below the raised area.

The dictators patronized tea, and the tea-master Rikyu made his house, Tai-an, for the antecedent of the Tokugawas, Hideyoshi, before a battle in 1582. The rough textures of the walls and the two-mats size mark Rikyu's attempt to impose an austere and rustic simplicity on an

event which is both a ritual ceremony, emphasizing the common status of host and guest where the unequal become equal, and an informal contract for the mutual exchange of pleasure far from the mundane world.

That the tea ceremony reflected the warrior household's etiquette may have indicated an increased awareness of the niceties of social appraisal. The tendency can certainly be observed in the conventions surrounding the use of architectural fittings such as waiting at doors before they are opened and permission is given to remove shoes, the precedence given by social status on entering rooms, and in the seating thresholds delineated

above
Main Shoins, Katsura Imperial Villa, Kyoto (from 1603). Posts stand on single stones, laterally stayed at floor line.

below
Farmhouse, Hida, Gifu Prefecture. The roof line was probably once much lower.

by the edges of mats. It is perhaps
no coincidence that the most secure
place for a warrior to sit, where he
could not be attacked from behind,
was in front of the main post of the
house or the support of the flower
alcove, itself a vestige of god's pillar
from at least the Yayoi period.

Indeed, that the powerful who
were not warriors should turn away
from extravagance and build
charming but magnificent rural
villas such as Katsura, and that
they should choose with such an
obsessively fastidious taste which
houses and items of scenery were to
be combined for whatever exquisite
parody of a landscape mentioned in
a famous poem or seen in a painting, can only have been stimulated
by the denial of a social outlet to
more ostentatious but more danger-
ous expression. 'The protruding
nail gets knocked in' as the proverb
goes.

Katsura is one demonstration by
an imperial prince of the flexibility
with which native materials and a
preference for unpainted wood and
white plaster might be combined
with the now completely
naturalized understanding of what
post and beam construction might
achieve. Despite the need for an
extra-high floor in case the neighbouring river were to flood, the

above
Mausoleum of Tokugawa Ieyasu,
Nikko, Tochigi Prefecture (1636):
structural orders are here merely
decorative.

above left
Interior of Shokin-tei informal Tea
House, Katsura. Each screen division
corresponds to a mat.

left
Exterior of Shokin-tei. A record of 1624
notes seeing from a pavilion mountains
on four sides, as is possible here.

residence avoided the heavy Chinese base by mounting the posts on single stones. The roof could now be shaped according to taste, unlimited by structural considerations.

The antithesis of Katsura is the tomb of the early dictators at Nikko. It illustrates a completely domestic strain of bombast, the architectural sloth of whose decorative but structurally redundant brackets testifies to a warrior mind emptied by war and family intrigue.

The final consequences of architectural change may be found where they began – in the domestic space. Despite their outward simplicity the Edo town houses were a complex synthesis of board floors and rice-matted main rooms, with roof-truss systems owing much to farmhouses but built by carpenters who had repaired temple roofs and

knew how to push up the roof line when desired. They became tiled only when the Edo authorities wanted to avoid fires.

In the country thatched roofs survived. In parts of the house a raised floor was inserted for boards and in parts rice mats were laid on it, particularly after the 1850s when clan sumptuary controls on the peasants were revised or could be ignored. The roof-truss system which had been added to a sometimes medieval core could be strengthened on re-thatching, and the roof lines lifted up from near or on the ground, so that light could enter a peasant's house via the new paper screens often for the first time. In short, the simple survived – a fitting conclusion built around an ancient farmhouse.

AMERINDIAN

About 40,000 years ago, during the last glaciation, the American continent was populated by peoples from Asia who migrated across the ice-covered Bering Straits and spread gradually southwards. The ice melted, leaving America isolated, and its inhabitants developed their own cultures without significant contact with the rest of the world until Columbus's arrival in 1492. But there can be no doubt about their architectural achievements: regularly laid-out towns and cities, huge pyramids, splendid temples and palaces, roads, bridges, irrigation systems and astronomical observatories, however strange to us, are ample testimony to their skills. These achievements are all the more astounding when we realize that they were built without the aid of metal tools or of the wheel, both of which were crucial to our own historical development.

One of the most striking aspects of Amerindian architecture is the constant emphasis on external rather than internal space. The chief focus of attention for both the general public and the architect was undoubtedly not the small, dark interiors but the elaborate profiles of the buildings and the monumental stairways and sculpted friezes of their facades. The principle of the arch was not discovered in America, and this probably did not happen by accident. A society and its architecture necessarily develop more or less simultaneously. Once a pattern of social behaviour has been established, it is unlikely that any major structural innovations will be made until those traditional patterns have been overthrown, or at least severely disrupted, and this tends to be a result of outside influences. Such influences were lacking in America, and so the Amerindian architects continued to devote their energies to exterior forms. Their architecture provides a setting on which and in front of which were enacted the numerous elaborate rituals that formed an integral part of their lives, while the interiors remained reserved for the use of small elites. Thus, not only the buildings but the plazas and wide processional roads that link them must be considered as vital parts of the overall architectural scheme.

The following examples have been selected to offer a variety of important forms and styles, but they merely hint at the immense richness of the architectural imagination of the native peoples of America.

The Pyramid of Quetzalcoatl, Teotihuacán

Almost all the great architecture of Central America owes something to the city of Teotihuacán. About a century BC a thriving township was established on the flat plain northeast of present-day Mexico City, a township which in the next five centuries grew into a great city, larger and more populous than Imperial Rome. The citadel, a large enclosed plaza overlooked on the western side by the Pyramid of Quetzalcoatl, marks the juncture between the commercial and the religious centres of the city.

The Pyramid of Quetzalcoatl was built around 300 AD. In Amerindian architecture a pyramid is a solid, man-made hill, faced with stone and with a flat top. On this platform, at the top of a grand stairway, stood a small temple, and religious rites were performed by priests at the top of the stairs and in the temple itself. From ground level the enormous stairway and tiny temple beyond create an exaggerated sense of perspective, and the temple must have appeared awe-inspiringly close to the heavens. A pyramid was generally oriented in accordance with certain celestial motions – at Teotihuacán the main facades of the Pyramid of Quetzalcoatl and of the older Pyramid of the Sun face directly into the setting sun on Midsummer's day – and at certain times of great calendrical significance the temple was ritually destroyed, a new layer of masonry laid over the old pyramid, and a new temple built on top.

No temple survives on the Pyramid of Quetzalcoatl, but the periodic process of renovation is obvious: an older pyramid has been partially excavated, and the ceremonial stairway and some of the richly sculpted facade can be seen behind the later addition. The overall structure of both pyramids is the same: a broad central stairway to the temple platform, flanked by the stepped facade so typical of Mexican architecture. Each giant step consists of two units, the lower part sloping inwards, known as the talud, is surmounted by the tablero, a vertical framed panel which projects out over the talud. This arrangement produces strong, dramatic shadows on the pyramid facade, and the impression of solidity created by the talud is counterbalanced by the tablero perched precariously above it.

The wealth of sculptural detail which survives on the facade of the earlier temple tells us something about the world view of the Teotihuacanos. The mask of the rain-god Tlaloc alternates with the head of Quetzalcoatl, the feathered serpent: hence the god of natural forces is balanced by the god held responsible for the introduction of culture and civilization. Perhaps the forces of culture had greater importance for the Teotihuacanos because Quetzalcoatl alone appears on either side of the great stairway; certainly the size and complexity of

their well-ordered city show them to have been a sophisticated and cultured people.

The Pyramid of Quetzalcoatl, Tula

Teotihuacán declined in importance from about the eighth century, and was surpassed by the city of Tula to the north. Here a powerful, aggressive race known as the Toltecs built pyramids similar to those at Teotihuacán, but the most important architectural innovation at Tula is the extensive and imaginative use of the pillar as a supporting member for roof-beams.

above
Pyramid of the Moon, Teotihuacán: the talud-tablero motif can be seen in the foreground structure.

below
View of the main street and the Pyramid of the Sun from the Pyramid of the Moon at Teotihuacán, Mexico.

left
Pyramid of Quetzalcoatl, Teotihuacán,
Mexico: this splendid facade was once
ritually buried under a later pyramid.

above
Pyramid of Quetzalcoatl, Tula,
Mexico: these stone warriors and the
piers behind once supported the temple
roof.

183

left
The Pyramid of Quetzalcoatl at Tula
was once decorated with carved and
painted stone friezes.

Traces of long ranges of pillars have
been found flanking the plazas,
forming porticoes, and linking the
chief ceremonial areas, while the
temple on the pyramid was constructed with eight richly carved
stone columns to support the roof.

The history of the Toltecs is not
yet fully known, but there was certainly internal conflict between the
adherents of the old cult of Quetzalcoatl and those who favoured the
war-god Tezcatlipoca. The remains
of the temple of Quetzalcoatl
demonstrate this tension. The first
four columns are carved in the
shape of men dressed in identical
uniforms, standing forever to attention, gazing out to the southern
horizon. The four square pillars
behind have shallow-relief carvings,
also of Toltec warriors, and all eight
are in marked contrast to the
remains of two more columns, decorated with the attributes of Quetzalcoatl, which apparently stood at
the entrance to the temple. These
were carved all over with feathers,
and each would have had a serpent's head at the base and a tail
curving outwards at the top to support a lintel across the temple entrance; Quetzalcoatl, the bringer of
culture, thus presides uneasily at
the doorway, while behind him wait
the implacable warriors, followers
of the new war-like cult.

Tula was the scene of regular
human sacrifice, not a part of the
cult of Quetzalcoatl, but for the
Toltecs and for the many other
cultures which did practise it, the
rite was considered essential if the
universe was to continue to exist.
Always an open-air, public spec-
tacle, it was inseparable from both
the spatial and structural architecture of the religious centre. After
dances and processions in the plaza,

left
Part of a decorative frieze from Tula's
Pyramid of Quetzalcoatl, showing a
rattlesnake with gaping jaws.

the priests would descend from the temple and accompany the victim back up the steep steps. At the top, in front of the temple, they turned to the crowd watching below; the victim was held down while a priest plunged an obsidian knife into his side and tore out his still-beating heart. The body was then thrown back down the steps, while the heart and blood were offered to the god whose statue was venerated in the temple. For this drama, the Toltecs did not require a sombre architectural setting; Tula's spacious plazas, its buildings, decorated with finely carved and once brightly painted friezes, seem an affirmation of the people's confidence in themselves and in their gods.

Temples I and II and the Great Plaza, Tikal

Away to the south in the tropical forests of the Yucatán peninsular and the Petén region of Guatemala a different pattern had emerged. Here the Mayan peoples built magnificent ceremonial centres, but archaeological investigations have proved that these were not proper towns with administrative and commercial functions. A few priests, nobles and servants remained there permanently, while the bulk of the Mayan population lived in scattered, disorganized hamlets, only journeying to these sites for important religious festivals.

The greatest architecture at the ceremonial centre of Tikal was built between AD 550 and 900, although the site was being used for ritual purposes over a thousand years earlier. The Great Plaza with the towering edifices of Temples I and II facing each other on the east and west sides dates from the eighth century, and to the spectator standing in the plaza between them there can be no doubt that these temples were designed to impress. The pyramid bases are very much steeper than Mexican examples:

from below, the flights of steps appear almost sheer, and the terraced stages are articulated vertically, producing a series of lines which lead upwards and inwards until they meet at the temple platform, focusing attention on the temple and at the same time

below
A mask of Tlaloc, the rain-god, from Tikal: carved in limestone and once finished in polychrome stucco.

right
The ring set into the wall below the Temple of the Jaguars at Chichén Itzá was used for scoring goals.

emphasizing its distance from the ground far below.

Temple I, the higher of the two, stands on a pyramid consisting of nine successive steps (nine being a number of great calendrical and ritual significance in Amerindian cultures); the talud-tablero motif is present in these steps, but is very understated compared with Mexican examples. The temple itself consists of three small rooms covered with the type of steeply pitched corbelled vault developed by the Maya. Its chief interest, however, lies in its exterior.

Here sculptural and architectural imagination fuse to produce a splen-did example of the greatest visual innovation of Mayan architecture: the roof-comb. This roof decoration is a wall of richly sculpted masonry, often a continuation of the back wall of the temple. In Temple I at Tikal it surmounted the roof above the vaulted chambers of the temple and was decorated with an image of a huge seated figure. Thus the temple and the roof-comb appear like an immense throne from which the god and his priests can preside over the ceremonies in the plaza below.

The Great Ballcourt, Chichén Itzá

Although the temple-pyramid-plaza

built a magnificent temple and colonnade similar to that at Tula, and, on the other side of the main courtyard, a ballcourt. Nearly 153 m (500 ft) long, with a small temple at either end and another grander temple overlooking the central playing area, this is the largest and most splendid ballcourt in America.

Finely carved panels depicting processions of richly dressed warriors and ball players decorate the walls and the interiors of the temples. The largest temple, known as the Temple of the Jaguars, has two well-preserved feathered-serpent columns at the entrance, their curved tails supporting the lintel and their gaping jaws facing the players below. They are similar to those at the entrance of the main temple, the Temple of the Warriors, across the courtyard, and to those which once stood on the Pyramid of Quetzalcoatl at Tula, and their presence here emphasizes the part played by the gods, and Quetzalcoatl in particular, in both Mexican and Mayan life.

The Kalasasaya Platform, Tiahuanaco

The ruins of Tiahuanaco lie 3962 m (13,000 ft) up on a bleak plateau just south of Lake Titicaca in what is now Bolivia. The land cannot support a large number of permanent inhabitants, and this means that the extensive ruins here must represent a ceremonial centre and not an urban settlement, and that the site must have been almost entirely contructed by labour from other regions, perhaps even by pilgrims coming to worship there. It was probably an important centre from before the time of Christ, but the major architectural remains date from about AD 600. They consist of two stepped pyramids – largely unexcavated – and a small sunken plaza overlooked by a rectangular platform, the Kalasasaya. There can be little doubt that these sites were closely related: all are oriented along the same axes and were once linked by straight roads. This grandiose architectural scheme must have formed an essential part of the religious rituals.

complex found throughout Central America is clearly an integral part of all religious practice, another architectural feature, the ballcourt, occurs at most ceremonial sites in both the Mexican and the Mayan areas, and the evidence suggests that this was not so much for recreational as for ritual purposes. The playing court is shaped like a letter 'I', with raised platforms and terraces at the sides, presumably for spectators, and miniature temples at either end.

The game involved teams of specially trained players, and, although the method of scoring is not yet fully understood, certainly the Mexican

version involved hitting a solid rubber ball through rings set high in the side walls, using only the elbows, hips and thighs. What is clear is that the game was accompanied by various rituals; early Spanish sources speak of priests carrying idols, leading processions from the main temple to the ballcourt, and officiating at the game, and the game itself often seems to have ended with the ritual sacrifice of some of the players.

In the north of the Yucatán peninsular, the Mayan centre of Chichén Itzá was conquered and settled by the Toltecs in the eleventh century AD. Here they

The most thoroughly restored parts of the ruins are the Kalasasaya Platform and the sunken plaza. The platform is faced with a high stone wall with huge, irregularly cut stones set at intervals and linked by walls of much smaller, roughly faced blocks. On the platform is a rectangular walled enclosure, and the only entrance is on the east side, up a monolithic stairway and through a stone gateway. The importance of this entrance is emphasized by the quality of masonry: the stones are smooth and perfectly jointed, and must have been laboriously worked with tools of harder stone or perhaps cold-hardened copper. There is evidence that copper clamps were used to hold the stones tightly together.

On the platform several huge stone statues have been found with blankly staring eyes and marks like tears on their cheeks. There is also a massive, free-standing gateway, cut from a single block of stone. It is known as the Gateway of the Sun because of a sun-like deity carved in shallow relief over the opening.

Sacsahuamán, Cuzco

The city of Cuzco, high in the Peruvian Andes and once the capital of the Inca Empire, is dominated by the huge fortress of Sacsahuamán. It was built towards the end of the fifteenth century AD at the height of Inca power, and was seen as a highly significant addition to their capital: they thought of Cuzco as the body of a puma, and Sacsahuamán as its head, overlooking the more mundane functions of the city below.

The north face of the fortress is the most impressive, consisting of three tiers of curtain walls, which zigzag like the teeth of a saw, both the upper levels offering protection for the level below. They rise from the flat land in front like huge, craggy, man-made cliffs. The conquering Spaniards were speechless with amazement at the quality of the masonry: each of the giant,

irregular blocks is fitted perfectly to those around it, despite the fact that the Incas had neither iron nor steel, nor the use of the wheel.

The solution to the question of how Sacsahuamán was built is to be found in the Inca political system which was a form of highly organized paternalistic welfare-state. Every able-bodied member of society had to do a share of communal duties, and in return received various benefits: food in times of famine, protection from hostile peoples, care when sick or old. Once a year the men had to spend a few weeks away from their villages, working for the Inca, building roads or bridges, temples or fortresses.

It is recorded that a work-party of this type consisting of 20,000 men was employed on the construction of Sacsahuamán for several years. They had to cut and shape the blocks at the quarry, using chisels made of a harder type of stone, and then, with the aid of ropes and rollers, the blocks were dragged up to the site. The perfect joints seem to have been achieved by hoisting the stones up into place, and then swinging them gently back and forth so that they were ground down tightly against their neighbours, using sand and water to increase the friction.

Sacsahuamán, placed as it is in the very heart of Inca territory, was built not so much for the practical defence of Cuzco, but rather as a symbol of the strength and security of the Inca Empire.

Machu Picchu
The Inca town of Machu Picchu is perched in the saddle of a craggy mountain on the humid eastern slopes of the Peruvian Andes, with the River Urubamba snaking between the rocks over 305 m (1000 ft) below. The site was only

above
This aerial view of Sacsahuamán, Cuzco, Peru, shows the zigzag pattern of the northern walls of the fortress.

discovered at the beginning of this century, and so it preserves intact a wealth of information about late Inca architecture and social organization at that time.

Houses, palaces, temples, granaries, a prison, a cemetery and an observatory are all neatly arranged around a spacious central square, while a wall divides the town from the main agricultural terraces which climb steeply up to the south-east. Everything seems to suggest that this inaccessible settlement was a retreat which could survive for long periods without

189

contact with the outside world. Excavations have revealed that a very high proportion of young women were buried here, and it has been suggested that Machu Picchu was a sanctuary for the young women who served in the Inca temples and who were known as the Virgins of the Sun.

The masonry of the main temples and palaces is of a very high standard, but what is most striking is not the buildings themselves but their careful positioning for maximum dramatic effect: the architects used the topography of the site to enhance the buildings in a truly imaginative way. Craggy outcrops of rock are deliberately incorporated into buildings even when it would have been easier to build beside them, or at least to have carved out a level surface. The result is that Machu Picchu looks as if it is growing out of the mountain itself. As at Sacsahuamán, the Inca architect did not attempt to disguise or transform his material: rather, he exaggerates its stoniness, suggesting that he wished to harmonize with nature rather than conquer it.

above left
Machu Picchu, Peru: this Inca retreat is perched high up in the Andes, between two jagged mountain peaks.

above right
The Inca architects of Machu Picchu did not disguise rough outcrops of rock, incorporating them into their work.

left
The giant, roughly-finished blocks of Sacsahuamán fit together as tightly as pieces of a jigsaw.

right
The fortress of Sacsahuamán formed a backdrop to Inca rituals enacted on the flat plain in front.

ROMANESQUE

The architectural history of Europe in the Middle Ages is distinguished by two major periods of rebirth. Each occurred in times of political and social change, and each found in the past achievements of the classical world fresh inspiration on which to found new artistic and architectural evolution. At the beginning of the ninth century, when order and enlightenment were returning to Europe with the establishment of the Holy Roman Empire of the West, a new dawning of civilization was to result in the architectural splendours of the Romanesque. For almost four hundred years Europe was to be enriched by its achievements in art and architecture, achievements which were to lay the foundations for that second outburst of creative energy in twelfth-century France, from which emerged the Gothic.

The origins of the Romanesque
The architectural inspiration in the ninth century was provided by the buildings of Rome, still surviving in monumental ruins throughout Europe; their structure, sculpture and decoration were the basis for the Romanesque. At the same time, the presence of Islam in southern Europe, existing in Spain for seven hundred years to threaten and so to unify western Christendom, provided a source for recovering the learning and technical skills of Byzantium and the Eastern Empire.

Perhaps most important of all, however, was the new vitality in building and the arts provided by those native races of north and central Europe who came to destroy Roman civilization but remained to advance and elevate the static qualities of late Roman architecture into the fullness of the mature Romanesque invention.

During this period, the Church was to dominate architectural and artistic evolution as it dominated all aspects of medieval life and thought, and an eleventh-century chronicler records the 'white wall of churches' rising across Europe in the spate of new building. The second and closely related factor in architectural patronage was the development of the feudal system and the provision of those buildings necessary for its institution and maintenance: the castles and fortified towns, the manor houses and the town houses of the wealthy citizens and merchants. Abbey, cathedral and parish church, castle and house, all share characteristics of architectural form, structure and enrichment, illustrating the basic concepts of the Romanesque in varying degree – its massive and permanent masonry structure based on round arch, vault and dome; its inward-looking, compartmented and defensive forms; its richness and vitality of sculpture, painting, glass and furnishing.

The earliest manifestations of a

new approach to architecture and art can be traced to those Dark Ages which followed the retreat of Rome from the West. Whilst sharing common Roman origins, and unified by the patronage of the universal Church of Rome, architecture during these early centuries developed strongly regional forms according to the traditions and skills of those native races who were providing the new building incentives and craftsmanship – Lombards, Visi-Goths, Franks and later the Normans. Because of these diverse origins, and its slow evolution over the centuries in different parts of Europe, the Romanesque developed differing national forms of expression which persisted even into the Gothic era, particularly in Germany and Italy.

From the fifth century onwards, the architectural awakening had been led by the Christian Church, spreading westwards from Rome to meet the survivors of Roman Christianity on the western fringes of Europe. Behind this movement lay the new monastic order of St Benedict, initiated in the sixth century at Monte Cassino in southern Italy and spread throughout Europe by Benedictine missionaries like St Augustine, who landed at Canterbury in England in 597 and immediately proceeded to build the first churches of his abbey there. St Benedict had always emphasized the importance of architecture and all the arts and their teaching, and in an age of violence and destruction the first monasteries played the leading role in establishing new forms of building and art.

The first churches to be built in western Europe at this time, often by craftsmen brought from Italy and the Mediterranean area, are however more closely related to Early Christian building in Rome than to the Romanesque. Most have succumbed to successive waves of destruction or to later rebuilding, but the basilican church which remains at Brixworth in Northamptonshire, England, built of local limestone with round arches of Roman-type brick, represents at least a major architectural advance on such Celtic churches as the monastery at Lindisfarne in Northumberland, which was 'built in the Irish fashion, not of stone but of cut oak and thatched with reeds'. Brixworth is a rare survival and merits its description as 'one of the most imposing architectural memorials of the seventh century north of the Alps'.

By the ninth century, the monastic church and community had already established a canonical form of layout which was to remain unchanged throughout the Middle Ages. It is first known from a plan of this date of the Benedictine monastery of St Gall in Switzerland, designed by Charlemagne's architect, Eginhardt. The ordered sequence of ancillary and domestic buildings around three sides of an arcaded cloister court, with the basilican church occupying the fourth side, is probably derived from the form of the Roman villa.

Carolingian, Ottonian and Lombardic Romanesque

Although the foundations of the Romanesque can be traced in these first centuries, it was not until political and social order had been reestablished in western Europe that the conditions which would stimulate architectural evolution could again emerge in full. The Franks were the first of the European nations to emerge as a political force and by the end of the eighth century

had succeeded in establishing themselves as the major power of Europe. Their defeats of both Muslims and Lombards had saved Europe for Christianity and gained for them the support of the Church in Rome. In 800, Charlemagne was crowned by the Pope as ruler of the new Holy Roman Empire, centred on the Frankish capital of Aachen, although Rome remained the religious centre.

In an empire that extended over France, central Europe and northern Italy, Charlemagne sought to restore the greatness of Rome, and in his new buildings to rival the splendours of Byzantium. A patron of the arts and architecture, he found support for his aims in the ideals of the Benedictines and a new wave of church building spread through Europe. At Aachen a new palace chapel was built by Odo of Metz to house the emperor's tomb. Now the cathedral, it was modelled on the plan of San Vitale, Ravenna, and its forms are entirely derived from Roman and Byzantine elements. (See page 81.)

Brixworth, Northamptonshire: the arcades of Roman-type brick formerly opened to an aisle in this 7th-century basilica.

The inclusion of Lombardy within the empire brought the Carolingian and, in the following centuries, the Ottonian builders into contact with the advanced work of the Italian masters, the Comacine masons. Their contribution to the evolution of new and improved structural forms, and in particular of ribbed cross-vaulting, was to be fundamental to the new way of building.

The Romanesque churches of north and central Italy retain the plan forms of the Early Christian basilicas, as in San Ambrogio, Milan. A new structural articulation of the plan is however evident in the subdivision of the nave into square compartments by the alternation of compound piers and columns, or by cross-arches as in San Miniato, Florence. Originally roofed in timber, the square-bay form adapted itself to the introduction of rib and panel cross-vaults, the first major advance on Roman building methods. In the earliest Romanesque churches to be vaulted in this way, each square nave-bay corresponded to two smaller aisle-bays. Over each bay, the use of half-round arches over different spans produced a domical form of vault, and this characterized both Italian and German Romanesque churches to the end of the period.

San Michele, Pavia, reveals a typical development of the basilican form with cross transepts and a full crypt under the apsidal choir, a feature developed from the Early Christian *confessio* which was to be

above
Pisa Cathedral (1063–92) is the finest
Romanesque church of northern Italy,
faced with marble and richly arcaded.

right
Abbey Church, Gernrode (958–1050):
Ottonian Romanesque with eastern
and western apses and wood-roofed
nave.

196

widely adopted. Externally, walls are articulated by flat pilasters or by rich arcading, seen in its most elaborate forms in the west fronts of such churches as the cathedral of Pisa, which, with its baptistry and campanile, form one of the most imposing groups of Romanesque building in Italy.

From the ninth to the eleventh centuries, these forms were widely adopted throughout the empire, particularly in Germany which retained Lombardic characteristics to the end of the Romanesque era, including the forms of bay division and vaulting and the arcading of external walls. The St Gall plan shows a distinctive treatment of the traditional basilican form, with eastern and western apses, and this double-ended plan is a feature of the greater Carolingian and later German Romanesque churches. Multiple-towered forms were also developed – there are six towers in the abbey church of Maria Laach – while the skill of the Rhineland builders in wood produced the distinctive forms of spires and also wooden roofs over wide spans.

In Saxon England, although outside the empire, similar forms at a more regional, vernacular level can

above
The palace chapel of Ramiro I of the Asturias, Santa Maria de Naranco, Spain (842–850), is barrel-vaulted on two floors.

right
Gernode Abbey, Germany: the nave arcades have alternating columns and piers.

be seen in the surviving churches, particularly in their towers and in the use of primitive forms of pilastering and wall arcading. Church plans, however, as at Bradford-on-Avon, retain elements derived from earlier building traditions in Britain. There is little surviving evidence of the greater churches of the period, but contemporary descriptions of the Saxon cathedral at Canterbury suggest that it was planned with the characteristic eastern and western apses. All such major buildings were swept away in the High Romanesque rebuildings of the Norman period.

High Romanesque

The ninth-century vision of a united Christian Europe disappeared with the death of Charlemagne, and, although the empire was re-established at the beginning of the eleventh century by Otto the Great, Germany and Italy were by then no longer in the mainstream of Romanesque development. That role was increasingly passing to France, in particular to Burgundy and to Normandy. Two events occurring early in the tenth century had contributed to this change of direction: the establishment by Duke William of Aquitaine of the new order of reformed Benedictines at Cluny, which reflected a revitalization of the monasteries; and, politically, the advent of the Norsemen, establishing themselves from northern France to southern Italy by conquest, and in 911 gaining recognition as Dukes of Normandy.

The reform of Church and society which these developments implied was to lead to a new fervour for church building. The development of the crusades, of pilgrimage and the veneration of relics brought new wealth and importance to the monasteries within feudal society. The need for new and vastly greater buildings involved developments in plan and structure, and Cluny played a major role in this. Burgundy was well placed to receive influences from all parts of Europe, while the architectural forms it sponsored spread rapidly along the pilgrimage roads of Europe. Of

above
A 10th-century Saxon church, St Lawrence, Bradford-on-Avon, with a small square-ended chancel and lateral porticus.

right
Barrel-vaulted St Sernin, Toulouse (1080–12th century): the largest pilgrimage church on the road to Santiago de Compostela.

198

below
Cluny, the third abbey church (completed by 1131): the most influential Romanesque church in France.

bottom
The apse and ambulatory with radiating chapels of Ste Foy, Conques (1045–1119), a typical pilgrimage church plan.

Cluny itself, the greatest of all Romanesque churches, little more than one transept has survived the destruction of the nineteenth century, but its unrivalled influence on architecture and religious art can be seen in many great churches of the order throughout Europe.

To satisfy new liturgical needs, the eastern arm of the traditional basilican plan was extended with choir aisles and choir terminating in three parallel apses, whilst the development of transepts established the cruciform plan. An alternative eastern termination was developed by taking the choir aisle around the eastern apse as an

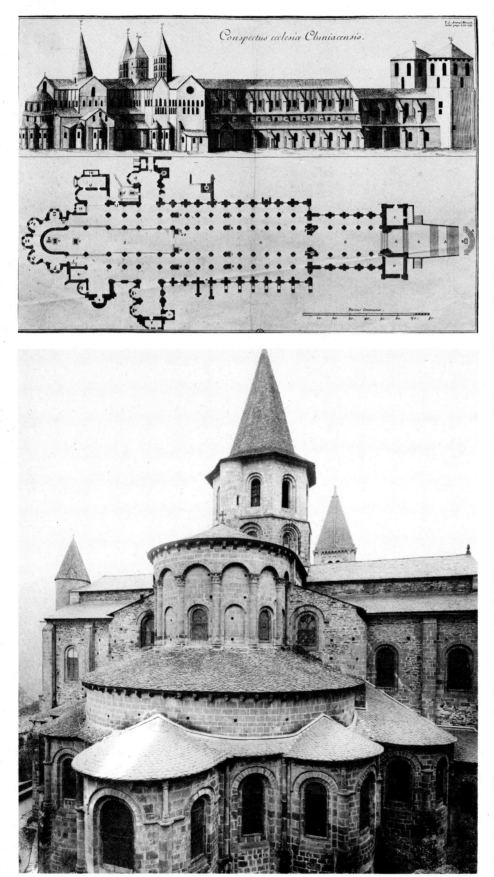

below right
The nave of St Savin sur Gartemps (11th century) is roofed with a richly frescoed barrel vault supported on tall 'classical' columns.

below
St Philibert, Tournus: early 11th-century Benedictine abbey combining cross-barrel vaults (nave) and groined vaulting (aisles).

ambulatory, from which radiated chapels, and this form was adopted for the third church of Cluny. It was to become popular in the greater pilgrimage churches, where it helped the free movement of pilgrims around the treasures of the church. In the vast programme of rebuilding which followed the Norman conquest of Britain, both forms are equally widespread – of the two great abbeys in Canterbury, the cathedral was built with the tri-apsidal ending while St Augustine's Abbey terminated in the apse and ambulatory, or chevet plan.

Vaulting was however the primary preoccupation of the High Romanesque builders, who were intent on producing permanent and fire-resisting structures. Considerable variations in form occur in different regions, whilst in western France naves are spanned by domes on pendentives, as in Angoulême Cathedral. In Burgundy and the south, the Roman barrel vault was widely adopted, articulated into bays by cross-arches on massive pier supports. The monumental splendour of this form can best be seen in the great pilgrimage church of St Sernin in Toulouse. The weight of the nave supports for these heavy vaults restricted lighting into the church, a necessary element in northern climates. To provide clerestory lighting, barrel vaults were set transversely as in the church of St Philibert, Tournus, or groined cross-vaults were introduced, again showing little advance on Roman building, as at the great church of Ste Madeleine, Vézelay. Externally, walls were relieved by flat pilasters, marking the divisions between the bays.

The Romanesque love of strong

above
Sculptured capitals in the cloister of
Santo Domingo de Silos demonstrate
the work of the Toulouse school.

right
Notre Dame la Grande, Poitiers (1130–
45): the sculptured screen of the
west facade is typical of Poitou's
churches.

colour expressed itself in painting,
which extended over walls, arcades
and vaults, as well as in stained
glass and in the rich decoration of
church furnishings. It is in this
period that the great tradition of
late Romanesque stone-carving
emerges, in schools distributed
through France, England and
Spain, producing both the geometrical patterning and rich figurative
carving which enriches so many
monastic cloisters.

It is however in Normandy and in
Norman buildings in Sicily and in
England that the final and most
advanced expressions of Romanesque structure can be seen. The skill
of the Norman builders was
developed both by contact with

above
The tri-apsidal east end of Céfalu
Cathedral, Sicily (1131), combining
both Norman and Islamic features.

left
Durham Cathedral Abbey (1110–33): the high vaults are probably the first use of pointed arches in a ribbed vault.

Islamic work in southern Italy and by ecclesiastical associations with Lombardy. The articulation of the Lombardic bay with alternating pier forms was widely adopted, as for example at Jumièges in France and Durham in England. Groined cross-vaults were initially used, often only in the aisles with richly painted wooden roofs to the main spans, as in Peterborough Cathedral in England. The ribbed cross-vault reached its highest level in the great cathedral abbey at Durham, the first church outside Lombardy to be completely roofed with ribbed vaults, whilst in Caen, Normandy, the subdivision of the quadripartite vaults by an additional cross-rib, producing the sexpartite vault, prepared the way for later Gothic developments.

The Romanesque was to take many different forms in different regions of Europe, with distinctive traditions of building, sculpture and painting established in Provence, Alsace, Poitou, Auvergne and elsewhere. In England, the Norman disposition of two western towers and a central lantern is varied by surviving Carolingian traditions to produce the central and western towers of Ely or the transeptal towers of Exeter. Many English church west facades, like Castle Acre Priory, are simply arcaded screens without towers, reflecting forms found in western France or northern Italy. There are many departures from the Norman division of nave arcade, triforium gallery and clerestory, as at Tewkesbury Abbey where the giant order of columns in the nave arcades is more

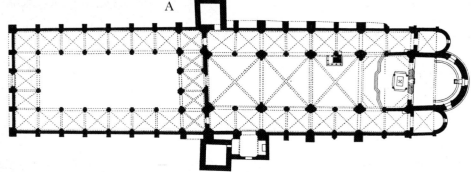

Romanesque church plans: (A) San Ambrogio, Milan (1088–1128); (B) Santiago de Compostela (1075–1128); (C) Durham Cathedral (1093–1133).

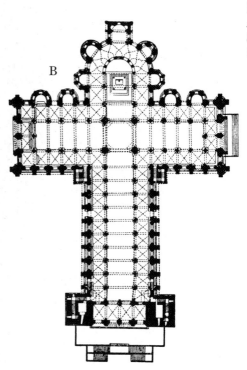

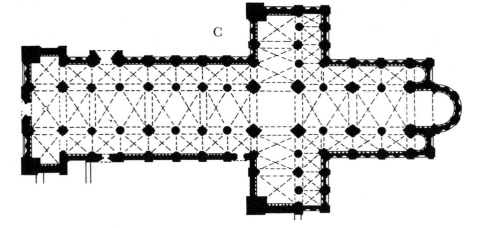

above
Zamora Cathedral (1151–74) is one of
several Spanish churches with ribbed
central domes, showing Islamic
influence.

below
Kilpeck parish church, Herefordshire:
rich carving represents a 12th-century
regional school of sculpture.

characteristic of central France than
of Normandy.

Such national and regional variations naturally find still greater
expression lower down the social
scale of building, in the parish
churches and domestic buildings.
The divisions of feudal society in the
eleventh and twelfth centuries, sep-
arating Church and State from
both peasantry and townspeople,
resulted in very clear distinctions
between their respective building
forms. This is particularly so in
England, where the gap between
the Norman ruling-classes and the
English-speaking people laid down
the foundation for that division
which has so characterized English
society, and which throughout the
Middle Ages was to divide its
architecture.

In France, the parish churches,
particularly in the north, are usually vaulted in stone and differ from
the greater churches primarily in
scale and degree. In England, however, the lesser churches retain clear
evidence of earlier pre-conquest
building traditions, as do the houses
of the peasantry and smaller gentry.
The strength of the timber-building
tradition survives in the general use
of open timber roofs in parish
churches. There are also significant
differences in plan and form, with
such features from late Saxon building as the square-ended chancel, the
western tower and the lateral entrances from north and south, contrasting with more usual Norman designs.

Secular building
Apart from the churches, little
remains of Romanesque building,
with the notable exception of the
castles. The castle is as important to
the Romanesque as is the abbey;
both are equally the product of the
social and political order of their
day. In an age of rebirth and re-
settlement, their roles were complementary in restoring peace and
order to Europe.

Although military architecture
had been developed to a high level

by the Roman engineers, their defences, like the earthwork fortifications of the post-Roman era, were entirely designed for the protection of communities in towns, encampments and burghs. The concept of the castle as an individually maintained and strategically sited strongpoint is probably Byzantine in origin. It was however the development of feudalism in the post-Carolingean period which gave full scope for its evolution in western Europe.

The feudal system occasioned the development of a warring aristocracy, holding land for themselves and their king by means of strongly defended buildings, serving both as personal dwellings and as military strongpoints. Private strongholds of this nature played an increasing role in the ninth century in defending the empire from attack by the Normans, and the Normans themselves subsequently played a major part in developing this concept in their conquests through Europe. In Britain in particular, the major programme of building following the conquest produced significant developments. The Normanization of the country was shared between the king and his feudal overlords, from their new castles, fortified manor houses, and *bastide* towns, and the equally feudal powers of the new monasteries and cathedrals from their defended enclaves in town and country.

The first castles were designed for offence as much as for defence, in forms which could be rapidly erected in hostile country. The

above
San Gimignano, Tuscany: tower houses of the 11th century and later, built by rival families and their adherents.

above left
The 12th-century nave of Peterborough Cathedral with richly painted wood roof. The aisles are cross-vaulted in stone.

motte and bailey castle, relying primarily on earthwork defences which could be erected by unskilled labour, appeared in France in large numbers in the eleventh century and spread to England even before the conquest. It comprised an artificial mound of earth – the motte – often of great size, surmounted by a tower of wood or stone, and approached from a court or bailey.

It is probably from this early form of vertical defence that the most notable feature of Romanesque military architecture emerged – the great tower, or *donjon*, now generally termed the keep. Of the many

forms developed, square and circular, the most impressive are the great stone keeps of London and Colchester, dating from the late eleventh century, together with such French examples as Loches and Houdan. The towers provided living quarters for the feudal lord and his family on upper floors above guard-rooms and cellars. The introspective character and architectural forms of these vast structures correspond to those of the greater churches, with massive walls and vaults enclosing compartmented and dimly-lit spaces, and presenting a monumental and vastly awe-

inspiring presence to the outer world.

The great towers were usually built in baileys, defended initially by massive earthern ramparts, such as still dwarf the great keep of Castle Rising in Norfolk, England. As times became more settled, the practice developed of strengthening the outer fortifications with stone walls, towers and gates, the Romanesque builders drawing on experience of the engineering achievements of Islamic builders in Spain and the Holy Land. The increased geometrical skills required to design such defences, and the complex polygonal tower

Oakham Castle Hall: the late 12th-century great hall of a fortified manor house or castle.

Château de Niort: a French donjon tower, with rounded angles to counter the practice of mining.

Castle Rising is a mid 12th-century keep in East Anglia within a ring motte and flanking baileys.

forms seen in Henry II's tower at Orford in Suffolk, England, certainly appear to reflect eastern influences, and these developments owe more to the approach of the Gothic era than to the Romanesque.

Within the enclosing defences of the bailey more spacious living apartments could be developed, assembled on the informal, com-partmented and additive principal which is itself so characteristically Romanesque. The apartments of the king or feudal lord would normally be within the great tower, while further halls and solars, built over vaulted ground-floor cellars, were provided for other members of the household. The most important element in the informally-planned group was the great hall, built at ground level and fulfilling many functions. The chapel, kitchen, service- and store-rooms completed the domestic apartments.

In the larger palaces and castles the great halls were of impressive scale and magnificence. That in the former royal palace of Westminster measured 73 m × 20.5 m (239 ft × 67 ft), and in its Romanesque form was aisled in timber, although re-roofed and reformed in the fourteenth century to its present appearance. Remains of English great halls of this date with timber roofs and aisle posts still stand at Lincoln Castle and in the bishop's palace of Hereford.

above
Wartburg Palace, Eisenach, is a rare survival of 12th-century palace architecture, with principal apartments at first-floor level.

The two concepts of living expressed within castles, the ground-floor halls and first-floor halls and private solars, were together to provide the basis for the domestic architecture of the Middle Ages. Because of great advances in domestic building in later centuries, surviving evidence is limited to a small number of town houses within the older cities of Europe and, in England in particular, to some surviving stone-walled manor houses of the twelfth century. The manor house was itself a further link in the chain of feudal control and in Norman England these were often built of stone and well defended. The usual arrangement includes a first-floor hall and adjoining solar, over a cellar at ground level, entered like the castle great towers at the upper level. The manor house at Boothby Pagnell in Lincolnshire is probably the most complete survival of this type, with a wall fireplace and cross-vaulted undercroft or cellar.

In France, possibly because of the destruction of the Hundred Years' War, there is little evidence of early manors. The more rapid advancement of urban society here and elsewhere in Europe meant that town building was more highly developed with town palaces and smaller houses built in stone for the noble families and rich merchants for the protection of themselves and their goods. Their poorer neighbours continued older traditions of vernacular building in timber. Throughout Europe, first-floor living was general in the eleventh and twelfth centuries, ground floors being used for storage or for commercial use, and commonly vaulted in stone for security and protection from fire. The twelfth-century houses remaining at Cluny are of this type, with ranges of round-arched windows to the first-floor rooms, and round chimneys in stone.

In the more autonomous cities of Italy, in particular, town houses and palaces are often extended by tower-like structures for reasons both of defence and ostentation. The palace towers of San Gimignano reached such heights that local ordinances had to be introduced to control the competitive aspirations of greater noble families.

Apart from such buildings, the towns of Romanesque Europe had little need for other works of architecture. Within the structure of feudal and ecclesiastical jurisdiction, church and castle between them provided all that was necessary for administration and justice, for education and welfare. It was left to the Gothic era and the increasing emancipation of urban society to produce a demand for new public buildings and to provide new architectural forms to satisfy this need.

GOTHIC

above
Autun Cathedral, Burgundy (1090–1132): transitional Gothic characterized by use of pointed-arched barrel vaults.

right
Noyon Cathedral (late 12th century): the apsidal end of the south transept, showing the four stages of the elevation.

The origins of the Gothic

In an outpouring of creative activity almost unparalleled in Europe since Roman times, Gothic art and architecture emerged in the mid-twelfth century in the region around Paris, with the Abbey of St Denis, lying at the point of origin, serving as one of the formative buildings in its creation. The guiding inspiration has been attributed to one of the greatest ecclesiastics and statesmen of the age, Suger, Abbot of St Denis and for a time Regent of France. His new buildings at St Denis marked the end of a short period of transition, in which Romanesque structure and planning had advanced to the point where they could be translated into Gothic, under the necessary conditions of political and social advancement.

In the twelfth century, such conditions prevailed in Europe only in the Île de France, the Royal Domain of the Capet rulers of France, of which Paris was the capital. The accession of Louis VII in 1137 had opened a new era of political evolution which, in the following century under the rule of Philip Augustus and Saint Louis, was to make France the greatest power in Europe. Within the Île de France, the union of political, religious and civic authority provided the stimulus as necessary for the creation of the Gothic as were the fine limestones of the region.

Although the name Gothic derives from the criticisms of medieval art by the writers of the Italian Renaissance, the later twelfth century was itself a period of renaissance as a result of a new and beneficial flowering of classical learning. Preserved by the Islamic conquerors of the Eastern Roman Empire, classical texts were being translated into Latin in Toledo, where Christian and Muslim worlds met, and so brought to Paris, where at the end of the twelfth century the University of Paris came into being. It was to be the focal point of European culture and learning, drawing scholars from all Christendom. Here was evolved scholasticism, the new school of philosophy from which Gothic art is inseparable, and in Paris also was conceived the Gothic of the cathedrals, described with justification as scholasticism in stone. For almost four hundred years, Gothic was to remain the art of western Christendom, reflecting in its splendour all the richness of the medieval world.

Gothic art and architecture were conceived as a total creative concept designed to enable the apocalyptic vision of the Heavenly City to be realized in the material forms of the greater cathedral church. Just as the works of the scholastic philosophers brought together all knowledge in their great theses or *summae*, so the cathedral was the *summa* of all known concepts of structure, form and enrichment, wherein architec-

tural elements such as the pointed
arch, the ribbed vault and the flying
buttress, all of which ante-date the
Gothic, take a sudden leap forward
in development to express with
absolute clarity a new theologically
and philosophically based ideal. A
new unity of space, a soaring verticality and a transparent luminosity
are achieved within a fully articulated and apparently weightless
structure, the whole providing the
setting for a complex iconographical
programme of enrichment to which
all the arts and crafts contributed.

Because of its central position,
the Île de France could draw on the
architectural experience of both
Normandy and Burgundy in the
development of Gothic structure.
From Normandy was adopted the
late Romanesque form of sexpartite
vaulting, but transformed by the
use of pointed arches. In Burgundy,
the adoption of the pointed arch
early in the twelfth century from
Islamic sources in southern Europe
had resulted in a distinctive, transitional style, which was transmitted
by the new monastic order of the
Cistercians throughout Europe in
buildings of great beauty and simplicity. The violent opposition
voiced by their leader, Saint Bernard of Clairvaux, to all aspects of
applied richness and beauty in
church architecture did much to
end the influence of Cluny and
indirectly to prepare the way for
cathedral Gothic. In contrast, Suger
provided a philosophical and
theological justification for material
beauty in declaring that 'the dull
mind rises to truth through that
which is material' and so established a basis for all Gothic art. In
the concept of beauty, the symbolism of light came to be regarded as
the primary source and essence.

Cathedral Gothic
The west front of the Carolingean
basilica of St Denis was rebuilt by
Suger between 1137 and 1140, but it
is in the rebuilding of the choir
which followed that the qualities of
Gothic emerge, in a continuous
sense of interpenetrating space
which permits the richness of coloured glass to transfuse the interior

above
Chartres Cathedral: introduction of the flying buttress made possible the 13th-century dissolution of solid walls.

above left
The ambulatory of Abbot Suger's new choir for the Abbey Church of St Denis, near Paris, built between 1140 and 1143.

with mystic and uninterrupted light. The new church was consecrated on 11 June, 1144, and Suger's own account vividly recalls the splendour of the occasion. With King Louis and his queen, there were present 17 archbishops and bishops, including Theobald of Canterbury, and within the next 75 years, all their cathedrals had followed the lead of St Denis.

The completion of Suger's work marked only the beginning of the realization of the Gothic concept within the Île de France. In subsequent cathedral building in and around the Royal Domain in the second half of the twelfth century, notably at the cathedrals of Sens, Senlis, Noyon, Laon, Mantes and Paris, and culminating in the building of Chartres, cathedral Gothic moved rapidly towards its classic phase. In each city, cathedral chapter and urban commune joined together to outdo their neighbours in the scale and magnificence of their great churches. In the spirit of

faith which characterized the age, it is recorded that peasants and noblemen alike contributed to the costs of building at Chartres, and joined together to draw the carts laden with stone, in scenes of rejoicing.

It is at Chartres, at the turn of the century, that cathedral Gothic reaches maturity. Of all the great cathedrals, Chartres has most perfectly preserved its original form and treasures, and here, perhaps better than in any other great church, can still be comprehended something of the meaning of Gothic. The incomparable beauty of the sculpture, the radiant luminosity of the stained glass, the spacious and classically composed proportions, all mark Chartres as one of the greatest achievements of the Gothic world.

The harmony of the proportions of the interior and of the western facade have been attributed to a classical and measurable order, determined by the application of 'sacred geometry'. In a period

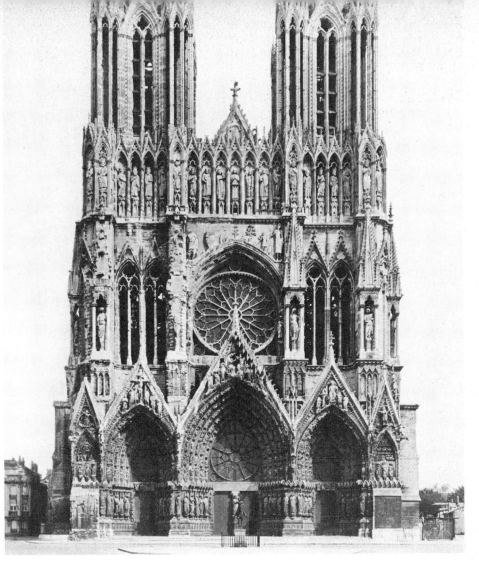

West facade of Reims Cathedral, begun after 1241 by Bernard de Soissons with towers completed in the 15th century.

Le Mans Cathedral: rebuilding of the choir began in 1218, omitting the triforium stage.

marked by the growing status of the architect, from that of anonymous master craftsman to one meriting the title of 'Doctor Lathomorum', as inscribed on the tombstone of the great Parisian master, Pierre de Montereau, it is evident that some system of geometric proportions was used in design, although there is no indication of a generally accepted method.

Structurally, the advances of Chartres, in the use of the flying buttress and the ribbed vault over a rectangular bay, were only the first step towards the achievement of still greater churches which followed in the first half of the thirteenth century. Bourges, Reims, Amiens and Le Mans, all extend the concepts of verticality and transparency into the development of Rayonnant Gothic and the almost total elimination of the solid wall, achieved most completely in the new nave of St Denis. When work was begun at Beauvais in 1247, the ultimate in cathedral Gothic was achieved in this, the loftiest of the Gothic churches, with the concept of vertical space being extended to the limits of masonry structure. The church was uncompleted, and the end of cathedral Gothic was at hand.

From its first emergence at St Denis in 1140, the evolution of Gothic was to be centred on the

Royal Domain for almost a hundred years. Its spread through Europe reflects the growth and influence of France in the thirteenth century. In both Germany and Spain, ecclesiastical links with France resulted in the direct importation of cathedral Gothic by both French and native masters in major cathedral-building projects. Amiens, nearing completion in 1248, and Beauvais, started the previous year, provided the inspiration for the cathedral of Cologne, which exceeds in scale any of the French churches and is second only to Beauvais in the height of its vaulting. In Castile, the cathedrals of Burgos, Toledo and León are also closely related to French classic designs. However, whereas in France the rapid completion of the cathedrals to the designs of their original masters ensured the unity of the concept, in both Germany and Spain building tended to extend over the centuries into periods when more national approaches to Gothic had emerged.

León however is a splendid exception, entirely French in conception and retaining its great areas of late thirteenth- and early fourteenth-century glass to create that sense of sublime weightlessness and rich luminosity which are the essence of cathedral Gothic.

From the outset, England developed a national approach to Gothic. English Gothic owes its origins both to the Anglo-Romanesque traditions which it shared with France and – through the Cistercians – to Burgundy. As in other countries of Europe, however, it was a direct infusion from the Île de France, at Canterbury, which was to end a long period of transition and bring England fully into the Gothic world. For the rebuilding of the choir at Canterbury Cathedral in 1175, a French master, William of Sens, was selected, whose familiarity with work in northern France is clearly shown in the forms of the new choir. There are however significant variations in plan form and

above
Vaulted crypt of the palace chapel of Louis IX, by Pierre de Montereau: Sainte Chapelle, Paris (1243–48).

right
Ambulatory of the Trinity Chapel, Canterbury Cathedral: rebuilding was begun in 1175 by William of Sens.

detailed design, possibly introduced by his successor, William the Englishman, which were to become part of the English Gothic tradition.

By the thirteenth century, in the new cathedrals being built at Wells and Lincoln, the influence of French Gothic had already been absorbed into a form of Gothic which is distinctively English – horizontal in emphasis, spatially subdivided, with strongly linear qualities, and exhibiting such features as the screen-like western facades and polygonal chapter-houses, which are to be associated with English greater churches. Salisbury Cathedral, begun in 1220, the same year as Amiens, is the most expressive of this national character, and unique

left
Cologne Cathedral: choir interior, begun in 1248 by Gerhard and modelled on French cathedral Gothic.

in England in that – apart from tower and spire – it was built in a short period of time and to a single design. Lacking the artistry and sculpture of Wells, or the structural invention of Lincoln, the horizontality and division of its interior spaces stress the different courses taken by English and French masters.

Late Gothic

By the middle of the thirteenth century, France and England had evolved the leading variants of High Gothic. In France, the cathedrals of Reims and Amiens were regarded as peaks of architectural achievement, perfected to the point where their unity of space, light, structure and enrichment could be regarded as a 'classic' solution. While later Gothic buildings continued the logical and often – as at Beauvais – daring exploration of High Gothic concepts, it was always within the limits of the classic solution,

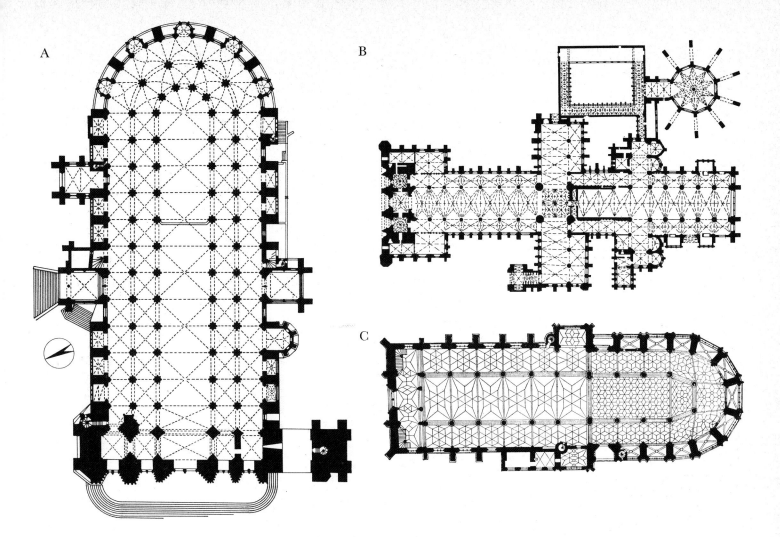

A

B

C

above
Early, High and Late Gothic church plans: (A) Bourges Cathedral (begun 1190); (B) Lincoln Cathedral (13th-century rebuilding); (C) Schwäbisch Gmünd, Holy Cross (begun 1317).

left
Salisbury Cathedral (1220–58): built by Elias of Dereham and Nicholas of Ely, with 14th-century tower and spire.

developing it to the ultimate refinement of the Rayonnant phase of the later thirteenth century and subsequently enriching and elaborating it in the Flamboyant style of Late Gothic.

Whereas the rationalism of the French architects came to restrict evolution, the imagination of the English masters was free to explore more radical forms of vaulting and spatial enclosure, which were to reach their peak in the Perpendicular period of the fourteenth and fifteenth centuries. There nevertheless continue to be clear principles common to both schools and shared by all manifestations of later Gothic throughout Europe. Above all was the desire to achieve greater unity of space, fundamental to Gothic since its inception but now to be developed in new forms generally described as Spatial Gothic.

The Hundred Years' War with England and the Black Death of the fourteenth century retarded architectural development in France, and leadership in the Gothic passed to England and Germany. From the fourteenth century onwards, cathedral building was no longer to be the only or even the primary vehicle for Gothic evolution in Europe. Although the largest of the Gothic cathedrals were still to be built, in Italy and Spain, the highest levels of Gothic achievement in religious architecture now appear in splendid chapels and chantries, in the town churches of the new orders of preaching friars, and in spacious parish churches, serving a populace increasing in numbers and in social importance.

In France, new development occurs not in the north, but in Languedoc and the south, which had inherited a strong tradition of Roman and Romanesque-Catalan building. Here, the traditional basilican form was replaced by a new form of aisleless church of great spaciousness. It is seen most impressively in the fortress-like cathedral of Albi, begun in 1282, and was widely adopted in the Late Gothic period, particularly in Spain.

right
The early 14th-century nave of Exeter Cathedral, by Thomas Witney: tierceron vaulting of the Decorated period.

below
Tewkesbury Abbey, Gloucestershire: the 14th-century lierne vaulting of the choir.

In England, the rebuilding of Westminster Abbey in 1254 for Henry III, himself a great patron of architecture, was probably inspired by the splendours of the Sainte Chapelle in Paris, and was to lead to the elaborate geometric forms of the Decorated period of English Gothic. Of particular significance to English building at this time is the development of tierceron vaulting, first introduced at Lincoln, but seen in its most perfect form at Exeter, the only English cathedral to be rebuilt almost wholly in this period. By the end of the thirteenth century, geometric forms were giving way to the curvilinear Gothic in which reticulated and flowing window-traceries are complemented by the net-like forms of lierne vaulting, creating a continuous and overall patterning which dissolves the solidity of walls and vaults.

The final phase of English Gothic, the Perpendicular, is represented by no complete cathedral, although many, like Gloucester, were rebuilt in part. Its most splendid expression, including the culminating forms of fan vaulting, occurs in a series of great sixteenth-century chapels of outstanding beauty, notably those at Windsor Castle, Westminster Abbey and King's College, Cambridge. This final period is marked by the almost equally splendid series of parish churches built throughout England, in numbers and richness unrivalled elsewhere. In form they are influenced by the town churches of the friars, now almost all destroyed in England. Endowed by wealthy merchants and the rising middle-class, they rival the mainstream of Gothic building, while retaining the interest of a remarkable variety of regional forms, including open timber roofs of great splendour.

Elsewhere in Europe, direct contacts with the High Gothic of France and with the spatial forms of southern France added to the Gothic vocabulary of growing national schools in Spain, Germany and Italy. Despite national differences, there is a remarkable consistency in the later phases of Gothic development in all these countries. The Perpendicular of England, French Flamboyant, German Sondergotik and Spanish Plateresque are all expressions of a common movement in style and intention.

In Italy, there is no major expression of the French High Gothic to compare with those of England, Spain or Germany. The great double church of the Franciscans at Assisi, begun in 1228, is an adaptation of French forms to traditional Italian Romanesque concepts. In the southern sunshine, the simplicity of the interior is enriched by the murals of Giotto and Cimabue, dissolving the solidity of the enclosing walls by their colour and decoration in a manner akin to that of the coloured glass in the churches of north-west Europe.

At the end of the eleventh century and later, civic pride in the independent cities of north and central Italy found expression in an ambitious programme of cathedral building, producing some of the greatest

above
King's College Chapel, Cambridge (1446–1515): looking east, with the fan vault built by John Wastell in 1512.

below
San Francesco, Assisi: entrance to the upper church of Franciscan monastery built between 1228 and 1253.

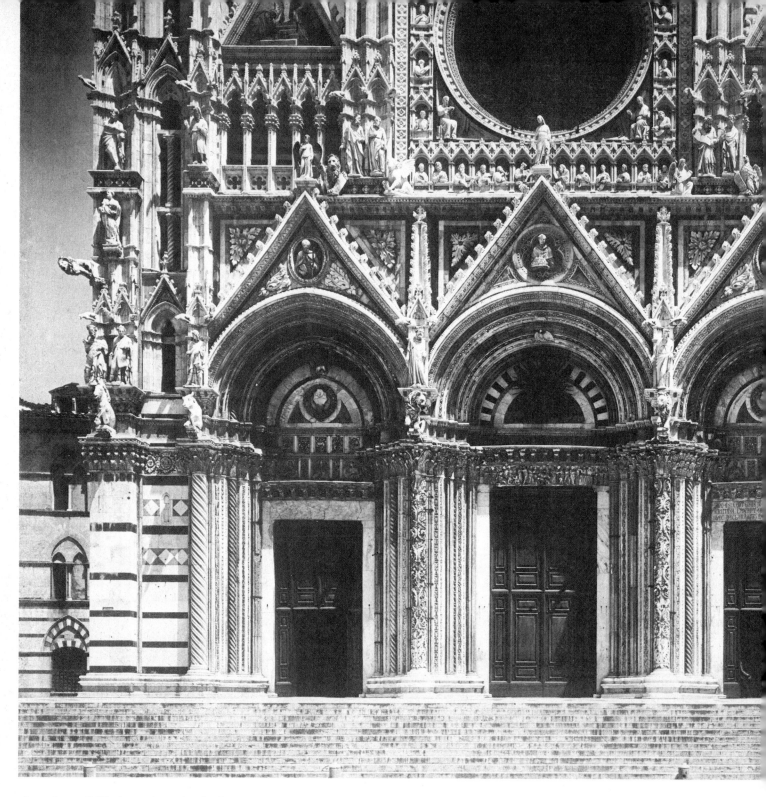

churches of Christendom, including the cathedrals of Milan, of Florence and Siena. Patronized by the ruling families, supported by church and populace, they called on the talents of all local artists for their enrichment. The greatest of these, second only to Seville Cathedral in size among the Gothic cathedrals of Europe, is Milan, begun in 1386 and the last great work of Gothic in Italy.

It is particularly in the Isabelline period of the late fifteenth century that specifically Spanish characteristics develop in Gothic building. In Catalonia, church building followed the same traditions as southern France, in broad, aisleless churches like the cathedral of Gerona, which has the widest vault of any Gothic church, spanning 22 m (73 ft). The aisleless form was adopted throughout Spain, distinguished by rich and superficial decoration. From its resemblance to the *plateria*, or work of the Spanish silversmiths, the style is called Plateresque and is seen at its richest in Salamanca Cathedral as well as in elaborate additions to Burgos Cathedral. The final phase of the Gothic in Spain was one of undiminished vigour in cathedral building. Seville was not begun until 1401, to be followed by the cathedrals of Salamanca and Segovia, and the latter, started in 1522, was the last great cathedral to be built in Gothic Europe.

In Germany also, Late Gothic building assumes distinctive and

national characteristics, arising
from the rich and individual imagination of such great masters as the
Parlers. The hall church, possibly
originating in western France, was
particularly popular with the friars
and it is probable that their
influence extended its use throughout Germany and central Europe. It
provided an alternative solution to
the requirements of spatial Gothic,
by which naves and aisles of equal
height were merged under a single
roof, the slender piers uniting space
rather than dividing it as in the
basilica. Particularly associated
with this form is the development of
lierne vaulting comparable with
that in England. Its use is notable in
the work of Peter Parler, who produced the first net-vaults in Prague
Cathedral at the end of the fourteenth century, creating a continuous, reticulated pattern of light ribs,
comparable with the English fan
vault in its reduction of the structural vault to the character of a
richly textured ceiling.

The final phase of German
Gothic, termed Sondergotik, expresses continuity of movement
through the unity of space, as
achieved within richly-vaulted hall
churches throughout north and
central Europe. Here the vaulting
ribs flow without interruption from
the piers, spreading their mobile
patterns in complete negation of
their original structural function.
The widespread use of brickwork,
often in conjunction with hall
churches, also contributed to the

Medieval fortified city of Carcassonne, with citadel and concentric fortifications (largely 13th century).

Fireplace in the Palace of the Counts of Poitou, Poitiers (1384–86), by Guy de Dammartin for John, Duke of Berry.

The great 15th-century castle of the Mendosas, Manzanares el Real, showing strong Mudéjar characteristics.

establishment of a Gothic style which was notable for its particular individuality.

Secular Gothic

As the Church dominated all aspects of life in the Gothic world, so all levels of society shared to some degree in the architectural forms it had created. The great churches were rivalled by the magnificence of royal and ecclesiastical palaces and later by civic and commercial buildings of almost equally palatial scale. Of secular buildings, the castles alone remain in numbers and scale sufficient to show that their designs reflected the developing concepts of the Gothic and played their part in its evolution.

Islam contributed to the great buildings of the age of chivalry from its long experience and advanced skills in military engineering. In particular, the concentric forms of curtain-wall defences, developed by the crusaders in such great Near Eastern fortresses as the Krak des Chevaliers, transformed the design of castles and town fortifications throughout Europe. Of equal importance to their development was the understanding of geometry. Conflicts within France and in England in the late twelfth and thirteenth centuries provided abundant scope for the design skills of the medieval masters and *ingeniators*. Among the results were such fortresses as the Château Gaillard, built by Richard I; the concentrically walled fortress towns of central France, such as Carcassonne; and, later in the thirteenth century, the magnificent series of castles and *bastide* towns built in support of Edward I's conquests in north Wales and Scotland, one of the very

above
Harlech Castle, north Wales: a late 13th-century concentric castle built by James of St George for Edward I.

below
House of Jacques Coeur, Bourges (1442–53): the town house of a merchant prince, built around a courtyard.

above
Stokesay Castle is a late 13th-century fortified manor house in the Welsh Marches with a great hall.

greatest building operations undertaken during the Middle Ages.

From the fourteenth century onwards, more settled conditions in Europe accelerated the transformation of the military stronghold into the palace and country house. Little remains of the greater palaces of the thirteenth and fourteenth centuries but it is clear that they provided halls and chambers of great scale and splendour, as can be still seen in the Palace of the Popes at Avignon. By the fifteenth century, castles throughout Europe had developed into stately mansions, with fine suites of apartments planned around courtyards, but often retaining the military trappings of mural towers, castellated battlements and machicolated galleries, their effectiveness now reduced by the advent of gunpowder and cannon, but still symbolizing feudal authority.

Throughout the Gothic era, welfare and education remained the province of the Church. These functions were originally served within the actual precincts of the greater churches, but hospitals, almshouses, colleges and schools were increasingly developed as separate buildings, their plans and forms

224

above
Urban Gothic of the 15th century in Louvain, Brabant: Town Hall (1448–63) by Mathieu de Layens and St Peter's Church (1425–97).

left
Town Hall, Audenarde, Brabant (1525–30): a rich example of Flemish civic Gothic, built by Jan van Pede.

clearly retaining evidence of their ecclesiastical origins. The universities of Oxford and Cambridge were developing distinctive collegiate forms of Gothic architecture as early as the fourteenth century, combining both the qualities of religious and domestic Gothic. Their splendid chapels and great halls place them increasingly in the forefront of architectural design in the fifteenth and sixteenth centuries, and buildings of such splendour as the Divinity Schools in Oxford, with lierne and pendant vaults of great richness, rivalled any ecclesiastical structure of the period.

Above all, however, it is within the prosperous mercantile towns and cities of later medieval Europe, advancing in wealth and independence, that Gothic building was most fully extended into new and secular architectural forms of a scale and splendour equalling the heights of religious building. Civic pride now found expression in the palaces and town houses of the nobility and the merchant princes, in town halls, guild halls, halls of justice, cloth halls and other civic palaces. The

225

mercantile palaces of Venice and other Italian cities are of particular splendour, looking forward to the Renaissance in their plan and form, although purely Gothic in character as in the unrivalled Doge's Palace in Venice. In Belgium, the commercial centre of Europe in the later Middle Ages, the greatest of the cloth halls, that at Ypres, survives only in rebuilt form, but almost equally fine public buildings remain at Bruges, Brussels, Louvain and in the Hanseatic cities of Germany and northern Europe, rich in tracery, sculpture, vaulting and coloured glass, and conceived in the full spirit of Spatial Gothic. But rich and splendid as are these greater secular buildings, the full concept of the Gothic can only be appreciated in the great cathedrals and churches which gave it birth, where full philosophical and theological understanding gives reason to the outward forms.

The late 14th-century facades of the Palace of the Doges, Venice, were designed by Giovanni and Bartolomeo Buon.

RENAISSANCE

Dominance of classical models
'Renaissance' is the English version of an Italian word meaning 'rebirth'. It was first used in the nineteenth century to describe a series of changes which overtook European society from the fifteenth century onwards. There has been considerable debate about exactly what took place during this period of change and even about when it started and finished. For our purposes the word will be used to describe buildings produced under the influence of Renaissance culture which appear quite different from any of those which had ever existed before.

In answer to the question of what exactly it was that was 'reborn' or 'renewed' during this period, it is helpful to see the renewal as one which took place on every level of society and involved reference to a common denominator of excellence. It was thought that the idea of what constituted excellence could be discovered in ancient civilization. For architecture this meant a conscious decision to uncover or rediscover the remains of antiquity, learn from them and apply this learning to building. Antiquity could teach lessons of various kinds: ruins were examined for structural laws, ancient theory books were perused and translated, visual motifs were copied and ideological principles were reapplied. Ancient buildings were seen as a series of examples and architecture was judged on its capacity to follow them.

Developments in building during the Renaissance took the form of a conversation held in the language of classical architecture. Exactly what defined 'classical' was not always clear and sometimes hotly debated but there was rarely any dissent from the basic principle that 'classical' equalled 'good'. In Renaissance Florence it was no compliment to refer to a building as 'modern' for this implied Gothic in style and therefore old-fashioned. The most prestigious architecture was designed *all'antica*, that is in the ancient style and in direct contrast to the barbaric Gothic. As more became known about ancient architecture it grew clear that 'classical' could mean an enormous variety of different things. This discovery reinforced the notion that constant reference to ancient buildings was a common denominator for architectural excellence.

The earliest developments in the culture of the Renaissance, including architecture, took place in the Italian city of Florence, and its buildings illustrate most of the major changes. The architects of fifteenth-century Florence formulated the classical language of architecture and learned some basic lessons from the remains of antiquity. Their productions demonstrate another important characteristic of Renaissance architecture, that

is its intellectual flavour. Very few of the really important early figures were, in fact, trained as architects. Filippo Brunelleschi started out as a goldsmith and Leon Battista Alberti was a gentleman and scholar. During the Renaissance architecture began to be more of a mental exercise than a manual exertion, viewed as a science controlled by literary theory and mathematical principle rather than the rules of thumb and traditional pattern duplication of the Gothic architects, who were invariably trained as masons.

Once the principle of the theoretical dominance of classical models had been adopted, it controlled developments at every turn. The dome of Florence Cathedral, the construction of which Brunelleschi supervised from 1420 to 1434, is an example at the level of structure. The fabric of the cupola is formed from an unusual pattern of herringbone brickwork and the commonly-held view was that Brunelleschi had learned about this pattern from his examination of the ruins of antiquity in Rome itself.

The dome was to become a potent symbol of the achievements of the Florentine people and they took particular pride in the fact that it had been constructed in such close sympathy with the ideals of Ancient Rome. In some ways the recognition that this might in fact be a myth is more important than

228

the actual origins of the technique used. Contemporary sources suggest that Brunelleschi was well aware that the problems involved in the hemispherical vault over the Pantheon were quite different from the eight-sided drum upon which he was forced to build in Florence. Here we have a typical example of the conflict between architectural theory and practice. The story of architecture built in the classical style is very much dominated by such tensions.

above
Brunelleschi's Florence Cathedral dome (1420–36): a technical experiment symbolizing a new era in architecture.

below
Pazzi Chapel in the cloister of Santa Croce, Florence: Brunelleschi's clever centralized plan of the 1430s.

Importance of rational systems

Another early building by Brunelleschi illustrates an important feature of what was to develop into the Renaissance style. This is the basing of architectural design upon the juxtaposition of pure geometrical forms. The chapel paid for by the Pazzi family, great political rivals of the Medici, and erected in the cloister of the Franciscan church of Santa Croce (1429–46) is an

example of the fascination which centralized planning continued to hold throughout the fifteenth century, an interest which culminated in the Roman designs of Bramante early in the sixteenth century. The Pazzi chapel is built around the relationship of cubes and spheres, or, in two-dimensional terms, squares and circles.

The environments which resulted from such experiments are rightly characterized as light, airy and graceful. For many they remain the epitome of the Renaissance as it affected architecture. Nevertheless it would not be doing these buildings justice to allow our appreciation to rest solely upon such aesthetic grounds as these. For early Renaissance architecture, controlled as it is by the definition of space in terms of proportion and harmony, reflects the influence of classical antiquity on an ideological level as well as in its good looks. The architects of the day had heard that the architecture of antiquity was based upon mathematical principles and were keen to emulate their ancestors.

It is doubtful whether the observer of an interior such as the Pazzi Chapel would immediately register the relationship of its parts, although its ground plan is exactly defined mathematically. However, once this is known to be the case he or she can interpret the building as an exercise in science and relate closely to the architect's intentions. The appreciation becomes intellectual rather than purely aesthetic, with the observer being offered a direct and quantifiable method by which to relate to the architecture. On this level too the question of size becomes less important. The history of the Gothic cathedral can be told in terms of natural growth and continuing process of expansion. In contrast to that, many of the centralized plans of the Renaissance are quite modest in their dimensions; questions of scale have inevitably become subordinate to those of proportion. Grandeur was frequently a by-product rather than an objective, the aim being to stimulate and inspire rather than overwhelm.

above
The 'classical' style in the columns and arches of Brunelleschi's nave of Santo Spirito, Florence (*c.* 1436).

Andrea Palladio

The harmonic disposition of the internal units and the repetition of external members in the villas and palaces designed later in the century by Andrea Palladio are thus manifestations of a wider desire to impose a rational system upon man-made environments. His particular formula was initially based upon a careful observation of the remains of ancient Rome and he even produced a guidebook to the ruins. Yet, he was also willing to invent motifs of his own and accept and expand upon the ideas of various other modern architects – Bramante, Michelangelo, Giulio Romano, Sansovino and others. These attributes

above
The facade of the Strozzi Palace, Florence, looks solid and well organized, as suited a merchant family.

above
Santa Maria della Consolazione at
Todi: an exercise in central planning of
c. 1500, well-placed on a hill-top site.

of antiquarian wisdom and acute
visual judgment were combined
with a flair for producing practical
solutions and an immense capacity
for hard work and satisfying his
clients. Palladio was thus able to
produce a huge corpus of designs for
both public and private commis-
sions. His work has only rarely been
rivalled in its variety, serenity and
integrity and never in the influence

it exerted on later architects. This
process was certainly aided by the
fact that Palladio's book, *Architet-
tura*, was not only illustrated by his
own designs but was so much more
useful than the often obscure
ancient text of Vitruvius, the late
first century BC Roman authority.

Palladio's main contribution was
a great series of palaces and villas in
and around Vicenza, a satellite city

of Venice in northern Italy, whose social structure included a large number of noble families. This group formed his private patrons for 30 years from about 1550. His first great success was, however, a public commission for the remodelling of the basilica in Vicenza with a design both grand and elegant. This task was one which required considerable structural expertise and Palladio always remained an architect of the highest professional standards. A later building near the basilica is the Loggia del Capitaniato (1571), which made use of the Giant Order – a column or pilaster embracing two storeys – a feature established by Michelangelo in his Capitoline palaces, built in Rome in the 1540s. Another motif extensively used by Palladio was the balustrade or bannister. This was not, in fact, found in antiquity either but in his hands looks absolutely at home in the classical canon of design.

In the villas and palaces of the Chiericati, Thiene, Valmarana and other families great emphasis was placed on the shapes and sizes of the rooms. These were characterized by the imposition of mathematically based proportion and the creation of dynamic sequences. The interiors of Palladio's buildings – symmetrical and generously proportioned – seem the perfect compliment to his elegant exteriors, which is, of course, exactly what he intended.

Synthesis of two worlds

Apart from this intellectual element in the whole movement, it also contrived, through the use of symbolism, to weld the physical and religious natures of man. Despite the value placed upon the examples gleaned from ancient civilization, Renaissance culture was, for the most part, an intensely devout, Christian phenomenon. Great emphasis was placed upon the ability to combine the pagan philosophies of antiquity with the god-centred world of fifteenth-century

Italy. As far as architecture was concerned, this synthesis could operate on several levels. For example, Christian churches came to be called temples during this period without complaint from the ecclesiastical establishment, who were, for the most part, as keen as any to show their sympathy for the new learning.

In one particular respect many of the attributes discussed so far combined as the result of a most ingenious solution. In their attempts to understand and illustrate a small passage in an ancient book on the theory of building, Renaissance architects discovered a means of expressing simultaneously their interest in imposing a rational system upon building designs based upon immutable mathematical principles within a system which

below
Palladio's Villa Rotonda at Maser, near Vicenza (*c.* 1550): a gracious exterior to the working centre of a country estate.

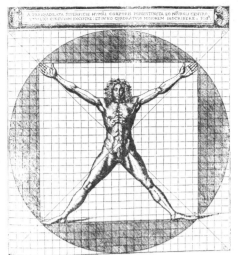

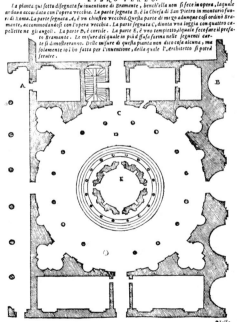

used perfect geometrical figures and a principle for relating architecture to man, which in turn transformed building into a form of worship.

The passage appeared in Vitruvius's *Ten Books on Architecture* and describes how the figure of a man could be disposed within a circle and a square with its limbs outstretched and touching the circumference. The numerous illustrations of this passage show the attraction of the principle, despite the practical problems which arose in achieving the effect whilst keeping the centre of both figures at the navel. The next stage in the process of synthesizing these theories was to turn the man-centred structure of the centralized plan into a glorification of God. This was achieved by the manipulation of the ancient Judeo-Christian dogma of man created in God's image. The dimensions of man thereby became a celebration of the perfection of the

above
Santa Maria Novella, Florence:
Alberti's carefully proportioned facade
was started in 1458 on earlier
foundations.

left
Loggia del Capitaniato, Vicenza
(1571), by Palladio: the unfinished
facade uses Giant columns through
both storeys.

godhead, which was in turn reflected in the purity of the basic geometrical forms.

Rules of structure and design
The concept of perfection in architecture raises important questions about the practical issues of design and structure. Alberti not only designed and supervised the construction of buildings but also wrote the first book on the theory of architecture to be produced in modern times, *On Building* (first published in Florence in 1485, a work very much on the model of Vitruvius). He argued that the roots of architectural beauty lay in attempting the 'perfect' design,

which he defined as: '... the harmony and concord of all the parts achieved in such a manner that nothing could be added or taken away or altered except for the worse.'

Within such an ideological framework, the organic aspects of Gothic building had clearly been rejected. We can observe Alberti's theory of beauty translated into stone on the facade he superimposed upon the much older west end of the church of S Maria Novella in Florence (1456–70). At S Maria Novella Alberti was working under the practical difficulty of completing a work started in an older style. The skill with which he

235

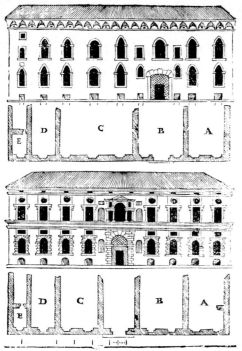

fulfilled his task shows not only his confidence in introducing classical motifs like pointed pediments and moulded string-courses into the composition but also his sympathy for the scale of the earlier arcade at ground level. To ensure the compatibility of the upper and lower parts of the facade Alberti introduced a visual pause in the form of a high attic running across the middle of the building. This horizontal emphasis offsets what would otherwise have been an excessive verticality in the arcade and columns below and the pilaster strips above.

The basic features of the classical style of building as they were adopted in the Renaissance were the use of vertical structural members, or columns, which supported horizontal beams, the entablature, and in turn rested upon bases. The horizontal surfaces were decorated by a variety of mouldings. Arches between the vertical members were round-headed rather than pointed and disposed symmetrically around a central point. The overall impression was one of balance, order and an organization of the parts in such a way that the essential structure, that is the fabric of the building that was responsible for it remaining upright, was usually arranged in an easily recognizable grid. The parts of the fabric which carried the weight had to be seen to be doing their job and also to seem well capable of taking the strain. The adoption of the language of classical architecture meant that importance was placed on the proportions of the different members one to another. Deviations from these rules tended to be interpreted as mistakes and criticized as such.

Michelangelo

The most profound rejection of the basic principles of Renaissance architecture came from Michelangelo, whose achievements in this field match his contributions to painting and sculpture. He not only invented new types of ornament but fundamentally changed the prevailing attitudes towards the nature of the wall surface and the enclosing of space. His capacity to master,

transcend and finally dispense with principles hard won by most of his contemporaries is demonstrated in all his designs.

The Medici mausoleum at San Lorenzo, Florence (slow progress from 1520), suggests that Michelangelo saw the wall surface as an organic entity – no longer an inert structural curtain. The nearby vestibule for the Library (1526) includes columns which are in fact weight-bearing, but apparently only decorative. Everywhere he rejects the dominance of the classical Orders. He also introduced a new compositional shape by adopting the oval as the central space in the reorganization of the Capitol, Rome (begun 1539).

These innovations, together with his control of mass and space (see his additions to St Peter's, Rome, on which he worked from the death of Antonio da Sangallo in 1546), were only fully understood in the Baroque period. Although many architects were directly influenced by details of his work, for example Vasari, the great biographer of artists (Uffizi, Florence, started 1560), there were many more who were unable to grasp the total impact.

With the passing of time and the growth of greater confidence on the part of architects, the value of the mistake designed to shock and stimulate the observer came to be recognized. In some way, it makes sense to understand the phase of Renaissance art known as Mannerism as a conscious breaking of the rules. Of course, those rules are simply sets of conventions existing between observer and designer, and the offering of potentially stimulating mistakes by the latter presupposes a willingness on the part of the former to learn and appreciate the *status quo*. Mannerism is even more intellectual than Renaissance.

Provincial Renaissance architecture

Renaissance architecture has so far been discussed mainly in terms of the mainstream of developments which took place firstly in Florence and subsequently in Rome. The

left
Vestibule of the Library in San
Lorenzo, Florence (started 1524):
Michelangelo's personal style is clear.

below
Courtyard of the Ducal Palace, Urbino,
designed pre-1468 by Laurana: the
inscription outlines the patron's virtues.

above
A magnificent facade for the Certosa, near Pavia (started *c.* 1490): the church served a Carthusian monastery.

left
Machuca's facade of the Palace of Charles V, Granada (started 1527): Roman High Renaissance in Spain.

right
Galerie de François 1, Fontainebleu, France (begun *c.* 1533), by Rosso and Primaticcio: decoration is Italian.

changes which architecture underwent as a result of the general cultural shift of the Renaissance have been described as of ideological interest only to an elite group. Thus the appreciation of architecture in the Renaissance could be seen as a game in which all those wanting to play – architects, patrons and observers – had to know the rules. It would follow, therefore, that for those who were unaware of the ideological foundations of the Renaissance style – the use of perfect geometrical forms, for example – its appreciation could take place on one level only: the adoption of stylistic motifs gathered together from a number of sources under the general label of classical. The

degree to which it makes sense to consider Renaissance architecture not only as a set of visual characteristics but also as a style with a 'meaning' is demonstrated by the forms of Renaissance buildings in provincial contexts.

Provincial forms of Renaissance architecture could relate to the prototypes established in High Renaissance Rome in a considerable number of different ways. In the same non-Italian location at the same period we can find examples of buildings where the influence of Italianate classicism is extremely strong alongside more conventional buildings where the knowledge of any Renaissance style is barely discernible. As we might expect, the

'purer' Italianate designs are more international in style whereas the 'corrupt' examples show a resistance to change and an adherence to traditional forms.

Two buildings under construction in Spain in the later 1520s make this point. The Palace of Charles V at Granada is entirely classical in spirit and is closely related to the style of the Roman High Renaissance. The plan places a circular colonnade or peristyle in two storeys within four ranges of walling, which in turn form a square. This circle within a square is a clear example of architecture based on geometrical purity. The fabric of the palace also shows a correct application of the Orders:

the architect, Pedro Machuca, has got his grammar right. On the other hand, the facade of the university building at Salamanca in Old Castile reveals a debt to the Renaissance style only in its surface appearances; an Italianate decorative vocabulary is employed as a veneer on a Gothic framework.

We do not have to go beyond Italy itself to come across provincial variations from the Florentine-Roman mainstream. Typically, Venice went very much her own way as we can see in a church like S Maria dei Miracoli, dating from the 1480s. Here we have examples of the classical vocabulary, like grotesque decoration in low relief, baluster colonnettes, fluted pilasters and so on, applied to a building some of whose characteristics derive ultimately from Venice's ancient and unique connection with the Byzantine culture at the eastern end of the Mediterranean.

The two Spanish buildings considered demonstrate the importance of knowing the exact nature of the contact between designer and prototype because this determines the extent of the sympathy for an influential culture which a building will eventually display. Machuca is known to have been in Rome during the High Renaissance period, and the ground plan of his Granada

above
University facade, Salamanca (1514–29): typical provincial use of Italianate Renaissance motifs on Gothic structure.

right
Lombardo's Santa Maria dei Miracoli, Venice (1480s), is a miniature church faced in coloured marble decoration.

palace is perhaps related to the
original scheme for the court of S
Pietro in Montorio, the Spanish
church in Rome, as it is shown in
Sebastiano Serlio's treatise, *L'Ar-
chitettura* (1537). The roots of
Machuca's inspiration are therefore
clear. But most architects working
throughout Europe and attempting
designs in the Renaissance style had
only secondary contact with either
the original remains of antiquity or
their offspring in Florence or Rome.

The invention of movable type-
faces in the mid-fifteenth century
was of tremendous importance for
the spread of both the ideology of
Renaissance architecture and its
visual character. Dozens of editions
of books on architectural theory
after the style of Alberti appeared in
most European languages throughout the sixteenth century. These
were usually related to Vitruvius –
translations, derivations or illustrated editions – and they could
explain the new style in considerable technical detail for those

above
Wollaton Hall, Nottinghamshire
(1580s), by Smythson: a grand,
Elizabethan 'prodigy house' with
imposing skyline.

right
Porch of Kirby Hall, Northants (dated
1572): 'stacking' of orders is typical of
English gateways of this period.

above
North wing of Bullant's Château
d'Écouen (1550s): severe Doric
columns and dormer windows with
round pediments.

right
North front of the Château de
Chambord (begun 1519): its character
is entirely French and largely medieval.

who were not able to go to Italy.

Nevertheless, there were inherent drawbacks in a situation where so much of what was known of Italianate style was derived from secondary sources. The unavoidably two-dimensional presentation inevitably resulted in the adoption of corrupt forms and a lack of understanding of, for example, the subordination of the decorative details to the harmonic qualities of the whole. The remedy adopted most frequently was for architects to visit the remains of antiquity and see for themselves, and Rome continued to be a source of inspiration for the new Baroque style created there in the early seventeenth century to succeed the Renaissance and Mannerism.

EUROPEAN BAROQUE

The classical tradition

Architecture has changed in two major ways during the Renaissance. Firstly, architects readopted a 'classical' language of shapes and details which they developed into the Renaissance style. Secondly, the architecture of the period was experienced in a totally different way. In the eras of the Baroque and Neoclassicism the buildings produced continued to use the classical language established in the Renaissance. Although the way in which we experience this later architecture is very different, it still refers back to classical antiquity and it was the antique which continued to supply the standard of excellence against which success was judged.

Matheus Daniel Pöppelmann, the designer of the bizarre and extravagant Zwinger, a palace outside Dresden, claimed that his construction was based upon the principles laid down by Vitruvius just as the architects of the early Renaissance had done. Alberti and his colleagues might well have been shocked by this claim: the architectural style which the Zwinger represents is, of course, very different in tone from the ordered, calm buildings of Renaissance Florence. Even

right
Der Zwinger, Dresden (1711–22), by Pöppelmann: a lavishly decorated grandstand for pageants and tournaments.

244

so it is best understood as a later development within the same classical tradition.

One of the reasons why a tremendous variety of styles could shelter beneath the one label 'classical' was that the definition of what constituted classical was changing all the time. It was often the case that the designers, patrons and connoisseurs of architecture during this period were also the sponsors of the massive project of reacquainting European society with the remains of antiquity through archaeological excavation and research. The latest knowledge of classical building was thus likely to influence current trends in architecture. As more

below
Juvarra's Superga, near Turin (1717–31), is a pilgrimage church set high on a hill and derives from the Pantheon.

became known of antiquity and its remains, it grew clear that an enormous range of styles, moods and types of architecture, often appearing to be directly in conflict with one another, could rightly be described as classical. It was this comforting fact that encouraged architectural designers to experiment with the forms or motifs to which they had grown accustomed during the Renaissance.

The particular selection made by an architect from the treasure-house of motifs which classical antiquity supplied was to a considerable extent dependent upon current taste. The use made of antique models by a Baroque architect like Borromini was different to that made by Alberti. In Baroque Italy, for example, it is the concave, scalloped cornice of the Temple of Venus at Baalbek which becomes a popular model; see, for example, the

turrets on Juvarra's Superga outside Turin (1717–31) or Borromini's S Carlo alle Quattro Fontane, Rome (1638–41). In the Renaissance period it was buildings such as the Theatre of Marcellus with its ordered arcaded storeys which had been most influential.

The meaning of 'Baroque'

The term 'Baroque' is typical in several ways of the labels used in the writing of the history of art and architecture. Firstly, it was applied originally to imply dissatisfaction with a change in style: Impressionism and Expressionism originally had similarly pejorative overtones. Secondly, it can be applied both to a style and to a period. And thirdly, it can all too easily mean very little.

As a description of a period I shall use the word to cover the architecture produced in the seventeenth and eighteenth centuries in

left
The exuberant decorative forms of The Sanctuary, Ocotlán, Mexico (begun *c.* 1745) typify Latin American Baroque.

above
The west facade of Santiago de Compostela, Spain (completed 1749), obscures the medieval cathedral.

Europe up to the moment when the Neoclassical movement started, roughly around the year 1750. Just as with the Renaissance, the Baroque means different things in different countries at different times. As a description of the style of the period, the word can be used confidently to cover Italy during the seventeenth century and part of the eighteenth, and the same applies in Spain, Germany and Austria. The story is a little more complicated during these same years in France. Britain and her colonial settlements in North America will be discussed in the following chapter.

The situation in France usefully highlights the inadequacy of the term Baroque, which is often used to indicate a style quite opposed to the true classical. This is a polarity which works well to distinguish the architecture of the seventeenth century from the 'classical' style of the Renaissance with its regard for regularity, straight lines, balance and so on. The Baroque style is most usefully characterized by its very different sense of mass, by its delight in expansive decoration, its use of curvaceous forms, its preference for spatial compositions that are complex and even confusing, and in some cases by an appreciation of the potential of large-scale and panoramic vistas.

Very rarely do all these traits come together in a single instance, and in general the Baroque styles of the European nations and their new colonies are particularly distinguished by their regional characteristics. This is especially the case when, as in Mexico for example, the imposition of a Baroque style becomes very much a question of the imposition of a Baroque decorative scheme upon a traditional form of structure: the polychrome tiles used on the facade of the church of S Francisco at Acatepec in Mexico are a good example. In France, however, the architecture of the period rarely if ever adopts a significant number of these style traits. It is therefore difficult to describe it as a true Baroque, and the apparently contradictory term Baroque Classicism has unfortunately been

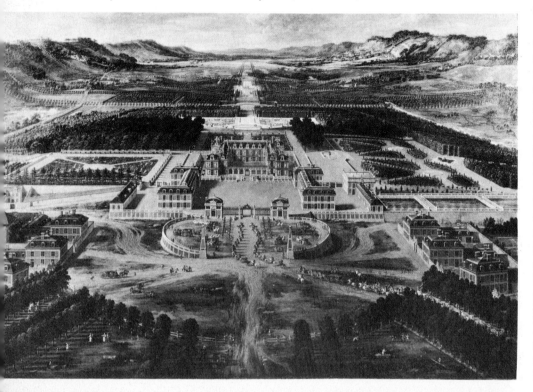

Patel's painting of Versailles, near Paris (1668), shows the buildings which form the nucleus of the whole complex.

left
Bernini's square before St Peter's, Rome (begun 1656): a vivid image of the embracing arms of the Church.

248

adopted to cover a whole tradition of French buildings.

During the Baroque era there was a continuing need for new churches, town palaces and country residences, but to these must be added other architectural schemes where the new style found expression in novel and exciting forms, as for example the massive monastic foundations of cental Europe, the schemes for urban renewal in Italy and France and the spreading complexes of palaces like that of Louis XIV at Versailles. It is in this context – of architecture as a series of functional types – that the role of these great buildings within the overall framework of society can best be understood. A large proportion of them reflect social requirements or religious emphases which architecture had not had to meet before.

Magnificent buildings had always been used to demonstrate and indeed establish the social order but those erected for the absolutist monarchies which rose to power during the course of the seventeenth century throughout Europe were unusual in their lavishness of scale. Many of the grander schemes of the period rely upon the capacity of the building to overwhelm the observer through size alone.

The east facade of the Louvre in Paris, designed by Claude Perrault in 1665, illustrates features of the Baroque style. Firstly, there is the dominance of classicism even within the Baroque mould, although Perrault, in fact, took the side of those who preferred a certain amount of

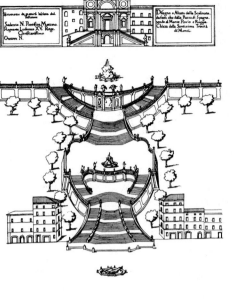

below
An urban development combining natural rock forms and a palace front: the Trevi Fountain, Rome (1732–62) by Salvi.

above
The Spanish Steps, Rome (1723–25), by De Sanctis: contemporary designs show the curves used in Baroque urban planning.

freedom in applying the rules of the ancients. It might seem strange to describe Perrault's design as anti-classical but there were aspects of the decorative detailing especially which singled him out for criticism from the purists – for example, the curved tops to the windows in what functions as the ground floor but appears to the eye as the basement.

A nationalistic note is being sounded here, a second feature of the Baroque style. Indeed, the social implications of a building like Perrault's cannot be over-emphasized. France during this period was passionately concerned with its own identity and its own progress. The State was organized by Colbert to maximize advancement in every walk of life and the arts were no exception. The potential of architecture to celebrate the monarch, the nation and the State was realized as never before. The standards to which good architectural design had to aspire were, like everything else, set by the State, and control was achieved by establishing the rank of royal architect in recognition of competence. The elegance, power and gravity of the Louvre facade perfectly expresses all these demands. The classical

vocabulary dominates but room is left for national preference.

Baroque churches

The church architecture of the Baroque period, especially that of the Catholic countries, was also meant to impress the onlooker – with the absolute power of the militant and often passionate church of Christ. Throughout the seventeenth century the Roman Catholic Church was engaged in a fierce rearguard action to defend its territory from the incursions of the

Borromini's San Ivo della Sapienza,
Rome (church begun 1642): the facade
makes interesting use of the concave
curve.

Protestant heresy. Where architecture was concerned, the process of spiritual renewal which accompanied the Counter-Reformation initially took the form of an attempt to steal the ideological thunder from the Protestant forces.

For many, a basic and early attraction of the Protestant faith was its rejection of the idea that Christ's church should reflect Christ's splendour in the fabric of its buildings. Even spending money on church building was considered a vain sin and some of the more extreme Protestant sects did away with formal buildings altogether. Throughout the whole movement, the accent was on simplicity and demystification. The Counter-Reformation recognized the truth of this point of view and initially at least attempted to acquire unto itself the attributes of modesty and sincerity.

Giacomo Vignola's Gesù (begun in 1568), the mother church of the Jesuits, the religious order created specifically to combat the Protestant threat, shows these principles applied to architectural design.

It was in Rome that the fully developed Baroque style first appeared in the middle years of the seventeenth century. In church building there was a reaction against the academic Mannerist style, of which Vignola's church was a representative. It is possible to make too much of the connections between the attitude of the Catholic Church and the stylistic changes undertaken by those who developed the Baroque style. Even so, it is clear that during the course of the seventeenth century there was a return to the traditional attractions of the Catholic Church and the astringent tone of the militant Counter-Reformation was abandoned in favour of a more popular, tolerant and gentle approach. Once again it was acceptable for the popes and cardinals of the day to celebrate their own and their Church's magnificence, and churches adopted a manner of decorative exuberance and visual mystification in marked contrast to the great severity of the Counter-Reformation period.

The church of S Carlo alle Quattro Fontane, started in Rome by Francesco Borromini in 1633, seems to have been designed to convey the mystery that surrounds the relationship of man with the godhead. The techniques at Borromini's disposal, many of them of his own invention,

above
Inside the dome of Borromini's San
Carlo alle Quattro Fontane, Rome
(1638–41): a highly patterned simple
oval.

all involve the manipulation of
space, interior and exterior, to con-
fuse the spectator as to the exact
nature of the building's structural
elements. The god reflected in and
worshipped by a Renaissance
chapel – the disposer of perfect form
within a rational plan – is here
replaced by the mover of great
forces, whose ways are not man's
and whose purpose it is not his
place to know. This is a complete
reversal of the role of structural
elements in Renaissance architecture, where good, strong columns
were seen to be supporting entabla-
tures which recede into space. In S
Carlo the senses are confused and
the spirit humbled at every turn.
Mystery replaces clarity. It is
impossible not to register the
intense and introspective quality of
the church, the mood of which
seems unavoidably pessimistic and
as explicitly neurotic as the
architect's own character.

Typically, the ground plan is an
exercise on the theme of the oval.
This was a favourite figure for the
architects of the Baroque, combining as it does both central and
longitudinal elements. Borromini
superimposes upon his central oval
space a set of bevelled, convex walls
which give the interior a swaying
rhythm and turn the structure into
a means by which to mould space.
This exercise is continued both in
the dome, contained along its edges
by a confusing series of straight and
curved lines, and by the facade. The
latter was added to the building in
the year of Borromini's suicide and
contributed an important idea to
the vocabulary of Baroque architecture. This was the notion of setting
whole walls in rhythmic motion.
The three vertical bays of the
ground floor take the form of a
convex central section flanked by
two concave units. These are not
like niches in their effect because
both the entablature and the bases
reflect the motion.

This sense of architecture in
motion was valued above all other
attributes during the Baroque
period and in some ways remains

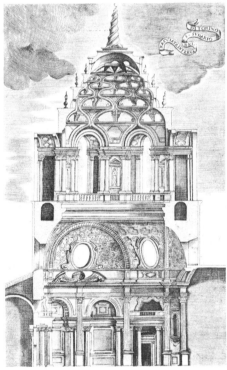

above
A sectional view of the Chapel of the
Holy Shroud, Turin (1667–90), by
Guarini, built to house a sacred relic.

above
Graceful curves in Longhena's design
for Santa Maria della Salute, Venice
(begun 1631), create light and space.

the unique contribution of the style. The range of effects was enormous. Borromini's use of undulating mass contrasts starkly with the more static grandeur of Bernini's colonnade before the Basilica of St Peter's in the Vatican (1656 onwards) and reminds us that the mobility of much High Baroque architecture and the extensive use of curvaceous form should not be confused with randomness. The latter is a quality which found its way into the history of architecture in the style called Rococo (after the French for 'shell-like' – a reference to a common decorative motif). There was always a system to Baroque architecture and the fact that it sometimes appears confusing does not mean that it was erratically planned. Baldassare Longhena's S Maria della Salute (started in 1630) introduces curved forms and a novel buoyancy to the pattern for Venetian churches established by Palladio. The facade of the palace of the Marqués de Dos Aguas in Valencia (1740–44) is built around an exuberantly decorated portal, but this is still located in the centre and the whole composition is conventionally balanced by the two short towers at either end.

Late Baroque

The Rococo style is well illustrated by a series of monastic and pilgrimage churches erected in central and southern Germany and Austria late in the seventeenth and early in the eighteenth centuries. In the course of a massive outbreak of building activity, architecture again treated the appreciation of spatial qualities as a genuine form of religious experience. Balthasar Neumann was the greatest master of this style and his interior at Vierzehnheiligen (started 1743) is a major monument to his skills. The complex relationships of the plan's component parts, again using ovals, were to some extent made certain by Neumann's acquisition of an earlier architect's foundations for the church. But the whole effect gives us no impression that his imagination was hampered in any way. The traditional spatial values of nave, aisles and so on are

above
Neumann's scheme for Vierzehnheiligen consciously seeks ambiguity in interior space.

below
Vierzehnheiligen pilgrimage church (1743–72), by Neumann: a chain of ovals creates the longitudinal interior plan.

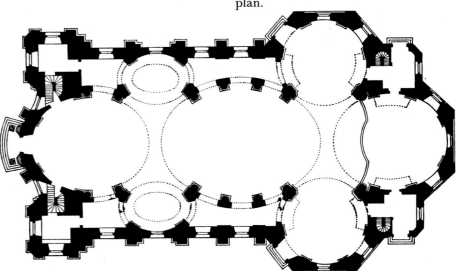

entirely dispensed with and the decoration demands an analogy with the movement of water as it foams and eddies around and above the observer.

Neumann is concerned that stone, paint, and stucco adequately express the Divine Presence, and a similar objective can be found in Narciso Tomé's *Transparente* for Toledo Cathedral (completed 1732). This elaborate construction took the form of an altar-setting on a massive scale – large enough to run from floor to ceiling in the ambulatory of a vast Gothic cathedral. Its function was to both protect and present the Holy Sacrament within a framework of decorated columns and very lavish sculptural ornament. The work also shows the familiar Baroque device of the hidden light source used to heighten and dramatize visual climaxes within the composition.

Neoclassicism

The visual devices of architects like Neumann and Tomé were of such intensity and sophistication that the speed of the reaction against the style in which they built was inevitably matched only by its range. In the age of Neoclassicism which followed the Baroque, archaeology and architecture come closer together than ever before. Indeed, the excitement generated by the extensive discoveries at Pompeii and Herculaneum was partly responsible for the Neoclassical fervour which gripped European culture from the mid-eighteenth century.

Whereas Borromini had been attracted to the sculptural qualities

above
Prandtauer's Melk Abbey, Austria (begun 1702): a massive complex for the Benedictines towers over the Danube.

right
Le Petit Trianon, Versailles (begun 1762), by Gabriel: clean lines and simple detail indicate Neoclassicism.

of a particular building, Neoclassical taste in architecture was for the clean lines and impression of ordered proportion which were also to be found in the remains of antiquity. Another innovation was the interest in and influence of ancient Greek buildings, most of which had hitherto been neglected in comparison to the later Roman works. These were particularly valued not only for their visual appeal but also as representatives of what was increasingly recognized as the major source or birthplace of European culture.

The Neoclassical revival was to a considerable extent a movement interested in moral renewal. The moral and heroic virtue of Periclean Athens and Republican Rome were greatly admired by the influential movement known as the Enlightenment and it was felt that the buildings of those periods must reflect that virtue in their arrangement. The complexity of the Baroque and Rococo styles was thus abandoned in favour of the 'purer' images of

Neoclassicism. But the purity of the new style was designed to impress the observer with its grandeur of sentiment and virtue as actively as the complexity of high Rococo had been planned to humble. Pure invention and the celebration of imagination in architecture were replaced by an emphasis on correctness and the capacity to obey the rules. Once again, the appreciation of these buildings demands considerable intellectual application and a willingness to appreciate the difference between the tameness of a merely academic copy and the excitement and stimulus of an interesting variation.

France's earlier unwillingness to abandon itself wholeheartedly to the excesses of High Baroque makes it not surprising that Neoclassicism was adopted more immediately and with greater commitment there than elsewhere. The Petit Trianon in the gardens of Versailles (begun in 1762) is hardly revolutionary in its appearance but gives a good impression of the economy of line

and idealization of proportion so characteristic of the new style. The architect, Ange-Jacques Gabriel, excluded curves and spatial recession from his vocabulary and instead concentrated on linear clarity and an exquisitely detailed finish. The result is a neat, static cube.

A later development in French Neoclassical architecture was the return to a primitive or archaic visual language. The buildings and design of Claude-Nicolas Ledoux and Étienne-Louis Boullée not only have a touch of meglomania about them but are usually stripped of decorative detail, planned around juxtapositions of simple geometrical figures, and rely upon silhouette and massivity of scale for their dramatic effect. This architecture evokes an atmosphere of feeling rather than reason: a shift away from the principles of Gabriel but still within the Neoclassical canon. The consequences of this change were most fully realized in the nineteenth century.

below
Tomé's *Transparente* altar in Toledo
Cathedral (1728–32): built to house the
Sacred Host, it uses dramatic lighting.

right
Rich stucco decoration by an unknown
artist for a functional interior: the
sacristy, Charterhouse, Granada
(*c.* 1725).

BRITISH
17th and 18th century

Effects of social change

The development of building in seventeenth-century Britain demonstrates once again the principle that the innovation of architectural types is often directly related to changing social circumstances. One of Britain's most important contributions to the history of building was the series of great country houses started in the Elizabethan period. This expansion was made possible by the dissolution of the monasteries and the transference of land ownership to those who had bought up the ecclesiastical properties.

After a period of consolidation these families started to build country seats which were designed not only to accommodate expanding households and supply centres of operations for agricultural estates but also to demonstrate newly-attained social status. Changes in the architectural style of these great houses reflected not only the vagaries of fashionable taste but also the fact that architecture could be used to express social information about the patron. In this period an educated knowledge of Italy, an adherence to a particular religious code or recently acquired political power could be, and indeed all were, communicated by the appearance of buildings.

The political stability of the realm during these years (with the brief exception of the Civil War of the 1640s) and the lack of foreign invasion meant that for the first time in centuries defence was no longer an issue in the planning of large domestic dwellings. Architects were thus given a new freedom from the stifling influences of vantage points, small windows and heavily rusticated walls in their treatment of exteriors.

The Reformation directly affected the pattern of church building too. Very little was done in the years following the break with Rome. So many medieval parish churches remained that church building was only seriously considered again late in the seventeenth century with public recognition of the need to replace or expand the facilities for worship. An Act of 1670 provided for over 50 new churches to replace those destroyed in the Great Fire of London and another Act, of 1711, ordered a further 50 to be built throughout the country, although few of these were in fact completed. During the eighteenth century all the major architects of the day included ecclesiastical building within their repertoire.

Inigo Jones

At the start of the period the royal court and its attendant circle of patronage were a powerful influence on architecture as in all fields of artistic endeavour. Early in the seventeenth century Inigo Jones, the first British architect to understand and master the High Renaissance style in all its details, was actively engaged in introducing the British aristocracy to the new Italianate architecture as part of a complete programme sponsored initially by James I and then by Charles I. Jones's most important debt was to Palladio's work, which was particularly admired for its combination of grandeur, elegance and a claimed adherence to the principles of classical antiquity. The influence of the Italian Renaissance had previously made itself felt in Britain only in the adoption of a style of surface decoration.

The designs Jones produced for his royal masters – the Banqueting Hall at Whitehall (1619–22) and the Queen's House at Greenwich (1616–35), both of which pay direct tribute to palaces in Vicenza by Palladio – had a revolutionary effect upon the development of British architecture. The Banqueting Hall must have appeared particularly striking in the early 1620s. Today it is surrounded by buildings showing many of its Palladian characteristics for Neo-Palladianism has been adopted the world over as the style most suitable for government and other 'establishment' architecture. But Jones placed his alternating pointed and segmental pediments, his elegant top balustrade, and his carefully detailed Orders of columns and pilasters on a facade in a still largely Gothic London.

So unusual were Jones's designs

above
Design of the south front of the Queen's
House, Greenwich (1616–35), by Jones
derives from a Palladio palace.

below
Double Cube Room in Wilton House
(*c.* 1649), by Jones and Webb: careful
proportions underlie rich decoration.

that it was not until the early years of the following century (during the Palladian revival) that his lead was followed by significant numbers of patrons and builders. Typically, Scotland provided something of an exception to this rule – in the work of Sir William Bruce who, during his Surveyor-Generalship in the 1680s, worked on the royal palace at Holyroodhouse and built a house for himself at Kinross in a style owing much to Jones's classicism.

Continental influences

Throughout these two centuries the relationship with continental Europe was of central importance in the development of architecture but the exact location of the source of inspiration tended to change with the passing of time and the shifting of taste. Architects regularly looked to Italy both as the heir of the classical tradition and as the venue for so much important innovation in the post-Renaissance period.

In the middle years of the seventeenth century northern European models became influential. The use of brick and the adoption of Dutch

gables were aspects of a style of comparatively modest pretensions recently christened Artisan Mannerism, which existed in various forms in the years between Jones and Neo-Palladianism. Originating in London, it was influential throughout much of Britain. The Dutch House at Kew Gardens (1631) is an important example. A more sophisticated version of this style, which is called Mannerist because of the licence it takes with the rules of classical architecture, grew up around the Stuart court just prior to the Civil War. This was also stimulated by northern European developments and especially the style of the painter Rubens. An example is the York Water Gate on the Victoria Embankment in London with its heavily rusticated columns and isolated segmental pediment, probably by Sir Balthasar Gerbier.

Wren and the status of the architect

Gerbier's architecture, like Jones's, was designed to appeal to court taste. The major figure in English architecture in the second half of the seventeenth century was Sir Christopher Wren, who built for the Restoration monarchy and a good many other patrons. His career shows how the court not only encouraged the introduction of new styles but also helped formulate the public view of the architect's role and character. Some idea of this can be gained from the criteria employed in the choice of the effective head of the architectural profession, the Surveyor of the Office of Works. This was the department of the royal household responsible for all royal buildings and was run by the Surveyor. At a time when the Crown was the source of the most prestigious patronage, it was clearly a highly desirable appointment.

In 1661 Christopher Wren was offered the post at a time when he had not built a single building. Wren was a professional astronomer and academic at this date; no less an authority than Isaac Newton considered him one of the three best geometricians of his day. He had also produced evidence of his capacity to come up with solutions to practical problems in his experiments in the field of the natural sciences. Once these qualifications were added to his academic skills as a researcher amongst contemporary and ancient sources, Wren apparently seemed quite suitable to fill the post. Clearly architecture was held to be a matter of planning and calculation – administrative rather than manual skills. His lack of practical experience was not seen as a problem, although it might well have caused some anxiety amongst those whose origins were more in the 'craft' end of the business.

Wren's appointment shows that an architect was required to be educated and education was mainly the preserve of the socially privileged. Gradually more and more openings appeared for those born as gentlemen to turn their hands to architecture. John Vanbrugh, for instance, came from a wealthy mercantile background via careers in the Army and as a playwright. Thomas Archer was the son of a country squire who undertook the Grand Tour before advising his social peers on the designs of their

above
The Dutch House, Kew Gardens, London (1631): typical of the Artisan style – built in brick with prominent gables.

above left
Jones's Banqueting Hall, Whitehall, London (begun 1619), shows a clear understanding of recent Italian design.

right
A standard mid 17th-century town house: Mompesson House, Cathedral Close, Salisbury, Wiltshire.

country houses. The acceptability of an interest in architecture had, in fact, been established quite early in the seventeenth century.

It was argued that architecture was, above all else, an exercise in the science of mathematics, the intellectual status of which was universally accepted. Architecture thus appeared to the layman not so much as an art, demanding genius and inspiration, but rather as a science, which could be learned from books and which depended upon rational solutions. This rise in status was assisted by the fact that architecture could point to classical antiquity for its precedents.

Seventeenth-century thought also held architecture's value to society in high esteem. The idea that architecture could improve the standards of the whole population by its capacity to transform and control the environment had been formulated by the Italian humanist and theoretician Alberti in the fifteenth century. Wren had close links with the Royal Society, a group of scientists who wished to further knowledge in order to 'assist familiarly in all occasions of human life', and it seems likely that he placed an involvement in architecture in this same tradition.

Great designer though he was, Wren was undoubtedly fortunate that his rise to power in the field of architecture took place in the 1660s, a decade which saw not only the return of a monarchy keen to patronize buildings but also the Great Fire of London (1666). The devastation offered Wren an unrivalled opportunity. St Paul's Cathedral alone would win for him a place amongst the great but the series of city churches shows the tremendous variety of solutions possible with different applications of his mature

style. St Paul's reflects Wren's education in architectural sources such as Bramante's High Renaissance Tempietto in Rome for the completed version of the great dome, and St Peter's, Rome, in the form of the final plan. Nevertheless the end result is a unique achievement and is more refined in its execution than some of the city churches, which were erected in rather a hurry and without Wren's closest supervision.

English Baroque

Wren's architecture was rarely truly Baroque in the sense of the word as it is applied to some of his followers. Around 1700 there was a brief flowering of an architectural style of a rather more personal tone led by Vanbrugh and Nicholas Hawksmoor and called the English Baroque. The accent here was on originality, caprice and a particular interest in dramatic effects of space. For many, their architecture is difficult to appreciate because of its uncomfortably meglomaniac grandeur and occasional lapses into dour heaviness. The buildings they cre-

below
Blenheim Palace, Oxon (begun 1705), by Vanbrugh: aerial view showing the importance of the landscape setting.

bottom
A severe and magnificent country seat for the great soldier Marlborough: Blenheim Palace.

right
Hawksmoor's St Mary Woolnoth, City of London (1716–27): impression of great grandeur achieved on a modest scale.

ated were certainly not what most would associate with an 'English' style. Vanbrugh's greatest works were a series of major country houses culminating in Blenheim Palace (1705). Hawksmoor's group of six churches for the 1711 Act were probably his most important contribution (including St Mary Woolnoth, 1716–27).

The period of the English Baroque saw architects once again making considerable use of Italian models, employing designs by near contemporaries. Wren had been particularly influenced by French and Dutch architecture. Thomas Archer designed his church of St Paul at Deptford (1712–30) as an exercise in this manner based upon Borromini's plan for Sant'Agnese in Rome. Occasionally French textbooks on architecture acted as intermediaries in this process.

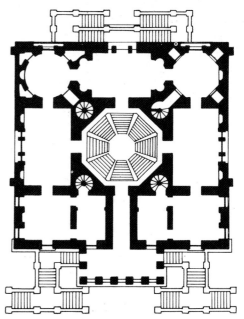

above
The plan of Chiswick House arranges rooms around a tall hall with a dome above.

left
A Neo-Palladian 'villa' derived from the Rotonda, near Vicenza: Burlington's Chiswick House, near London (begun 1725).

left
The Assembly Rooms, York (1730), by Burlington: reconstruction of an Egyptian Hall after Palladio and Vitruvius.

Neo-Palladianism

The reaction against the Baroque style, the movement known as Neo-Palladianism after its Italian hero, was closely linked to the philosophies of the second generation of Whig politicians who came to power with the Hanoverian monarchs. Palladio's buildings appealed to a whole generation of men of 'taste', who saw architecture as a means to improve society by exerting a moral influence on the observer. Pure lines in architecture were linked to purity of spirit. The taste of the Whigs rejected, amongst other things, those architectural forms which had been sponsored by the Stuart court, their own political rivals the Tories, and anything which smacked of foreign Popery. They therefore spurned the Baroque style, which had made extensive use of Roman High Baroque models. Instead they turned to the style of Palladio, which was considered 'purer' because it was thought closer to the antique originals and clearer in its lines. It was an architectural style which did not rely on deceiving the eye for its effects and was therefore considered more honest morally. It was also argued that Neo-Palladianism was a style with a particularly British appeal and the contribution of Inigo Jones, 'the British Palladio', was often cited as evidence of this.

Through a series of appointments, the adherents of the Palladian style assumed the reins of architectural power. A leading figure in this process was Richard Boyle, 3rd Earl of Burlington, a powerful politician with a passion for architecture. Burlington not only employed Colen Campbell, William Kent, and others but also designed buildings himself. His house at Chiswick (started 1725) was inspired by Palladio's Villa Rotonda on the hills outside Vicenza, whilst his Assembly Rooms at York are an attempt to realize Vitruvius's description of an Egyptian hall using a treatise by Palladio.

With the Neo-Palladian reform of the 1720s–30s closely linked to the moral attitudes of the Whig party, British architecture at this time took on a political tone and styles were connected to political creeds. Opposition to Neo-Palladianism was eagerly supplied by a Tory Scot, James Gibbs, who was unique among his contemporaries in this country in having been partly trained under an authentic Italian master, Carlo Fontana. He remained faithful to the more 'decadent' Italian styles and avoided Neo-Palladianism. His Radcliffe Camera in Oxford (1739–49) shows particularly Mannerist leanings. The constant interruption of the vertical accent from the corners of the rusticated basement through the

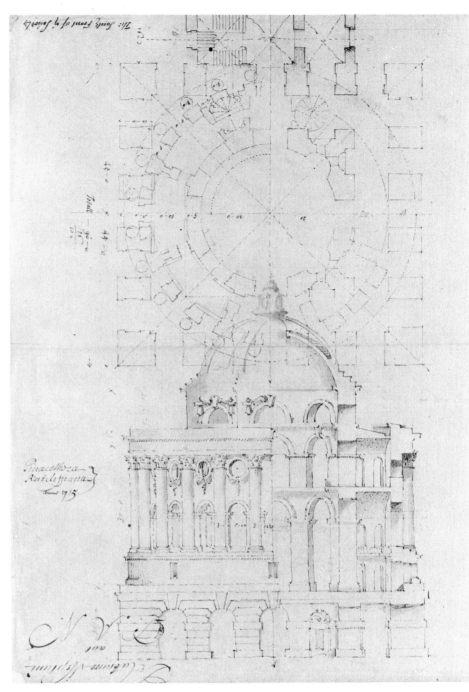

above
Gibb's project for the Radcliffe Camera, Oxford (1739–49), shows a central plan and domed space.

269

order of coupled columns to the buttresses of the dome is worthy of note: none are in line.

The Gothick Revival

Many buildings showing medieval features continued to be put up during the course of the seventeenth century. Italianate fashions were not to everyone's taste; nor were they suited to perform certain jobs. It is interesting that Scotland did see a deliberate eradication of Gothic detail in church building after their Reformation of 1560 but in England Gothic was still considered most suitable for churches, chapels and monastic-style cloisters in the universities. These buildings had hardly ever been built in any other way. Thus Wren, an other-

above
Senate House, Cambridge (begun 1722), by Gibbs: originally the plan included three ranges of buildings such as this.

right
The Palladian Bridge, Stowe, Bucks: landscape schemes often included details like this bridge after Palladio's plan.

below
Strawberry Hill, Twickenham, near London (remodelling begun 1748): the facade and statues add a Romantic tone.

wise highly 'latinate' designer, occasionally built in the Gothic manner, or at least with Gothic elements in his style, in the spires of several city churches and at Oxford (Tom Tower, 1681–82).

The tradition of building in the Gothic style in Britain lasted right through the period until it overlapped with a new antiquarian interest in all ancient forms of architecture, not just those of the classical world. This movement lay at the roots of the revival of interest in Gothic architecture, previously despised as anti-classical. The medieval contribution came under close scrutiny and its architecture was copied. It was at this point that the tradition which had guaranteed the Gothic survival was transformed into a conscious 'Gothick' revival, with

the great wealth of medieval buildings in Britain as inspiration.

One of the final stages in the development of styles that followed the Renaissance through to the Baroque was the formation of the Rococo style. In England this coincided with the Gothick revival to form Rococo Gothick, which employed Gothic forms as decorative devices. Buildings erected in this manner range from the interiors of country churches like that at Shobdon in Herefordshire to major houses. The accent was on a mixture of traditions and the movement was particularly refreshing in the way it broke down the barriers between the styles which had been erected by the antiquaries, who were especially impressed by purity as an aesthetic goal. The result was

a series of novel inventions and in some quarters the eclecticism displayed in the gathering of source material was quite remarkable. Gothic, classical and even Chinese elements were combined with tremendous freedom. Horace Walpole was important as the promoter of the new Gothick style and had his home at Strawberry Hill (by the banks of the River Thames, started 1749) designed as a sequence of consciously revivalist and imitative architectural environments. The spirit of the final result is that of an antiquarian caprice which takes full advantage of the possibilities of evocative imitation.

The romantic view of architecture exemplified by Rococo Gothick became the fashion during the second half of the eighteenth cen-

tury and was an important stimulus for the architecture of the period whatever its type or style. The placing of buildings within the landscapes created around so many country houses was invariably designed to evoke some such response. Fleeting glimpses of carefully located structures, or parts of structures, or even ruins, were played off against vistas which tried to appear 'natural' but which were actually artificial creations. A bridge in Stowe Park, Buckinghamshire, a reduction of a Palladian design on a triumphal scale, functions in just this way.

Neoclassicism
The powerful literary element in the background of architecture and the stylistic eclecticism accompanying

271

it certainly played some part in the tremendous variety of buildings erected. Every major architectural style adopted in the eighteenth century was accompanied by publications of designs and theory and sometimes the influence seems to have been even more direct as the contents of books actually caused new developments.

In the second half of the eighteenth century one of these movements came to particular prominence as part of a wider European phenomenon, namely Neoclassicism. This development was encouraged by such established British interests as archaeological discovery and the common currency of classicism remaining after the Neo-Palladians. It was also stimulated by contact with antiquity gained

through the Grand Tours undertaken by the well-to-do and the fashion for collecting antique works of art. The houses designed for these connoisseurs and their collections, those by Robert Adam for example, are particularly interesting for the emphasis they place on interior decoration and the visual effects of finely worked materials.

Adam's style was created from a unique combination of sources: an interest in a varied skyline, giving a sense of movement and derived from Neo-Palladianism; the influence of published books on archaeological discoveries; and Italian Renaissance and French decorative details, especially the types known as grotesque and arabesque. Not only did Adam work as an architect but he also

published books of archaeological interest, for example his scenes of the Roman palace at Split in 1764. Adam's great contemporary and rival, Sir William Chambers, also created an eclectic Neoclassical style but was especially interested in Chinese architecture, bringing out a book of *Designs* in 1757.

The rediscovery of the architecture of the ancient Greeks contributed an important theory to Neoclassicism. This was the basing of all architectural design upon so-called first principles. The implications of this resolution were twofold: firstly, the rejection of the vocabulary of motifs compiled since the rediscovery of antiquity during the early Renaissance; and secondly, that the role of intuition (in the establishing of the first principles) was now

above
The plan of Ickworth House, Suffolk, includes curving wings and a rotunda with decoration after Flaxman.

left
The impressive hall at Kedleston, Derbyshire (*c.* 1761), illustrates Adam's domestic Neoclassical interior style.

above
Chambers's Pagoda, Kew Gardens, near London (*c.* 1760): an early view of the fashionable Chinese style.

admitted. This placed the theoretical development of Neoclassical architecture within the framework of the whole philosophical apparatus of the Romantics.

Provincial Britain

The architecture of Britain in these two centuries is not entirely a matter of sophisticated taste and changes in fashion. The period offers many examples of local variations, eccentric exceptions and the adherence to old traditions. At the same moment that Inigo Jones's Queen's House at Greenwich was receiving its finishing touches, one John Abel, King's Carpenter, was erecting the Town Hall at Leominster far away near the border with Wales. Jones's inspiration was a

273

patrician palace in Vicenza whereas Abel simply fell back on the experience of generations of timber-framed buildings and added the minimum of 'modern' detail.

Provincial England also saw local versions of the fashionable productions of the big cities. The gatehouse of Tilbury Docks of the 1670s shows a rather cluttered form of the style used by Wren. A comparative lack of social prestige in provincial architecture could be expressed in a number of ways. The adherence to an old structural system, the insensitive application of a new language of motifs and also the use of lesser-quality materials. Local stone was cheaper than imported marble but often just as effective. Almshouses, frequently erected as a personal monument by a local man-made-good, are often built of local materials and appear rather grand in their modest surroundings.

Colonial North America

The European nations sharing the Atlantic seaboard transmitted Renaissance architecture to America as they developed their colonies. This produced a rich variety of Renaissance forms that was further diversified in response to variations in climate and natural resources. South America was colonized principally by the Spanish and Portuguese, who developed Baroque forms that are described in Chapter 16. In North America English colonies were ranged along the east coast, although Florida was Spanish and there were Swedish and Dutch settlements in the north. French influence extended from the central plains and the Great Lakes down the Mississippi to the sea. Relatively little still surviving eighteenth-century American architecture corresponds with French Renaissance forms, but the gridiron plan of New Orleans is a French legacy, as is the distinctive tradition of colonnaded, externally-

right
Market Hall, Leominster, Hereford (*c.* 1630): traditional materials and techniques continued to be used.

below
The 'Town Hall', Gatton, Surrey: an elaborate architectural satire mourns the loss of democratic rights.

left
This interior at Osterley Park, near London (*c.* 1775), shows the Etruscan style which Adam was to make so popular.

275

above
Monticello, Virginia (remodelled 1796–
1808), by Thomas Jefferson,
statesman and amateur architect.

top
Drayton Hall, South Carolina (1738–
42): its pedimented, projecting
portico and superimposed orders are
Palladian.

success of the colonies and closely
followed English forms up to the
advent of Neoclassicism.

The first fully mature example
of Renaissance architecture in
the English states is the College of
William and Mary (1695–1702) at
Williamsburg, Virginia. The design
has been attributed to Wren and
has features consistent with this.
Williamsburg became the second
capital of Virginia and other important buildings soon followed, e.g.,
the Capitol (1701–1705) and the
Governor's Palace (1706–20), the
latter being a characteristic 'Queen
Anne' house. Numerous country
houses in Virginia were built in a
similar vein and one of the most
notable is Westover (c. 1726), for
which various features and fittings
were imported from London. This
metropolitan influence can be seen
also in several churches whose stee-
ples and towers are reminiscent of
either Wren's city churches or
James Gibbs's St Martin-in-the-
Fields (1722–26), such as respec-
tively Christ Church (Old North),
Boston (1723), and St Michael's,
Charleston (1752–61).

Architectural books were readily
available and Palladianism soon
supplanted the previous mode.
Drayton Hall, South Carolina
(1738–42), is a striking example of a
plantation house which closely follows Palladian precedents, particularly in the design of its projecting,
two-storeyed, galleried portico with
superimposed Doric and Ionic
columns.

Thomas Jefferson, America's
third president, was an able and
scholarly amateur architect. His
own house, Monticello, Virginia,
remodelled 1796–1808 to a design
of 1779, in its form acknowledges
one of the most famous Palladian
buildings, the Villa Capra, Vicenza
(1552). Jefferson, when serving as
ambassador to Versailles, became
familiar with Neoclassical sources
and in 1785 designed the new
Capitol for Richmond, Virginia,
after studying the Maison Carrée at
Nîmes (see Chapter 4). He therefore
introduced into America the new
values and classical forms that
severed the Georgian tradition that

galleried houses that exists in
former French territories: Parlange,
Pointe Coupée Parish, Louisiana
(1750), is a classic example.

A remarkable architectural
flowering occurred in the English
states, although here too there were
wide regional differences. Timber
was the staple building material in
New England and remained in use
even for elaborate houses, whereas
in Virginia a tradition of fine brickwork grew. Here, also, the warmer
climate suited expansive, colonnaded designs, but architecture
generally of the northern and southern states reflected the wealth and

had flourished with such distinction in his own state. America thus embarked upon its architectural independence.

Towards the new century

Two final topics introduce architectural dilemmas which the nineteenth century would have to confront. Firstly, the need for large numbers of dwellings expressing some aesthetic character. This had been partly met in the eighteenth century but only on the refined level of the elegant complexes like those built by the John Woods, father and son, in Bath. Like many Georgian town-planning schemes, these cast the architect in the role of speculator and contractor as well as designer. Although the development of fashionable Bath resulted in blocks of town houses being treated as monumental units and the creation of the crescent as an urban compositional type, these grand schemes left the nineteenth century with no really valuable precedents to follow in the accommodation of an expanding urban population.

The second issue is closely related. It is the question of the reaction of architecture to the Industrial Revolution. The changing economy placed new demands on builders in two ways. Not only were new sorts of buildings required – factories for example – but new possibilities were offered too, as with the developing technology of the iron industry. Abraham Darby's Iron Bridge (1779) at Coalbrookdale in the west Midlands exemplifies the tensions of this new challenge. The bridge is certainly one of the first built of cold-blast iron but a new span was only required at that point over the River Severn because of the expansion of the local industries. The changing relationship between architectural design and materials and between design and function is a nineteenth-century development.

below
Early view of the Royal Crescent, Bath, Avon (1767–75), by Wood, showing the elegant scheme and its setting.

above
The Iron Bridge, Coalbrookdale, West
Midlands (*c.* 1779): new materials and
techniques for a new purpose –
industry.

278

NINETEENTH CENTURY
in the western world

The threads of continuity
In comparison with other periods when architecture found a more uniform expression, western architecture in the nineteenth century seems freakish. How, it may be asked, can this large-boned, polychromatic, stylistically hydra-headed phenomenon contribute to the world's great architecture?

Stylistic variety is not peculiar to the nineteenth century. It was a part of its legacy from the previous age when some wealthy patrons, especially in Britain, indulged in extravagant architectural whims, particularly for the design of country houses or landscape features, erecting a Chinese pagoda at Kew (see page 273), Greek temples at

below
The Royal Pavilion, Brighton (1815–21), by Nash: some interiors are designed in Indian and Chinese styles.

Shugborough, Staffordshire, and numerous Gothick castles, towers and follies, as at Fonthill Abbey, Wiltshire. This eccentric vein of architectural patronage, inspired by an enthusiasm for the Picturesque and a rapidly growing interest in antiquarianism extended into the early decades of the nineteenth century. John Nash was the grand master of the Picturesque on any scale. At Blaise, near Bristol, in 1811 he built a pretty, toy-like village of richly varied cottages; but for the Prince Regent at Brighton he created an exotically decorated, onion-domed, oriental palace, the Royal Pavilion (1815–21), that is both informal and grand. It best represents the capriciousness, inventiveness, ebullience and sensibility of the opening phase of the nineteenth century in Britain.

This fantastic architecture may be seen as a reaction to the classical tradition, the established architectural language of western Europeans for three centuries; but although classicism represents continuity, it also provided variety because its formal vocabulary was constantly evolving. The arrival of Neoclassicism in the mid-eighteenth century and the revelation that Greek architecture preceded Roman virtually ended the Renaissance tradition of design, although it survived to emerge occasionally in the nineteenth century as in the rebuilding and extension of the United States Capitol, Washington DC (1851–65), which were under-

above
Arc de Triomphe de L'Étoile, Paris (1806–35), by Chalgrin and others.

top
The Consols Office, Bank of England, London (1794–99), by Soane.

left
Edinburgh New Town, where a series of interlinked formal spaces stand on the edge of the Dean Valley.

taken by Thomas Ustick Walter.

By 1800 Neoclassicism was supreme. It offered three principal avenues: a modern reinterpretation of classicism as a radical and rational system, based on M A Laugier's idea that classical architecture had evolved from the elementary construction of a primitive hut and should be emulated; second, a revival of architectural forms from Roman antiquity; and similarly, a revival of the architecture of Ancient Greece. Exponents of the first were C-N Ledoux in France and Sir John Soane in England. Ledoux's works belong to the eighteenth century but Soane's work at the Bank of England (demolished) from 1788 to 1833 illustrated this aspect of Neoclassicism and showed great originality in the handling of space and in the invention of a system of abstract decoration using incised lines. Antiquarianism, however, was more widely practised: Roman forms were favoured in France, as in the grandiose Arc de Triomphe de l'Étoile (1806–35) by J-F-T Chalgrin, but Greek models inspired major works of grave dignity and restraint in America, Britain and Germany, e.g. the Altes Museum, Berlin (1828), by C F Schinkel.

In America and Britain the Greek revival constitutes an important phase that lasted until about 1840, although in Scotland it survived much longer. Edinburgh saw some of the finest Neoclassical urban design of the period, e.g. the development that included Ainslie Place and Moray Place designed by Gillespie Graham, and neo-Greek was still acceptable for the design of a prime public building such as the National Gallery by W H Playfair as late as 1850.

Industrial technology

Britain played a significant part in the development of nineteenth-century architecture. The industrial revolution transformed society and with it the architectural world. As the first nation to experience extensive industrialization and the urban expansion this necessitated, Britain was the first to be affected architecturally and the first to react vigorously to the new conditions. Whilst the classical tradition persisted abroad, technical innovation, the need for new or enlarged forms of building, new wealth and, above all, Romantic ideals shaped British architecture differently, and a voluminous technical press and the mass production of books ensured that architectural ideas were widely circulated. Throughout, however, Paris maintained its influence as an international centre of classicism and architectural education through academic institutions.

British influence lasted in varying degrees throughout the century. In 1826, Schinkel, the great German architect, visited England and was impressed by Telford's suspension bridges and the industrial scenes of Birmingham and Manchester. In contrast, in 1904–5 his compatriot Hermann Muthesius, in one of the most exhaustive studies of the English house, gave prominence to the ideas of two downright critics of industrialism, John Ruskin and William Morris. Technical development and the profound reaction the new industrial society inspired are both important factors in nineteenth-century architecture.

In technical as in stylistic matters the nineteenth century was debtor

above
The Palm House, Kew (1845), by Burton and Turner, is notable for its smooth, curved, glass and metal skin.

below
Crystal Palace, London (1851), by Paxton: a great achievement in design and technology.

281

to the eighteenth, and the new
structural techniques most extensively employed were inherited. The
structural use of iron had been
demonstrated spectacularly in 1779
with the construction of the world's
first iron bridge, at Coalbrookdale,
Shropshire (see page 278), and the
widespread use of iron for building
followed in an attempt to provide
fire-resistant construction for the
new manufactories. In the 1790s
northern millowners experimented
with iron columns supporting iron
beams that in some instances carried shallow, segmental vaults (jack
arches) to give fire-resistant floors.
This was consolidated in the building in 1796 of a flax mill at Shrewsbury, the first building constructed
with an entirely metal internal
frame, and the multi-storeyed, iron-
framed building with masonry
external walls rapidly became a
stereotype.

A further use of cast iron was for
the framing of the large hot-houses
so popular in nineteenth-century
gardens. Curvilinear forms were
adopted from 1815, and one of the
few to survive is the Palm House at
Kew (1845), designed by Decimus
Burton and the engineer Richard
Turner. The most famous ferro-
vitreous structure, the Crystal
Palace, was built for the Great
Exhibition of 1851. Designed by
Joseph Paxton, it was brilliant in
concept and, covering 7 hectares
(18 acres), unprecedented in size.
Exceptional for the speed and
efficiency of its prefabricated construction, it was designed, tested
and built in nine months and was
the crowning achievement of early
Victorian constructional technology. It survived on a new site until
burned down in 1936.

Wrought iron, being malleable
and strong in tension and com-
pression, is superior to cast iron,
which is liable to sudden fracture. It
has a long history of use in building
but until the end of the eighteenth

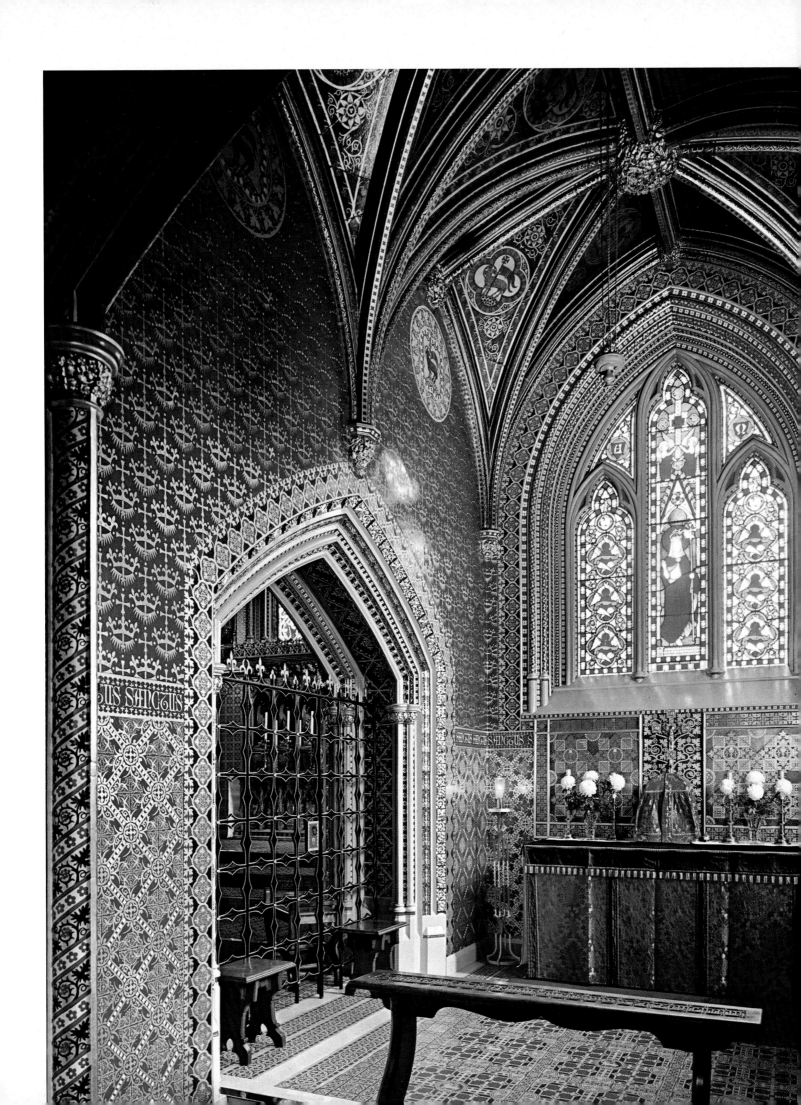

century was too expensive except for small essential components. Through inventions patented in 1784–85 this restriction was removed and it was soon used for wide-span structures. Cheap steel superseded it for building purposes in the 1880s. One early use of wrought iron was for the chains for a magnificent series of suspension bridges. Telford's Menai Bridge (1819–24) and Brunel's Clifton Suspension Bridge (1829–64) are fine examples by engineers with a strong sense of architectural design. Later achievements with wrought iron are the great arches of St Pancras Station, London (1863), by W H Barlow and the erection of the Eiffel Tower, designed by Gustave Eiffel for the Paris Exhibition of 1889.

Cast iron and wrought iron, combined with traditional masonry techniques including various forms of the arch, provided the standard constructional systems for nineteenth-century architecture. More advanced techniques employ-ing steel and reinforced concrete (a combination of steel bars with concrete that is exceptionally strong, versatile, and economical in the use of steel) appeared late in the century. Although their use was specialized, with surprising swiftness they were given distinctive forms of architectural expression which have been widely influential.

Gothic reform

The booming post-Waterloo era produced a rapid urban expansion and an equally rapid decline in architectural standards. New patrons indiscriminately aped the old, and the exotic novelty that was

left
The suspension chains of the Menai Bridge, north Wales (1819–24), by Telford, were of wrought iron.

below
Houses of Parliament, London (1836–65), by Barry assisted by Pugin.

permissible in an eighteenth-century landscape became an absurdity in towns where cheapness and pretentiousness prevailed. One of the critics of the new age was A W N Pugin, an architect with a gift for satire and a passion for architectural reform. At 20 he was an acknowledged authority on Gothic architecture and from it he formed his architectural principles. Medieval architecture and society seemed to him so superior that at 24 he became an ardent Catholic and with this his ideals, architectural, social and religious, fused in one inspired vision.

'Does locality, destination [purpose], or character . . . form the basis of a design?' was the radical Puginian test of contemporary architecture. Current forms of Neoclassicism failed outright. Further, classicism, he argued, was pagan in origin and therefore inappropriate to a Christian country. Architects, Pugin urged, should forget the Grand Tour and study the rich variety of indigenous buildings, Gothic and vernacular. Pugin can easily be dismissed as a crank, but he breathed life and fire into the Gothic revival. Before his emergence Gothic was *a* possible style which had become sufficiently accepted to be used for the rebuilding of the Houses of Parliament after the fire of 1834. A decade later to build in Gothic had become an article of faith, stylistic pluralism was no longer beyond question and the long line of the classical tradition was irrevocably broken in England.

Ironically, the most famous work with which Pugin is associated is the Houses of Parliament, for which Charles Barry was officially responsible. Barry, a most successful pluralist, won the commission in 1836 in a competition that required the designs to be Gothic or Elizabethan. Aware of his weakness in designing Gothic, he obtained Pugin's assistance, and it was Pugin who was the designer of all of the Gothic detailing. Barry was responsible for the planning and the overall form of the building, which show the discipline of classicism

despite the picturesque disposition of the towers and the irregularities in the plan made necessary by the surviving parts of the old palace. This building very clearly portrays the changing tides of the 1830s. Within its form classicism, Picturesque values and Gothic scholarship are reconciled.

Many of Pugin's buildings were designed for the newly emancipated Catholic Church and were marred by financial stringency, but he found a generous patron in the Earl of Shrewsbury, for whom he built the fine church of St Giles, Cheadle, Staffordshire (1841–46). It has a memorable tower and spire and is in the Decorated style of the fourteenth century, but the interior, rich with colour and pattern, is a Puginian *tour-de-force*.

The Anglican Church, served by architects such as William Butterfield, George Gilbert Scott and G E

above
All Saints, Margaret Street, London (1849–59), by Butterfield, reveals Ruskin's influence.

Street, adopted Puginian-Gothic principles wholeheartedly, and Protestantism generally followed suit, although with proper regard for biblical authority. John Ruskin's *Seven Lamps of Architecture* (1849) resolved any problems of conscience posed by the Catholic associations in which Pugin gloried, and thereafter the Gothic style became national in use.

Ruskin scorned English Gothic but enriched both literature and architecture with his perceptive interpretation of continental Gothic, especially that of northern Italy and Venice with its magnificent coloured marbles. In such an architecture it could be seen that

Nature, Truth and God, devoutly valued contemporary concepts, were simultaneously served.

Victorian architects, by adopting strong colour through natural materials and by giving their buildings powerful, cliff-like forms, satisfied a deep hunger for an emotionally expressive architecture after the long reign of taste and classical convention. Their response created the unmistakable character of High Victorian Gothic architecture. All Saints, Margaret Street, London (1849–59), and Keble College and Chapel, Oxford (1867–83), by William Butterfield, are examples of Victorian Gothic that demonstrate an individual character that far outruns historicism, and Manchester

Town Hall (1868–77) by Alfred Waterhouse is another, although in monochrome. Much of its structure is arcuated, and vaults and jack arches ensure that it is fire-resistant. In this and many other ways style and function are united in the design.

Victorian Gothic gained international acceptance and in 1844 George Gilbert Scott won the competition for the Lutheran Nikolaikirche, Hamburg, with a fine design with a well-proportioned tower and spire that still survive today. Many notable Gothic designs followed from continental architects, of whom E E Viollet-le-Duc is the most important. He made significant contributions to

the structural theory of Gothic design and in 1864 was awarded the Gold Medal of the Royal Institute of British Architects.

American architects were also caught by the Gothic vision. Ruskin's influence is particularly evident in the National Academy of Design, New York (1862–65), by P B Wright, closely modelled on the Doge's Palace, Venice; and it appeared too in the heavy, bold detail of the Provident Life and Trust Company Building

(demolished), Philadelphia (1879), by Frank Furness. Elsewhere, wherever there was a British colony, it is likely that a Victorian Gothic church will be found, illustrating how far some of Pugin's successors had departed from his catholic principles.

Classicism

In Europe classicism continued generally as the architectural mainstream. In Paris first the École Polytechnique and then the École des Beaux-Arts instilled into succeeding generations of architects classical principles of design, axial planning, symmetry, the discipline of the bay and the use of proportion. Classicism, thus maintained, proved sufficiently elastic to meet modern needs. After the Neoclassi-

cal phase there was a revival of
interest in Italian Renaissance
architecture. Its style was adapted
to northern use by the addition of
ranges of large, semicircular-headed
windows, and its regular rhythm of
bays perfectly accommodated the
new framed construction. In France
this combination resulted in a work
of great clarity and distinction, the
Library of S Geneviève, Paris
(1843), by Henri Labrouste, who
further developed the use of iron for
the National Library, Paris (1862–
68), where the interior is top-lit
through lanterns set in shallow
domes supported on slim columns,
producing an effect of extraordinary
structural lightness. True to precedent, the Renaissance revival proceeded to progressively richer
designs until a form of Neo-Baroque
was reached, as in the Paris Opera
House of 1861–74 by J-L-C Gar-

nier, where the grandiose planning of grandiose spaces is complemented with fantastically elaborate but fully coherent ornament in a supreme architectural gesture to the theatre.

In Britain such richness was never paralleled. The Renaissance revival was introduced into London in 1829 by Charles Barry with his design for the Travellers' Club, Pall Mall, modelled on an Italian palazzo. Barry followed this with the neighbouring Reform Club of 1839, but just previously had produced a very similar design for the Athenaeum, Manchester (1836–39). Manchester was then the wealthy commercial capital of the cotton industry. Numerous warehouses were needed, expressing civic, not merely utilitarian, functions. The suitability of the highly flexible palazzo mode was immediately grasped and exploited. It imposed no size restrictions and functioned perfectly. It was economical, urbane, and carried social connotations that were not unflattering to the new merchant princes. Up to c. 1860 it was very popular in Britain and was widely used too for commercial buildings in America. As with High Victorian Gothic, the historical references proved merely a starting point for a new genre.

The 'Battle of the Styles', the prolonged hostilities between Gothicists and classicists, lasted for 50 years from the 1830s and reached a virulent climax about 1860 when Lord Palmerston, the incoming prime minister, rejected Scott's previously approved design for proposed government offices in Whitehall. He demanded that Scott should produce a Palladian design or resign the commission. After long parliamentary wrangling, Scott, the professed Gothicist, 'ate his leek' and, without altering the plan, made a Renaissance design that is now admired. This incident discredited both sides although this was not fully apparent architecturally for a further decade.

Emancipation

The dependence on precedent that sometimes appeared as outright his-

toricism and at others as a convenient eclecticism irked many perceptive architects and critics from the 1830s. Architects were constantly looking for 'an architecture of our period, a distinct, individual, palpable style of the nineteenth century' (T L Donaldson, 1847). After the Scott/Palmerston fiasco, aspiring young architects were neither

above
Barry's suave, scholarly Reform Club, Pall Mall, London (1839), adjoins his Travellers' Club (1829).

below
The Foreign Office, London (1857–73), by Scott.

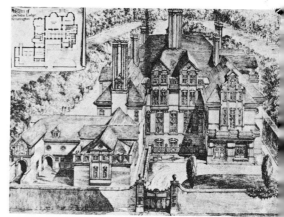

left
Red House, Bexleyheath, Kent (1859), by Webb for his friend William Morris.

bottom
Shaw's Leyswood, Groombridge, Sussex (1868–69), is a skilful exploitation of the form of a traditional manor.

below
Lowther Lodge, Kensington (1873–74), by Shaw, illustrates the Queen Anne style it helped to introduce.

convinced Gothicists nor classicists, nor were they pluralists of the old school. Each architect created his personal solution, and the architecture of the following decades in Britain and America is marked by pronounced individualism. In Britain this can be seen most clearly in the work of architects such as Philip Webb, R N Shaw and E W Godwin, and in America H H Richardson and Louis Sullivan reflect a similar attitude.

Architects ranged far beyond the traditional styles in their search for ideas and motifs. In Britain attention turned to vernacular architecture, including the classically influenced forms of the late seventeenth century. This led to the so-called Queen Anne style, a manner far removed from the original and so eclectic as sometimes to include decorative motifs from Japan. In contrast, Philip Webb's Red House, Bexley Heath, Kent (1859–60), commissioned by William Morris, shows Gothic inspiration, but the efficient sash windows, segmentally-headed under pointed arches, express a stylistic union contrary to the dogmatic temper of the recent past.

Stylistic versatility was carried to the furthest lengths by R N Shaw, a highly influential designer. Leyswood, Groombridge, Sussex (1868–69), is one of his numerous houses that draw upon Jacobean motifs. His Lowther Lodge, Kensington (1873–74), ably represents the Queen Anne revival, and his New Scotland Yard, London (1887–88), shows him at his most idiosyncratic in creating something entirely new from a wide variety of sources, British and foreign. Shortly after this, Shaw led a revival of formal eighteenth-century values, but whatever style he chose he made his own.

If Webb's eclecticism was practical and Shaw's playfully versatile, that of E W Godwin was aesthetic, inspired by the most advanced contemporary idea of art, i.e. that its essence lies in the appreciation of abstract aesthetic qualities. His design for the White House (demolished), Chelsea (1878), built for his friend J M Whistler, the painter, shows his intention of avoiding superfluous ornament and association with past styles. Partly frustrated in the former by outraged officialdom, he still succeeded in producing a building that can be interpreted only by reference to function and abstract qualities of design.

H H Richardson working from Boston, Mass., also broke away from historicism, creating his own powerful vocabulary drawn partly from American vernacular buildings. His Stoughton House, Cambridge, Mass. (1882–83), is in the 'Shingle' style, i.e. it adopts the loose form of timber houses clad in wooden shingles. His Crane Library, Quincy, Mass. (1880–83), is equally free but is constructed in powerfully expressive masonry.

above
New Scotland Yard, London (1887–88), by Shaw, fully reveals his brilliant idiosyncracy as a designer.

below
Crane Library, Quincy, Mass. (1880–83), by Richardson: it vigorously proclaims its stylistic freedom.

The Skyscraper

Louis Sullivan, cited already as an architectural emancipator, is associated particularly with skyscraper design and brilliant, Art Nouveau-like decoration. The skyscraper was only possible through advances in building technique which Sullivan and other American architects converted into an expressive architecture. Its evolution stems from the palazzo warehouses of the 1850s with their cast-iron frames and is indissolubly linked with Chicago.

In 1871 Chicago, a new and hastily-built boom town, was devastated by a terrible fire. Reconstruction began immediately and for several decades the town was the scene of great architectural developments. Land values provided a powerful incentive for the construction of tall buildings, and this was facilitated by two technical innovations: first, the lift, or elevator, which was made safe for public use; second, steel, which came into cheap production in 1855 but was not manufactured in rolled sections suitable for building until the 1880s. Whilst the building of the first skyscrapers was not dependent on steel (a skyscraper is defined not simply as a tall building, but as one in which all loads are carried by a structural frame), the full potential of the form could not have been realized without it.

American commercial buildings of 10 or more storeys were constructed in the 1880s using either masonry throughout or combined with iron framing internally. The most distinguished in the first category is the Monadnock Building, Chicago (1889–91), by D H Burnham and J W Root. Its striking, upswept form rises through 16 storeys, but its ground-floor plan reveals a crippling disadvantage: the principal walls are 1.8 m (6 ft) thick and wasteful of space. In neither category, the Leiter Building I, Chicago (1879), by William L Jenney has brick piers faced with cast-iron panels but in general character clearly expresses the spare lines and disciplined pattern of a structural grid. Jenney and his partner W B Mundie are credited with having produced unintentionally the first skyscraper. Their Home Insurance Company Building, Chicago (1883–85), was designed with masonry external walls attached to an internal frame. On demolition it was discovered that the frame carried the walls. Burnham and Root simultaneously were working in Chicago on similar lines as were others. The 16-storey Reliance Building, Chicago (1895),

left
The Leiter Building I, Chicago (1879), by Jenney, has metal cladding that anticipates the grid of the skyscraper.

below
The Monadnock Building, Chicago (1889–91), by Burnham & Root: a fine masonry structure but not a skyscraper.

by Burnham & Company perhaps most clearly demonstrates the logical, sensitive development of the new technique. Its steel frame is neatly sheathed in terracotta.

In a series of buildings that includes the Wainwright Building, St Louis (1890–91), the Guaranty Building, New York (1894–95), and the Gage Buildings, Chicago (1898–99), Sullivan expressed the grid of the structure, giving pronounced emphasis to the continuous verticals and treating the horizontals as panels. In each case the grid formation is made the principal feature of the elevation, but it is framed by wider piers, a base, and a deep frieze and cornice. The frieze provided a ground for his richly inventive decoration, and the bold cor-

nice a deep shadow to arrest the vertical emphasis of the columns. These became Sullivanesque hallmarks. In about a decade Chicago witnessed a technical and architectural transition of immense significance. Many skyscrapers were built elsewhere in America but no other city saw such a concentration of creative achievement.

The turn of the century

The advent of the skyscraper is the most dramatic event in nineteenth-century architecture, but it was by no means the only one at the turn of the century when indications of architectural change were generally abroad. On the European continent, in reaction to the current ponderously elaborate stage of classicism, a new, self-conscious, artistic cult swept through Belgium, France, Austria and Germany: it was Art Nouveau, a highly contrived decorative style based on the reflex, or S, curve. It sprang into architecture, fully mature, in 1893 in the interior of the Tassel House, Brussels, by Victor Horta, where in the hall and staircase principal elements were designed in ornamental curved forms and decorated with sinuously flowing lines. This short-lived style had no substantial architectural effect, although a few buildings appeared with unexpected undulations, e.g. Horta's Maison du Peuple, Brussels (1896–99). Its historical significance outweighs its architectural importance because it marks a distinct break with the past.

One architect with at least nominal associations with Art Nouveau who cannot be lightly dismissed is the Catalonian, Antoni Gaudi. He made architectural plasticity truly

structural. The unfinished church of the Sagrada Familia, Barcelona, with its sugar-loaf shaped towers is Gaudi's great work. It was designed as a Gothic revival church of cruciform plan in 1882 and taken over by Gaudi in 1884. Only one transept is complete and this shows, stage by stage, a progressive departure from Neo-Gothic to Gaudi's strange idiom; even this was finished after his death.

In Britain the extremes of Art Nouveau were shunned as morbid excesses, but the individualism of the 1870s continued to flourish. It found rational expression in modestly-scaled domestic architecture for new, educated, middle-class patrons. Careful planning for sunlight, view, and general convenience became a norm, and the infinite variety of vernacular architecture gave a wide choice of form and materials at a time when rural life seemed ideal to those compelled to work in a city.

The arts, crafts, and applied design were vigorously revived and brought to prominence in the 1880s through the Arts and Crafts Movement inspired by William Morris and John Ruskin. Architects were

left
Sullivan's Wainwright building, St Louis (1890–91): the first in which he used skyscraper construction.

right
The Guaranty Building, New York (1894–95), is considered Sullivan's master work.

above
The Forth Bridge (1882–90), by Fowler
& Baker, was a model of design to some
architects at the turn of the century.

left
Gaudi's extraordinary, sculptural
church of Sagrada Familia, Barcelona
(1884 onwards) defies categorization.

right
The library of Glasgow School of Art
(1909), by Mackintosh, shows his
command of space and abstract design.

Art Nouveau is evident in almost every line in the entrance hall to the Tassel House, Brussels (1893), by Horta.

below
Designs like Voysey's Sturgis House, Hogs Back, Surrey (1896), were influential outside England.

actively involved in its promotion through exhibitions and the commissioning of craftwork for the new houses and churches that were then the foremost vehicles for architectural advancement. C F A Voysey, M H Baillie Scott and C R Mackintosh were the best known of the many architects whose work was widely published abroad at this time. Pugin's ideal of an architecture responding to locality, destination, etc., had come to a late fruition, and houses like the Sturgis House, Hog's Back, Surrey (1896), by Voysey, represent the radical stream that Pugin had inspired.

Domestic architecture in America flourished similarly on free, experimental lines. Frank Lloyd Wright's 'prairie' houses built around Chicago in the early 1900s personify this, with the Robie House, Chicago (1909), outstanding among these (see page 297). It differs from contemporary British houses in its more open interior arrangement, with the main spaces gathered around a massive hearth and chimney stack. The high standards achieved in house designs, British and American, enlarged the concept of domestic living and inspired in Britain the domestic architecture of the new garden-city movement, so that the ideals of Ruskin and Morris for a truly social art found practical expression.

Simultaneously, on both sides of the Atlantic a revival of the formal values of classicism was occurring. In America the École des Beaux-Arts had always maintained a following through Paris-trained architects, but in Britain a new start had to be made. In continental Europe, however, the classical tradition had survived. Art Nouveau quickly evaporated, and architects turned to the formal and abstract qualities of the rectilinear volumes so brilliantly exploited by C R Mackintosh, as in his Glasgow School of Art (1897–1909). Its library reveals the importance of Godwin and the Japanese inspiration of 40 years earlier.

Classicism reduced almost to diagrammatic essentials gave a basis for both the structural frame and the spare lines and abstract geometry that Mackintosh's architecture had introduced. 'Modern' British architecture remained largely domestic, but by these means continental European architects such as Otto Wagner, Peter Behrens and Adolf Loos were able to find, without recourse to historicism, a satisfactory solution to the stylistic problem of the large urban building. Other architects built on similar uncompromising lines with another relatively new material, reinforced concrete. It had been experimentally introduced into building in the 1880s and patented in the '90s and was promptly developed in France, first for a Gothic-like church in Paris, St Jean de Monmartre (1894–97) by Anatole de Baudot, and then by August Perret for strictly rectilinear buildings conforming to the classical discipline.

In all of these innovatory structures new materials are frankly and architecturally used, but invariably the buildings are static in their expression because a fundamental principle of nineteenth-century architecture persisted: buildings were meant to express stability. It is the departure from this tradition rather than any technical advance that marks the end of the epoch. Once buildings began not only to express structure but to exhibit modern technical virtuosity as an end in itself, then a new era in the history of architectural expression had begun.

TWENTIETH CENTURY

Frank Lloyd Wright

'The machine by its wonderful cutting, shaping, smoothing and reinterpretive capacity has made it possible so to [produce] without waste that the poor as well as the rich may enjoy today beautiful surface treatments of clear strong forms that . . . Sheraton and Chippendale only hinted at, with dire extravagance, and which the middle ages utterly ignored.' With these words, given in a 1901 speech, the American architect Frank Lloyd Wright introduced two of the key themes of twentieth-century architecture: machine production and the notion of extending the benefits of architecture to everyone.

To any English-speaking architect of Wright's generation, the two ideas were combined in a complicated and sometimes contradictory way. The great nineteenth-century designer and theoretician William Morris had urged that art should pervade every aspect of life; that quality and beauty should be part of everyone's daily existence; that art, instead of being locked in the galleries, should be the product of a simple response to everyday living. For him, art had to be '. . . made by the people and for the people, as a happiness for the maker and user'.

To a young Morrisian of reforming rather than revolutionary temperament like Wright, acceptance of the machine and the concomitant horrors of the workplace was more than balanced by the benefits it conveyed in offering products to many more people than had previously been possible. Once the machine was accepted, it dictated a new aesthetic – the smoothness and repetition that Wright welcomed so enthusiastically. However, Wright's architectural work in the first decade of the century was not particularly distinguished by the use of the machine. Certainly his joinery was simple, smooth and repetitive. But so was that of English contemporaries like C F A Voysey. And Wright was one of the first architects to marry the spaces of his houses into a flowing continuum. But in this, he was matched and preceded by another Englishman, M H Baillie Scott.

Both Voysey and Scott belonged to the English Arts and Crafts Movement and their work had been widely published in Europe. By the time Wright's architecture was extensively illustrated by Wasmuth of Berlin in 1911, it was as a distinguished Arts and Crafts architect that he was hailed. His long, low-sweeping prairie houses, with their wide eaves supported on rows of close mullioned windows and their stretched-out spaces interlocked round a central group of fireplaces, were acclaimed as an American version of the English movement,

below
Wright's Robie House, Chicago (1906–9): its sweeping planes were widely imitated in Europe.

showing just how the New World could produce architecture largely free of the references to vernacular building to which most British architects were devoted. It was not for another two years that machine construction became overt in Wright's work – in, for instance, the patterned concrete blocks produced by primitive machinery for the elegantly ornate Midway pleasure gardens, Chicago (1913).

left
Design for Città Nuova (1912–14), by Sant'Elia: architectural embodiment of the Futurists' worship of the machine.

The machine as originating image

By 1911, Europeans were making their own terms with the machine. In 1909, a group of Italians, headed by Fillipo Tomaso Marinetti, founded the Futurist group. Antonio Sant'Elia, one of the architects of the group, proclaimed in 1914, 'The new architecture is the architecture of cold calculation, of reckless daring and of simplicity; the architecture of reinforced concrete, of iron, glass, cardboard, textile fibres and all those surrogates of wood, stone and brick which enable us to obtain the maximum of elasticity and lightness. . . . As the ancients drew inspiration from the elements of nature, so we – who are materially and spiritually artificial – must find this inspiration in the elements of this totally new mechanical world we have created, of which architecture must be the most beautiful expression.' Sant' Elia's Città Nouva, a series of designs produced in 1914, proposed a city of flats and offices in towers of glass and concrete with etiolated upper storeys, in style vaguely reminiscent of some Mackintosh designs or Wright at Midway Gar-

left
AEG turbine factory, Berlin (1908–9), by Behrens: the reality of the machine age.

below
Gropius's Bauhaus, Dessau (1925–26): school, design and products were vastly influential.

above

Rietveld's Schröeder House, Utrecht (1925): the interpenetration of interior and exterior, defined by horizontal and vertical planes.

dens; but in Sant'Elia's case, the towers were gigantic. Tied together by electric advertising, they straddled the network of vast roads and railways.

In the same pre-war years, a new attitude to machine production had grown up in Germany. Hermann Muthesius, a Prussian architect who had been attached to the German Embassy in London from 1896 to 1903, returned home full of enthusiasm for the simplicity and directness of Arts and Crafts design. In 1907, he helped found the Deutsche Werkbund, a group of artists, craftsmen and industrialists devoted to improving the quality of German design. In the same year the architect Peter Behrens was appointed as design consultant by Allgemeine Electricitätsgesellschaft (AEG).

Both moves were intended to make German-designed products more attractive abroad; both had an almost immediate effect on architecture at home. Behrens's AEG Turbine Factory in Berlin (1909) was one of the first expressions of the idea that a building in which machines are produced should share the machine aesthetic of simplicity, smoothness and repetition. The factory was basically a long thin shed, up and down which a mighty gantry crane could move, carrying parts of massive machines. The great columns on which the gantry rails were carried divided the side elevation into a series of identical flat bays simply filled with glass. Only at the corners, where the concrete was given recessed bands in an echo of classical detailing, was the simplicity compromised. Unimportant though they may seem, those recessed bands are symptomatic of a strand of twentieth-century architecture; Behrens was essen-

tially a Neoclassicist (one of his offices was devoted to producing Schinkelesque designs).

Six years after the turbine factory was completed, Behrens was at his most Neoclassical in his main hall for the Deutsche Werkbund exhibition held in Cologne in 1914. The stars of the show were Behrens's ex-pupil Walter Gropius and his partner Adolf Meyer. Their machine hall was a smoothed-out version of the AEG turbine factory: a potentially endless long space. Their administration building was symmetrical too, with floating flat-roof planes, reminiscent of some of Wright's work. At each end of the front elevation was a circular staircase neatly wrapped in conservatory type glass, which, at the first-floor level, tucked itself round the sides and formed a continuous band along the back. At Cologne, Gropius and Meyer showed how glass could be dramatically combined with opaque brick and concrete to form spaces of great complexity and ambiguity – one of the twentieth-century's great contributions to architecture.

After World War One, Gropius became head of the Bauhaus at Weimar, a school for architects and designers of all kinds. Under him, it aimed to weld together arts, crafts and industry and so produce the unification of art and life for which Morris had longed. But it was in style, not social message, that the Bauhaus was most influential. Its smooth Euclidean products, obviously of machine origin, were an inspiration for generations of designers. When the Bauhaus moved to Dessau in 1926, Gropius translated the style to architecture in the school's new premises: rectilinear buildings were arranged in an assymetrical layout. They were pierced with rectangular windows which emphasized their concrete structure or were wrapped in glass, echoing the administration building at the Cologne exhibition.

No architect is original; everyone feeds on images from the past. Usually, these are images of past architecture, sometimes of painting, occasionally of nature. The post-war continental architects were extraordinary in that their sources of inspiration were sometimes painting (mainly Cubism) and often the products of engineering – machines and simple structures like grain silos which had rarely been considered worthy objects for artistic or architectural consideration.

The movement was Europe wide. In Germany, Erich Mendelsohn built the Einstein Tower, Potsdam, which was intended to hold the great man's astronomical laboratory. It was built partly of brick but made to look like a smooth casting, a component waiting to mesh into a vast machine. In Holland, painting was more the source of the impetus.

A group of artists and architects founded the paper *de Stijl*, which propounded a mixture of Frank Lloyd Wright and Cubism – spaces which ran into each other, surrounded by glass and planes of colour which, by shooting out from the perimeter of the house in overhangs, balconies and upstands, extended spatial complexity and further broke down the difference between inside and out. The masterpiece of *de Stijl* was Gerrit Rietveld's Schröeder House, Utrecht (1925). In Berlin, Mies van der Rohe, who like Gropius was a former pupil of Behrens, produced a series of brick houses, the most celebrated of which (1923) remained a project. In plan, it was a series of planes of brick and glass which whizzed from exterior to interior and out again – the resulting diagram had much in common with works by Mondriaan and other painters attached to *de Stijl*.

Le Corbusier

It was France that produced the most plangent architectural voice of the 1920s and 1930s – Charles-Edouard Jeanneret, who, after extensive travel before the war (he too worked for Behrens), settled in Paris under the name of Le Corbusier. In a series of articles and books, the most famous of which was *Vers Une Architecture* (1923), Le Corbusier sang the virtues of the machine with missionary fervour. At the same time he pursued an art of planes and simple forms based on Cubism.

As far back as 1914, Le Corbusier had produced a design, Dom-ino, for a house in which the only fixed elements were the flat slabs of the ground and first floors, the roof and two flights of stairs. The elevations could be applied as a skin, just as Gropius and Meyer wrapped their skin of glass round the upper storey of their administration building at

above
Concrete, brick and plaster forced to resemble a machine component: Einstein Tower, Potsdam (1921), by Mendelsohn.

right
Le Corbusier's Dom-ino house design (1914): by concentrating on structure it liberates facades and spaces.

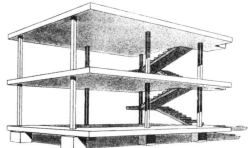

left
Lutyens's Viceregal Lodge, New Delhi (finished 1930): Neoclassicism was as ubiquitous as striped trousers.

the Cologne Werkbund exhibition. In *Vers Une Architecture*, Le Corbusier developed the theme, displaying his Citrohan House (a pun on Citroën), '. . . a house like a motor car, conceived and carried out like an omnibus or ship's cabin. . . . We must look upon the house as a machine for living in or as a tool.'

The image was all important: 'There is no shame in living in a house without a pointed roof, with walls as smooth as sheet iron, with windows like those of factories,' sang Le Corbusier. In the 1920s and 1930s he built a series of elegant white villas in which white rectangular solids were hollowed and carved to give spaces of great complexity and subtlety.

Parallel with his theories of building, Le Corbusier was developing a programme for town planning in which the ancient European maze of interlocked streets was to be

left
Weissenhofsiedlung, Stuttgart (1927): the modern movement's repost to Neoclassical architecture.

below
State Light Industry Centre, Kharkov, USSR (1926–30), by Serafimov and Kravets: classical planning meets 20th-century structural technology.

razed and replaced by a Cartesian grid of 213-m (700-ft) towers and motorways. All was to be set in 'clear air, trees and grass'.

Neoclassicism v. the International Style

The skyscrapers really being produced while Le Corbusier sang the praises of towers were far from his images of simple concrete structures infilled with glass. In Chicago's Loop and on Manhattan Island, gigantic steel-framed structures were being built in the first two decades of the century, but all were

clad in stripped versions of Neo-Gothic or Neoclassicism. The tallest, the Empire State building by Shreve, Lamb & Harmon (finished in 1932), was nearly 0.4 km (44; ft) high and over its 85 storeys was stretched a stone cladding in the severest stripped Neoclassical motifs.

For all the innovations of a few continental architects, the chief style of the twentieth century before World War Two was classicism. It reached splendid heights in the Delhi Viceregal Lodge by Edwin Lutyens (finished 1930), where the

302

architect combined Indian motifs with a tough doricism. It fell to batholic depths in the same architect's offices and flats in Park Lane, London, where Neoclassicism's little brother, Neo-Georgian, was stretched to meaningless triviality. It rose to histrionic grandeur in the people's palaces of Nazi Germany and Stalinist Russia, where it was favoured as an architecture that ordinary people could understand as the symbol of order.

The architects of the new movement were determined to prove that their way of building was just as universal and international as Neoclassicism. The opportunity for a major demonstration was offered by the Deutsche Werkbund, which in 1925 gave Van der Rohe overall control of a housing estate, the Weissenhofsiedlung on the edge of Stuttgart. He invited contributions from Le Corbusier, from Dutch architects J J P Oud and Mart Stam and from the Belgian Victor Bourgeois; Gropius and Behrens were among the German architects called in. When the estate was opened in 1927, many differences could be seen between the work of individual contributors. But the similarities were more obvious: standardization

and repetition of parts; simple rectilinear shapes; flat roofs; smooth wall surfaces, either white or in plain colours; and horizontal strips of metal windows. Weissenhof was the manifesto of the modern movement's International Style.

The Depression, the Nazi conquest of Germany and of most of western Europe precluded any vigorous development of the social and aesthetic ideals of Weissenhof until after World War Two.

The architecture of democracy

In Europe, the two decades after 1945 were dominated by the need to reconstruct and to evolve an architecture of democracy, in which the demobilized giant armies could be properly accommodated. Britain was still the richest European country and took the lead with a massive housebuilding programme. The New Town programme was an integral part of British post-war reconstruction. Completely new and theoretically self-sustaining communities were built outside the great cities so that population pressure could be reduced and green space introduced.

Initially, efforts were concentrated on development of traditional

forms. In Frederick Gibberd's Harlow New Town, for instance, most of the housing was in brick terraces, usually with tiled roofs and gables. Harlow's housing was not great architecture but it was a vigorous example of the European tradition of building in brick and timber, which had continued throughout the century as a quiet counterpoint to the dominant Neoclassical and the forceful modern styles.

A Finn, Alvar Aalto, had produced some of the most lively white International Style architecture of the 1930s but by the end of the war he had changed to brick as his chief medium. In 1953, he completed his masterpiece, a civic centre for the tiny town of Säynätsalo in mid Finland. Säynätsalo was virtually free of references to traditional architecture. It incorporated many effects of lighting and space evolved by pre-war modernists yet it rejected the machine image and the aesthetics of Cubism. Gentle but gem-like, it stands in the middle of the forest, a monument to real, unpompous democracy.

By 1952, the British housing programme was taking a new form. Britain's first tower block of flats

called his long corridors *rues inter-ieures* and, about halfway up, he provided a street of shops, which now includes a supermarket and a hairdresser to service his 'vertical garden city'. The Unité was one of the most dramatic examples of the twentieth-century architect's tendency to take over a housing programme for ordinary people and turn it into a monument of art. His imitators forgot the Unité's shops and turned Le Corbusier's village in the air into the stereotyped slabs and towers which in the last decade have come to be regarded with greater and greater disfavour.

above left
Unité d'Habitation, Marseilles (finished 1952), by Le Corbusier: a vertical garden city of great influence.

left
Van der Rohe's Crown Hall, Illinois Institute of Technology: the supreme translator of Euclid into architecture.

below
The high point of structural architecture is Nervi's Palazetto dello Sport, Rome (1958–60).

was completed by Gibberd in Harlow in 1951. The need to economize in land and a dearth of bricklayers suggested to architects and politicians that a new form of housing, high-rise and based on concrete and machinery, was needed. When the London County Council completed its estate at Roehampton in 1957, a complex of terraces and tall towers and slabs was revealed with the tall buildings set in an English park-like landscape of trees and lawns.

The towers owed much to the efforts of many Swedish architects in the 1940s. But the slabs originated in the work of Le Corbusier, who between 1947 and 1952 built the Unité d'Habitation at Marseilles. The Unité was a terrace of piled-up double-height flats, supported on great columns (*pilotis*), so that the whole slab hovered above a ground surface which was in theory able to sweep uninterrupted beneath. Inside, Le Corbusier

By the 1950s van der Rohe had evolved his own equally potent version of the modern aesthetic. A refugee from Nazi Germany to the USA, Rohe taught at the Illinois Institute of Technology, Chicago, for which he built the campus. A series of apparently steel buildings emerged in which the obvious structure (often false, because the Chicago fire regulations required encasement of real bearing members in concrete) framed panels of glass and brick, laid with machine-like precision. It was an architecture of pure proportion untroubled by petty human individualism and its simplicity was enormously influential. The smooth, metallic, Euclidean geometry of Rohe's campus was first brought to the heart of the city by Gordon Bunshaft of Skidmore, Owings & Merrill, whose Lever House office building, New York (1952), poised a tall thin vertical rectangle neatly wrapped in glass over a long thin horizontal rectangle. The structure of the tower was in essence a stack of Le Corbusier's Dom-ino houses.

The architecture of pure Euclidean form reached its apogee in Oscar Niemeyer's designs for Brazilia, the federal capital of Brazil. Brazilia's Congress building consists of a vast rectangular podium on which sit two segments of spheres housing the assemblies; the composition is set off by two linked towers of offices of Bunshaftian smoothness and elegance. Brazilia's pomp was the 1950s counterpart of the grandeur of New Delhi.

Equally elegant and almost as pure was Pier Luigi Nervi's Palazetto dello Sport, Rome (1958), in which a dome is supported on factory-made concrete ribs which are themselves propped by great Y-shaped flying buttresses. The Palazetto was one of a generation of buildings which set out to explore the curvaceous qualities of concrete. That reinforced concrete does not have to be forced into rectilinear moulds was well understood by English and German architects of

above
Spiralling interior of the Guggenheim Museum, New York (1943–59), by Wright, reveals new understanding of concrete.

below
Saarinen's TWA terminal, New York (1962): the new concrete space.

the first two decades of the century. But it was not until the late 1950s that the theory and practice of concrete building allowed a new monumental architecture not based on past geometries.

New monumentalism

Early in this field were those polymaths of twentieth-century architecture, Frank Lloyd Wright and Le Corbusier. Wright's Guggenheim Museum, New York (1943–59), was a hollow spiral of gallery, tapering downwards from the top: a shape that could scarcely have been built before the properties of concrete were properly understood. Le Corbusier produced a little pilgrimage chapel at Ronchamp in the Vosges, France (1950–53), with a great curved concrete roof of such complex geometry that it has been likened (by the architect) to a crab's carapace and (by others) to everything from a boat to a piece of cheese.

Almost as complex, but much larger, was Eero Saarinen's TWA terminal for Idelwald (now Kennedy) Airport, New York (1956–61), where the curved forms were likened (with the architect's approval) to a great bird. Equally evocative were the curved shells of Danish architect Jørn Utzon's Sydney Opera House (1957–74), where the white concrete concavities float above the harbour like a set of sails. The opera house strained the technology of the time to its limits, for it was only after thousands of hours of computer calculation that engineers Ove Arup & Partners managed to make the pre-cast concrete structure buildable. However, other non-Euclidian techniques began to be exploited in the same years. For instance the roof shapes of Kenzo Tange's gymnasium for the Tokyo Olympic Games (1964) were determined by the properties of hung cables – a principle which had long

above
Perfect shapes in Niemeyer's design for Brazilia's Congress building: the apotheosis of Euclidean architecture.

below
The gymnasium built for the Tokyo Olympic Games (1964), by Tange: a new approach to structure using tensile steel ropes.

right
The complex and ambivalent imagery of Le Corbusier's chapel at Ronchamp (1950–53): impossible without a new understanding of material.

been well known to bridge builders but rarely used in the context of architecture before.

While the Arup computer was pounding away on the Sydney Opera House, a new approach was emerging, based on exploiting a much wider range of technology than structure alone. In 1961 a group of students and teachers at London's Architectural Association school published the first edition of the magazine *Archigram*. Its editor Peter Cook explained that inspiration came from '. . . the space-comic; its reality is in the gesture, design and natural styling of hardware new to our decade – the capsule, the rocket, the bathyscope, the Zidpark, the handy-pak.' Like the Futurists, *Archigram* produced a wealth of visionary projects, the most famous of which was Plug-in City. This urban machine had a gigantic diagonal grid of tubes incorporating services and lifts, on to which were to be plugged prefabricated metal boxes to provide flats, shops and offices. A key element of the design was the overhead crane which could pick up the boxes and rearrange them in any pattern that the whim of society (or Big Brother) should demand.

In the early 1960s the closest building to Plug-in City was the Leicester University Engineering Building (1963) by James Stirling and James Gowan. It shared *Archigram*'s diagonals and gawky structure and was even topped by a crane (though it was for window cleaning, not moving parts of the building). At Leicester, the architects did what virtually every architect since Pugin has preached and allowed form to follow function. Lecture theatres, offices, workshops, laboratories were each wrapped tightly in skins of glass, brick and tile, producing such a variety of shapes that many architects of the older school were profoundly shocked.

New directions

But it was not until the 1970s that *Archigram* began to have an obvious effect on buildings. Kisho Kurokawa's Nakagin capsule build-ing, Tokyo (1972), a craggy pillar of habitable boxes looks like a detached chunk of Plug-in City. The Pompidou Centre, Paris (1976), by Renzo Piano and Richard Rogers is a great steel cage supporting theoretically infinitely flexible spaces. Round and through the cage are laced tubes for conveying people and services, forming a brilliantly coloured tartan counterpoint to the rigid rectangles of the steel structure. Equally sophisticated technology was used by Norman Foster in the Willis Faber office, Ipswich, England (1975), but there the tubes are exposed inside whereas the exterior wall, which curves amoebically round the site, is a smooth skin of dark glass uninterrupted by even simple frames.

The architecture of high technology was by no means the only form of expression in the 1970s. American architects like Michael Graves and Peter Eisenman rediscovered and reinterpreted Cubism, producing houses which play elaborate, arcane jokes on the work of Rietveld and other 1920s designers. James

Stirling's most recent designs show an almost exact reversal of his position at Leicester. His Stuttgart Staatsgalerie project, for instance, was an exercise in arranging simple shapes, almost as austere as the work of the late eighteenth-century Neoclassicists like Boullée.

Philip Johnson, who was one of the most respected practitioners of the International Style in the 1940s and 1950s shocked critics by adding a Chippendale top to one of his skyscraper projects of the 1970s and a set of pinnacles to another. In doing so, he was following a course pioneered by Robert Venturi, who advocated the use of simple, widely understood architectural features – a pediment to symbolize entry for instance – in an effort to make architecture much more universally appreciated.

In Britain, parallel attempts to popularize architecture resulted in Trad – a return to vernacular sources for inspiration. Widely used in housing, the style has been applied to at least one large building – the Hillingdon Civic Centre by Robert Matthew, Johnson-Marshall & Partners (1978), where a large conventional open-plan office is wrapped in an elaborate brick and tile garment, its details owing

much to the surrounding suburbs.

The difficulty of communicating with the real users of buildings, rather than client committees, caused some architects to try working directly with user groups. Ralph Erskine, for instance, opened an office in a shop on the site of his Byker housing scheme, Newcastle (continuing), to which local residents could come with their problems. The estate is plainly designed by architects but is said to be more popular than most because of the participation process.

Lucien Kroll, in his student accommodation for the University of Louvain near Brussels (1974), was much more radical, encouraging groups of students to become involved in designing different parts of the building. Kroll's task was to knit the elements together to form a whole in which each part could speak eloquently. The result, in which glass, wood, tiles, brick and concrete crash together in what is at first sight an entirely random fashion, is upsetting to those brought up in the cool Euclidean certainties of the International Style but it is surely one way of democratizing architecture.

Yet adopting popularly understood forms, like Venturi and

above
Byker, Newcastle (still completing), by
Erskine: high architecture but with a lot
of input by the users.

above right
The architecture of structure is taken to
the ultimate in Utzon's Sydney Opera
House (1957–74).

right
Plug-in City by Cook and others: the
Archigram designs celebrated machine
worship anew.

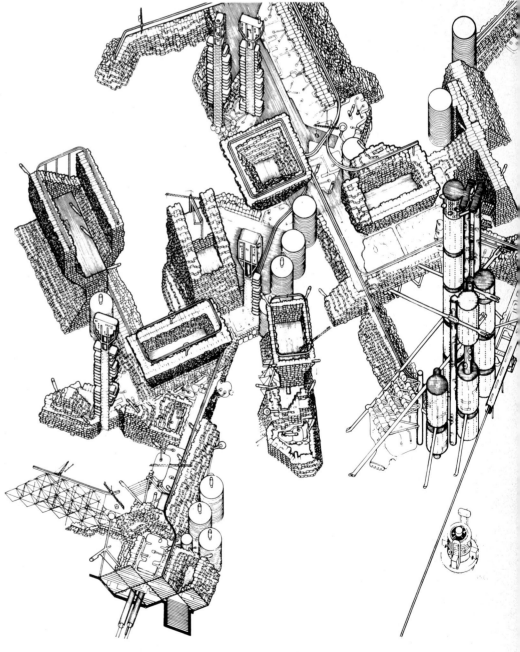

Matthew Johnson-Marshall, or
involving users in design, like Erskine and Kroll, are not the only
ways of encouraging popularity.
That temple of high technology and
high architecture, the Pompidou
Centre, is the most visited public
building in Paris and many visitors
are said to go just for the pleasure of
riding constantly up and down the
escalators.

Architecturally, the 1970s was
one of the most exciting decades of
the century. Now there are no certainties except that architects will
continue, as they have for 80 years,
the struggle to come to terms with
machine technology and the ideal of
an architecture for everyman.

above
The Pompidou Centre, Paris (1976), by Piano & Rogers: a wildly popular celebration of high technology.

left
Big bureaucracy wrapped in popular clothing: Roger Matthew, Johnson-Marshall & Partner's Hillingdon Civic Centre, London (1978).

Perspectives for the future

In July 1972 the Pruitt Igoe flats in St Louis were blown up. They had been designed in 1951 and erected between 1952 and 1955. There were several slab blocks, 14 storeys high, with play spaces, laundries, creches, and places for meeting and talking. They had received an award from the Amercian Institute of Architects. They had been vandalized, defaced and mutilated, and were said to have a higher crime-rate than any other development of their type.

In September 1979 two multi-storey blocks of flats near the River Mersey in England were similarly demolished. They had been built in 1958 and had a similar record of vandalism.

Such demolitions could be seen, said a critic, to mark the end of the modern movement in architecture. And it will probably not be the last time that modern buildings are demolished soon after they have arrived. Nor is it surprising that some of the first of the modern movement's buildings to be demolished should be housing because housing took the place in the twentieth century of building types that dominated architecture in earlier periods. The demolitions did not however mark the end of the modern movement as such: they marked the end of a major phase of it.

Inherent in that phase was the rejection of traditional aesthetics, conventions about beauty and style – a deliberate rejection of values which were thought to belong to an earlier privileged minority. What was thought to be central were human needs – the needs of a very large number of people. How ironic that now seems to be. But in architecture ideology has to be represented by hard facts.

What is now emerging as the next phase is something very different. The needs of people may not be the large scale, the concentration, but the very opposite – buildings on the scale of small human groups.

Modern man is part of an increasingly sophisticated and technologically orientated society. And his role in that society is certainly changing. For modern man is himself characterized by two things which have not always been dominant in the past – his access to information and his mobility.

He has access through the media to more information, more attitudes, more dislikes, more expressions of wants and needs than at any time before. His mobility is well known; he can move more often, go further, visit more places, travel faster, see more new environments, have more unprecedented perceptions than at any previous period in history. That means that with every year he himself becomes an increasingly important agent in the change of things.

How does this apply to the design of new buildings? It may be that if participation is to be a reality for everyman, buildings should be more incomplete than we make them at the moment – and designed in such a way that they provide people with opportunities for change and addition, the freedom to be themselves and to modify their environment.

There are many different ways of doing that. It could mean that houses will be strong, very solid and very permanent, so that the inside can be altered, or it could mean that a house should be very imperma-nent, light and flexible, so that the whole thing can be shifted around. It could mean that the environment as a whole should be more incomplete than it has been, more like a fairground than a housing estate – so that people can add things, move them and throw them away. Inspired more by personal choice, they might be places like caravan sites, factory sites, playgrounds. A modern architecture might look erratic but have a very profound order of a non-immediate kind, like the structure of plants and living organisms – very informal, often changing, capable of many different interpretations.

Growing from a new vernacular tradition, forming part of a chang-ing landscape, and made practic-able by the new technology, the new architecture may be an architecture of organic order. It may seem random or haphazard. If so, it will be deceptive; for organic order is not random; its underlying reality has to be studied and discovered.

Perhaps things will be the reverse of what we have often taken for granted. It may be that planning layouts will become more irregular, impermanent and changing, and that buildings will look more incom-plete, both outside and inside – an external simplicity, an internal architecture of light and colour and growth, of glass and plants and space and air. If that is so, the examples from which a future architecture will be developed are likely to be buildings by Gaudi rather than the repetitive flats of St Louis. Gaudi may indeed be an exemplar – an architect who under-stood nature's structures and had a grasp of solid geometry, who was able to express in his work the continuity of nature and to make a personal art from it.

In any event, the new technology gives more control to man in a man-made environment and a man-made society. It is control not only on a huge scale: it is control of the small things which are a part of the immediate environment of the ordi-nary person. It may be that the new architecture will be more continu-ous, transparent, and ambiguous, requiring a new kind of vision to understand it, an appreciation of things that are moving and chang-ing and being adapted all the time. At least one of the great lessons of architectural history is that there is no end to it. There is no reason to think that modern architecture has proceeded further than a very short way along its path.

Glossary

Abacus. The slab on top of a *capital* directly supporting the *architrave*. See *orders*.

Acanthus. A plant with sharp pointed leaves, copied in the *Corinthian* capital.

Acropolis. The citadel of a Greek city where the temple of the patron deity was usually built.

Agora. In Ancient Greece, a public space for assemblies; same as a Roman *forum*.

Aisle. In *basilican* buildings, one of the lateral divisions parallel with the *nave* but not as high. Sometimes used to include the nave as well (e.g. 3-aisled = nave and two aisles; 5-aisled = nave and double aisles). Transepts and chancel may also be aisled.

Ambulatory. A continuous *aisle* forming a processional path round some larger enclosed space. In Europe the east end of a cathedral, in India the shrine of a temple.

Amphitheatre. A round or oval arena with tiers of seats all round.

Apse. Part of a building that is semicircular or U-shaped in plan; usually the east end of a chapel or *chancel*.

Arcade. A line of arches supported on piers or columns.

Arch. A structure built over an opening to hold together when supported only from the sides, the downward pressure being transformed into lateral thrust. CORBELLED ARCH. So-called 'false arch', consisting of blocks of stone each laid slightly overlapping the one beneath until the gap can be bridged by a single slab. DIAPHRAGM ARCH. A stone arch built across the nave of a church when the roof is of wood (i.e. where there is no vault). HALF-ARCH. An arch from the *springing* to apex only. See *flying buttress*. HORSE-SHOE ARCH. A round or pointed arch shaped like a horseshoe, so that the diameter at its widest point is greater than the distance to be spanned. PARABOLIC ARCH. An arch whose curve is a parabola, one of the conic sections (the intersection of a cone and a plane parallel to its side). Used only recently in architecture. POINTED ARCH. An arch consisting of two curves meeting at an acute angle. RELIEVING ARCH. A concealed masonry arch built over another arch or a *lintel* to carry the weight. ROUND OR SEMICIRCULAR ARCH. The commonest and most elementary arch, consisting of a simple semicircle of wedge-shaped blocks. SEGMENTAL ARCH. An arch consisting of a segment only, not a full half-circle. In appearance flatter than a round arch. SQUINCH ARCH. An arch built diagonally across the corner of a rectangular space to be covered by a dome or spire, converting the rectangle into a circle or octagon. The alternative method is by *pendentives*. TRANSVERSE ARCH. An arch across a vaulted space at right angles to the walls. TRILOBE (OR TREFOIL) ARCH. With two *cusps*, dividing the arch into three lobes. A decorative, not a structural form.

Architrave. The lowest part of a classical *entablature*, the stone *lintel* above the columns. See *orders*.

Arcuation, arcuated. Having arches and supports.

Art Nouveau. Style of decoration popular in Europe *c.* 1890–1910, avoiding traditional motifs and basing itself on curving lines and vegetation-like forms.

Ashlar. Trimmed, regular masonry with flat surfaces and squared edges.

Axial planning. The placing of several buildings along a single line.

Balustrade. A line of balusters, or miniature pillars, supporting a handrail.

Barbican. Fortified outwork guarding the gateway of a medieval city or castle.

Baroque. Style after *Mannerism* in Italy, *c.* 1600, and later spread over Europe; characterized by dynamic lines and masses and the free use of classical motifs.

Basilica. (1) In Roman architecture, a large public hall where lawsuits were heard. (2) In early Christian and later architecture, a building consisting of *nave* and *aisles*, with windows above the level of the aisle roofs (*clerestory*).

Bastion. A projection from the *curtain wall* of a castle or defensive work, placed so that a zone of wall may be swept by fire from the bastions.

Bay. A compartment of a large building, consisting, e.g., in churches, of the space between one column or pier and the next, including the wall and the vault or ceiling over it. By extension, any unit of a wall-surface divided by large vertical features or (on exteriors) by windows.

Bracket. Member projecting from a vertical surface to provide a horizontal support. See also *corbel* and *cantilever*.

Buttress. Masonry built against a wall to give additional support, or to resist the thrust of a vault or arch. FLYING BUTTRESS. A *half-arch* leaning against that point in a wall where the lateral thrust of an arch or vault is being exerted, and transmitting this thrust to a body of masonry at a lower level. A characteristic of the *Gothic* style.

Byzantine. Style evolved at Constantinople about the fifth century AD and still in use in some parts of the world. The round arch, segmental dome and use of marble veneers are characteristic.

Calidarium. The hot-water room in a Roman public bath.

Canopy. Decorative covering over a small open structure such as a tomb, pulpit or niche; often supported on columns.

Cantilever. A beam or girder supported in the middle or along half its length and weighted at one end to carry a proportionate load on the other.

Capital. The upper part of a column. See *Doric, Ionic, Corinthian* and *orders*. In non-classical architecture capitals may be of any design.

Carolingian. Style originating under Charlemagne *c.* AD 800 and leading to *Romanesque*.

Caryatid. Pillar in the form of a sculptured female figure.

Cenotaph. Monument to a person buried elsewhere (Greek: 'empty tomb').

Central-plan. A plan symmetrical, or nearly so, in all four directions.

Chancel. Space in a church reserved for the clergy, including the altar and the choir.

Chevet. The combination of *apse, ambulatory* and *radiating chapels* at the east end of a large Gothic church.

Choir. The part of a church where the choir sits. Normally the west part of the chancel. The term is often loosely applied to mean the same as chancel, although in large medieval churches the choir sat under the crossing or west of it.

Classical. Greek or Roman and their derivatives, especially the use of the *orders*.

Clerestory. The upper window-level of a large enclosed space, rising above adjacent roofs. In particular the upper window range of a *basilican* building above the *arcade* and *triforium*.

Cloister. A square court surrounded by an open *arcade*.

Coffering. Treatment of ceilings and domes consisting of sunk panels (coffers).

Colonnade. A row of columns.

Column. A circular pillar, a cylindrical support for part of a building. Also erected singly as a monument. See *Doric, Ionic, Corinthian* and *orders*.

Columnar and trabeate. Using the column and 'beam', or lintel, only, i.e., not using the principle of the arch.

Composite. An *order* invented by the Romans, combining the acanthus leaves of the *Corinthian* with the volutes of the *Ionic* capital.

Concentric walls. Fortification introduced from the East by the crusaders, consisting of one complete defence system inside another.

Corbel. A *bracket*, a block of stone projecting from a wall as a horizontal support or as the *springing* of a rib. See *arch* and *vault*.

Corinthian. The last of the three classical *orders*. Characteristics: (1) high base, sometimes a pedestal; (2) slender fluted shaft with fillets; (3) ornate capital using stylized acanthus leaves.

Cornice. (1) The top, projecting section of a classical *entablature* (see *orders*). (2) In Renaissance architecture, a projecting shelf along the top of a wall supported on ornamental *brackets*.

Cove, coving. Concave surface connecting a wall and ceiling.

Crossing. The central space of a cruciform church where the *nave, transepts* and *chancel* meet.

Cruciform. Cross-shaped.

Crypt. Underground space below the east end of a church, originally to house the remains of saints (Greek: 'hidden').

Cupola. Sometimes means the same as *dome*. More usually in English a miniature dome or turret with a lantern-top.

Curtain wall. (1) In castles, the wall between *bastions* or towers. (2) In modern architecture, an exterior wall serving as a screen only, bearing no load. In *steel-frame* buildings all the walls are curtain walls.

Cusp. A projecting point on the inner side of an *arch*, window or roundel.

Cyclopean. Walling in very large irregular stones without mortar.

Dagoba. A Singhalese form of *stupa* or relic-chamber (lit: 'dhata' = relics; 'garbha' = womb).

Dais. Raised platform at the end of a hall.

Decorated. Style of architecture in England following *Early English*. Characterized by elaborate curvilinear tracery, unusual spatial effects, complicated rib-vaulting, cusping, naturalistic foliage carving.

Dome. A concave roof, roughly hemispherical, on a circular base. A section through a dome can be *semicircular, pointed* or *segmental* (see *arch*). A dome with segmental section is called a saucer-dome. Most west European domes have drums. Onion- or bulb-domes are external features only.

Doric. First and simplest of the classical *orders*. Characteristics: (1) no base, (2) relatively short shafts meeting in a sharp arris; (3) simple undecorated echinus and square abacus. See *orders*. The Roman Doric was similar but had a base.

Dormer window. Vertical window in a sloping roof.

Dromos. (1) A race-course. (2) A passage or entrance-way between high walls, e.g. to a Mycenaean tomb.

Early English. First phase of English *Gothic*, beginning *c.*1180. Characterized by lancet windows or (later) geometrical tracery, rib-vaults, emphasis on thin linear articulation instead of mass and volume, sharp mouldings and the clear distinction of architectural members.

Eave. The lowest part of a sloping roof that projects over the wall.

Ecclesiasterion. The public hall or council-chamber of a Greek town.

Echinus. The lower element of a *Doric* capital – a circular cushion-like member under the *abacus*. Also the corresponding member of an *Ionic* capital, partly obscured by the *volutes* and carved with egg-and-dart moulding.

Engaged. Bonded into a wall; not free-standing.

Entablature. In classical architecture, everything above the columns – *architrave, frieze* and *cornice*. See *orders*.

Entasis. Slight bulge given to a column to correct the optical illusion that it is thinner in the middle.

Exedra. An apsidal recess or alcove with seat; in Renaissance architecture any niche or small apse.

Facade. The exterior of a building on one of its main sides, almost always containing an entrance.

Ferro-vitreous. Iron-and-glass, as e.g., the Crystal Palace.

Flamboyant. Last phase of French *Gothic* (lit: 'flame-shaped'), characterized by complex curvilinear tracery and profuse ornament.

Flute, fluting. Channels or grooves, carved vertically down the shafts of classical columns. See *orders*.

Forum. Roman market-place or open space for assemblies, normally surrounded by public buildings.

Free-standing. Open on all sides, not attached to a wall.

Fresco. Strictly, painting applied to a wall while the plaster is still wet. Sometimes loosely used of any mural painting.

Frieze. Part of a classical *entablature*, above the *architrave* and below the *cornice*. In Doric it was divided into *triglyphs* and *metopes*. See *orders*. Often used for a band of figure-carving; hence in Renaissance architecture it means a continuous band of relief round the top of a building or room.

Frigidarium. The cold-water swimming pool in Roman public baths.

Gable. The triangular end of a *gable-roof*; in classical architecture called a *pediment*. By extension, a triangular area over a doorway even when there is no roof behind, as e.g., over French Gothic cathedral portals. GABLE-ROOF. Roof with two sloping sides and triangular gables at the ends.

Gallery. (1) An upper floor open on one side to the main interior space of a building (e.g. galleries over the aisles of a church) or to the exterior. (2) In medieval and Renaissance houses, a long narrow room.

Giant order. Pilasters or half-columns used to articulate a facade and extending through two or more storeys.

Gothic. Name given to medieval architecture in Europe from about mid-twelfth century to the Renaissance. Characterized by the *pointed arch*, the *flying buttress* and the *rib vault*.

Groin. The ridge or arris formed by the meeting of two vaulting sections.

Half-arch. See *arch* and *flying buttress*.

Half-column. A column divided vertically and attached to a wall, either as decoration (e.g., the Colosseum) or as the respond of an arch.

Hip. The line formed by two sloping roofs meeting. HIPPED ROOF. A truss roof with hips instead of gables: that is, the *ridge-beam* is shorter than the walls parallel with it, so that the roof slopes inwards on all four sides.

Hippodrome. In Ancient Greece, a stadium for horse and chariot racing.

Horseshoe arch. See *arch*.

Hypostyle. A hall or large enclosed space in which the (usually flat) roof rests on columns throughout, not just along sides.

Inlay. Small pieces of some rich material set into a bed or background of another.

International Style. Name given to the style of architecture evolved in Europe and America shortly before the First World War. Characterized by an emphasis on function and rejection of traditional decorative motifs.

Ionic. The second of the three classical *orders*. Characteristics: (1) elegantly moulded base; (2) tall, slender shafts with flutes separated by fillets; (3) capital using the volute, or spiral.

Joist. Horizontal beam supporting a floor or ceiling.

Kando. The main sanctuary of a Japanese Buddhist temple.

Keep. The innermost stronghold of a castle. Originally the only part built of stone, later surrounded by *concentric* walling.

King-post. Upright beam of a roof supporting the *ridge-beam* and resting on the centre of the *tie-beam*.

Lantern. (1) A tower open to the space underneath and with windows to admit light downwards. (2) Small turret with windows crowning a dome or cupola.

Lintel. Horizontal beam or slab spanning an opening. In classical architecture the lintel is called an *architrave*.

Loggia. A roofed space with an open *arcade* on one or more sides.

Longitudinal plan. Church plan in which the *nave-chancel* axis is longer than the *transepts* (as in all English cathedrals).

Mannerism. Style coming between High Renaissance and Baroque. Characterized by the idiosyncratic use of classical motifs, unnatural proportion and stylistic contradictions.

Mastaba. In Ancient Egyptian architecture, a flat-topped tomb with sloping sides, the forerunner of the pyramid.

Mausoleum. A rich and elaborate tomb, so-called from the tomb of Mausolus' at Halicarnassus.

Megaron. The principal hall of a Minoan or Homeric house (e.g., Tiryns, Mycenae).

Metope. Part of the *frieze* of a *Doric entablature*, one of the spaces between the *triglyphs*, at first left plain, later sculptured. See *orders*.

Mihrab. In Muslim architecture, a niche in the wall of a mosque, showing the direction of Mecca.

Mimber. The pulpit in a mosque.

Minaret. Tower built near or as part of mosque, from which a muezzin calls the faithful to prayer.

Module. A measure of proportion to which all the parts of a building are related by simple ratios. In classical architecture it is usually half the diameter of the column immediately above its base.

Mosaic. Small cubes of glass or stone (tesserae) set in a cement bedding as decoration for wall-surfaces or floors.

Mosque. The Muslim's place for prayer and exhortation.

Moulding. Decorative profile given to an architectural member; often a continuous band of incised or projecting patterning.

Mudéjar. Late Spanish Romanesque, strongly influenced by Muslim architecture (fourteenth to fifteenth centuries).

Mullion. The vertical member dividing a window of more than one light. (The horizontal members are called transoms.)

Naos. The principal chamber or sanctuary of a Greek temple, where the statue of the deity was kept.

Nave. (1) The central space of a *basilica*, flanked by the *aisles* and lit by the *clerestory*. (2) All of a church west of the crossing, or if there are no transepts, west of the chancel.

Neoclassicism. A style coming after the Baroque, characterized by a more academic use of classical features.

Niche. A recess in a wall usually for a statue or ornament.

Norman. Name given to the *Romanesque* style in England.

Obelisk. A tall stone, square in section, tapering upwards and ending pyramidally.

Orders. Columns and their entablature, especially the various designs followed by Greek and Roman architects: *Doric, Ionic, Corinthian, Composite, Tuscan*. SUPERIMPOSED ORDERS. In Roman architecture, the orders came to be used as ornamental features, attached to walls and facades, two, three or four storeys high. The sequence from bottom to top was always Doric, Ionic, Corinthian, Composite.

Orientation. Strictly, alignment east-west, but used loosely for any deliberate placing of a building in relation to the points of the compass.

Orthostat. A large upright slab of stone.

Pagoda. A multi-storeyed Chinese or Japanese building with wide projecting roof at each storey.

Pediment. Originally the triangular *gable*-end of a Greek temple with pitched roof. Later used as a monumental feature independent of what is behind it. See *orders*.

Pendentive. The curved triangular surface that results when the top corner of a square space is vaulted so as to provide a circular base for a dome. A *coved* corner. It fulfils the same purpose as a *squinch arch*.

Peripteral. Having a single row of columns all round; a temple surrounded by a single row of columns.

Peristyle. A row of columns (1) round the outside of a building (usually a Greek temple) or (2) round the inside of a courtyard (e.g., in a Greek or Roman house) and by extension the space so enclosed.

Perpendicular. The last phase of English *Gothic*, replacing Decorated during the second half of the fourteenth century and lasting into the seventeenth. Characterized by light airy proportions, large windows, straight lattice-like tracery over both windows and wall-surfaces, shallow mouldings, four-centred arches and fan-vaults.

Pier. Free-standing masonry support for an arch, usually composite in section and thicker than a column, but performing the same function.

Pilaster. A flattened column, rectangular in section, attached to a wall as decoration, without structural function, but still obeying the laws governing the *orders*. PILASTER STRIP. Vertical band of stone serving roughly the same purpose as a pilaster, but unconnected with the classical orders.

Pilotis. Posts or 'stilts' (French 'pilot' = pile) supporting a whole building, leaving the ground storey entirely open.

Plateresque. Early Renaissance style in Spain from about 1520.

Plinth. The base of a pillar, pedestal, statue or of a whole building.

Podium. Stone platform on which a temple is built.

Portico. Colonnaded porch or vestibule. In Neoclassical houses the portico (columns and pediment) often merges into the facade.

Propylaeon. (Greek: 'in front of the gate'); a monumental entrance to a sacred enclosure.

Purlin. The horizontal beam running midway along a sloping roof, resting on the principal rafters and supporting the subsidiary ones.

Pylon. Ancient Egyptian monumental gateway, usually composed of two masses of masonry with sloping sides.

Pyramid. Regular solid with a square base and sides sloping inwards to meet at a point.

Queen-posts. Two upright beams in a roof, standing on the *tie-beam* and supporting a principal *rafter* and *purlin*.

Radiating chapels. Chapels added to an *apse* and fanning out radially.

Rafter. The sloping beams of a pitched roof, carrying the battens for the tiles.

Relief. Carving on a surface so that figures and objects are raised against a background. High relief (haut relief) is deeply cut; low relief (bas relief) is shallower.

Reticulated. Net-like. Tracery with openings like the meshes of a net; is characteristic of the Decorated period in English Gothic.

Revetment. (1) A veneer or facing of stone over rubble or concrete. (2) A sloping wall holding back earth.

Ridge-beam. Beam running along the top of a pitched roof. RIDGE-END. The end of the ridge-beam, the top of the *gable*.

Rococo. Characterized by flowing lines, arabesque ornament, ornate stucco-work and the obliteration of separate architectural members into a single moulded volume.

Romanesque. Style following *Carolingian* and preceding *Gothic*, characterized by massive masonry and thick proportions, the round arch, and the re-discovery of vaulting – first the barrel vault, then groined and finally the rib-vault.

Rotunda. Any round building, not necessarily domed.

Rustication. Method of leaving the outside surface of stone building-blocks rough, to give an impression of strength; the edges are normally cut back, leaving deep grooves between the blocks.

Sanctuary. The most sacred part of a church or temple.

Screen. A dividing wall having no function of support, e.g., in medieval churches surrounding the *choir*. SCREEN-WALL. An exterior wall not part of the structure. Same as sense (2) of *curtain wall*.

Semidome. Half a dome leaning against part of a building (often a complete dome) and acting as an extended *flying buttress* (e.g., in Hagia Sophia).

Shingles. Pieces of wood used instead of tiles.

Springing. The point of an arch where the curve begins.

Squinch arch. See *arch*

Steel-frame. A skeleton of steel girders providing all that is structurally necessary for the building to stand.

Stoa. In Greek architecture, an open colonnaded space for public business; a long *loggia*.

Stucco. Plaster or cement applied with moulds, usually to make interior decoration (e.g., Rococo), but also on exteriors and occasionally to simulate whole facades in stone (e.g., by Palladio).

Stupa. Originally a Buddhist burial mound; later a chamber for relics surrounded by an *ambulatory*.

Stylobate. The continuous base on which a *colonnade* stands.

Suspension bridge. A bridge in which the path or road is suspended from chains between towers or pylons.

Temenos. In Greek architecture, a sacred precinct enclosed by a wall and containing a temple or altar.

Tepidarium. Part of a Roman public bath containing the warm water, intermediate in temperature between the *frigidarium* and the *calidarium*.

Terracotta. Clay burnt or hard-baked in a mould; harder than brick; may be either natural brown, or painted or glazed.

Thermae. Roman public baths, containing large halls with water at various temperatures (*frigidarium, tepidarium, calidarium*) and many other amenities.

Tie-beam. A beam (or rod) across the base of a pitched roof, holding the two sides together and preventing them from spreading.

Tokonoma. In Japanese houses, a niche for the exhibition of paintings or flowers.

Trabeated. See *columnar and trabeate*.

Tracery. The stone framework holding the pieces of glass which make up a large window – in practice the word means *Gothic* window tracery almost exclusively. Plate-tracery, the earliest type, is basically solid wall in which holes have been cut for the glass. Bar-tracery (tracery proper) uses stone ribs to form complicated patterns. See also *reticulated, flamboyant*.

Transept. Part of a cruciform church at right angles to the *nave* and *chancel* (the north and south arms are always called 'north transept' and 'south transept'). Some cathedrals have an additional transept east of the crossing.

Triforium. The middle storey of a Romanesque or Gothic church elevation, between the *arcade* and the *clerestory*.

Triglyph. A block with three vertical strips divided by two grooves, forming (together with the *metopes*) the *frieze* of a *Doric entablature*. See *orders*.

Truss. A rigid triangular framework designed to span an opening and to carry tile or lead. Most wooden roofs are trussed.

Turret. A small tower, often built over a circular staircase, or as ornamental feature.

Tuscan. A Roman addition to the classical *orders*, resembling the *Doric* but with a base and without *flutes* and *triglyphs*.

Vault. A stone ceiling. BARREL VAULT. An arched vault, either semicircular or pointed, having an identical section throughout, without intersections, and resting continuously on the supporting walls. Longitudinal barrel vault: a barrel vault running down the length of the building, like a tunnel. Transverse barrel vault: a vault consisting of a series of barrel vaults across the building, at right angles to the walls. FAN VAULT. A decorative type of rib-vault, in which the bay divisions and vaulting compartments are ignored and the ribs fan out from the wall-shafts in the shape of everted semicones each with the same curvature. The ribs have no structural function and are in fact often simply carved on to the slabs. Confined to English Perpendicular. GROINED VAULT. A quadripartite vault in which the compartments meet at a *groin*, not a rib. QUADRIPARTITE VAULT. A vault in which each bay consists of two barrel vaults intersecting at right angles, making four triangular compartments. The lines where the planes meet may be ribbed or left as a *groin*. RIB VAULT. A development of the groin vault, in which the line of the groin is marked by a stone rib. The ribs can then be built separately like a skeleton and the spaces in between filled in, the weight being taken by the ribs. Can be quadripartite, sexpartite, or with any number of compartments. SEGMENTAL VAULT. A barrel vault whose section is a *segmental arch*. SEXPARTITE VAULT. A quadripartite vault with the addition of an extra *transverse arch* in the middle of the bay, passing through the intersection of the two diagonal arches. TUNNEL VAULT. The same as a *barrel vault*.

Verandah. A small open gallery outside a house, with a roof supported on posts or pillars and the floor raised a few feet off the ground.

Vihara. A Buddhist monastery or hall in a monastery (originally a cave).

Volute. The spiral scroll, especially as it occurs in the Ionic capital.

Ziggurat. Stepped pyramid supporting an altar or temple, built in Ancient Mesopotamia and Mexico.

Acknowledgments

Colour illustrations

Architectural Association, London 306 bottom; Nigel Atkins, London 211; John Bethell, St Albans 11, 262, 263 top, 267 top, 270–1; British Tourist Authority, London 279; Camera Press, London 34–5; J Allan Cash Library, London 162; Bruce Coleman, Uxbridge 51; W F Davidson, Penrith 66; J E Dayton, Guernsey 95; Doeser Photos, Laren 299; Olga Ford, Leicester 115; Werner Forman Archive, London 30, 167 top; French Government Tourist Office, London 202 bottom; Photographie Giraudon, Paris 63; Richard and Sally Greenhill, London 150; Hamlyn Group Picture Library 38 centre, 74, 134, 182, 199, 206, 223, 246, 266–7, 274, 278, 283, 295 bottom; Lucien Hervé, Paris 307; John Hillelson, London 190 top; Michael Holford, Loughton 10; Angelo Hornak/Vision International 67 top; Martin Hürlimann, Zurich 131; Prem Chand Jain, Delhi 119 top; A F Kersting, London 215; Michael Macintyre, London 139, 142, 147; R J Mainstone, St Albans 82 bottom, 86 top, 87 bottom, 90, 91 top; Manchester Town Hall 286; Eric de Maré 295 top; Mas, Barcelona 294; Robert Matthew, Johnson-Marshall and Partners, Welwyn Garden City 310 bottom; George Michell, London 123 top; Orion Press, Tokyo 174–5; Colin Penn, London 158; Antonello Perissinotto, Padua 23; Pictor International, London 15; Picturepoint, London 50 top, 183; Josephine Powell, Rome 27, 110, 111, 126, 127, 138; *Realités*, Paris 203; Sakamoto, Tokyo 171; Scala, Antella 7, 83, 195, 226–7, 230 top, 231, 234, 238 top, 239, 258, 259; Spectrum, London 146–7, 282; Sean Sprague, London 186 top; Tony Stone Associates, London 179, 206–7, 214, 222 bottom, 242–3, 254; William Taylor, Oxford 42, 46 top; Vorderasiatisches Museum, Berlin 22; John Warren, Horsham 94, 98, 103 top left, 114; Roger Wood, London 31, 39; ZEFA, London 18–19, 43, 47, 75, 151, 194 bottom, 219 bottom, 302, 306 top, 310 top; Joseph Ziolo – André Held, Paris 78.

Black and white illustrations

Aerofilms Ltd, Boreham Wood 208 bottom, 266, 280 bottom; Alinari, Florence 59, 60 top, 60 bottom, 62–3, 69 top, 84, 194 top, 230 bottom, 232, 233 bottom right, 237 top, 240, 245, 251 bottom; Alinari-Giraudon 248 bottom; Almasy, Paris 184 bottom; American Academy in Rome 65 top; Wayne Andrews, Grosse Pointe, Michigan 276 top, 291 bottom; John Archer, Stockport 287 top, 290 top right, 296 bottom; Archives Photographiques, Paris 200 bottom, 222 top; B Arthaud Editeur, Grenoble 40 bottom; Ashmolean Museum, Oxford 269; Bauhaus-Archiv, Darmstadt 298 bottom; Paul Bijtebier, Brussels 296 top; Janet and Colin Bord, Montgomery 13, 205 bottom; Bord Failte, Dublin 14; Jean Bottin, Paris 61, 145 bottom; E Boudot-Lamotte, Paris 26 bottom, 36 top right, 99, 100 bottom left, 112 bottom, 114, 257; Andrew Boyd 159A, 159B, 159C; Brecht-Einzig Ltd, London 308 bottom; British Library, London 155 top; British Tourist Authority, London 208–9, 224–5, 261 bottom, 263, 281 top; Buffalo and Erie County Historical Society, Buffalo, New York 293 right; Bulloz, Paris 64 top, 251 top; Camera Press, London 8 top, 8 bottom, 102, 284 bottom, 309 top; J Allan Cash Library, London 101, 152 top, 161, 284 top; Central Office of Information, London Crown Copyright reserved 16 bottom; Ceylon Tourist Board, London 143 bottom; Chevojon Frères, Paris 287 bottom; John Clark, London 169 top, 169 bottom, 177 top; Commission on Chicago Landmarks, Chicago, Illinois 292 right; *Connaissance des Arts* (R Guillemot), Paris 256; Conzett and Huber, Zurich 137; *Country Life*, London 12 bottom, 268 top left, 272, 301 top; Courtauld Institute of Art, London 202; Denis Crompton, London 309 bottom; Crown copyright – reproduced with permission of the Controller of Her Majesty's Stationery Office 224 top; Denbee Studios, Leominster 275 top; Department of Archaeology, Government of India 106 left, 119, 121, 137; Deutsche Fotothek, Dresden 244; Dyckerhoff and Widmann, Berlin 300 top; Egyptian Ministry of Tourism, Cairo 38 top; Arpad Elfer, London 129; Chris Fawcett, London 177 bottom; Werner Forman Archive, London 26 top, 29, 156 top, 156 bottom, 157, 167, 174, 178 top, 178 bottom; Fototeca Unione, Rome 65 bottom, 72 top; Gabinetto Fotografico Nazionale, Rome 73 top, 88, 196, 220, 237 bottom; Leonard and Marjorie Gayton, East Grinstead 241 bottom; Photographie Giraudon, Paris 155 bottom, 200 top; Jean Guyaux, Brussels 308 top; Hamlyn Group Picture Library 21 top, 21 bottom, 24 bottom, 36 top left, 46 bottom, 52 top, 62A, 62B, 62C, 62D, 68, 69, 73 bottom, 80A, 80B, 80C, 92 bottom, 96 top, 100 top, 100 bottom right, 108 bottom, 109 top, 113 top, 117 right, 152 bottom, 176 top, 187, 208 top, 217A, 233 top, 233 bottom left, 236 top, 236 bottom, 250, 264 right, 268 top right, 270 top, 273 bottom, 277, 280 centre, 285 top, 288 top left, 295 bottom, 305 top; Robert Harding Associates, London 149; Hastings and Chivelta Architects, New York 293 left; Hedrich-Blessing, Chicago, Illinois 297, 304 centre; Lucien Hervé, Paris 300 bottom, 304 top; Hirmer Fotoarchiv, Munich 16 top, 17, 20, 24 top left, 32 top, 32 bottom, 36 bottom, 37 top, 37 bottom, 38 bottom, 196 bottom, 197 bottom; Historic American Buildings Survey 292 left; Mark Hobart 132 top; International Freelance Library Ltd/Laurie Sparham 308–9; Japan Information Centre, London 165 top, 165 bottom; Thomas Jefferson Memorial Foundation, New York 276 bottom; J Jeiter, Cologne 252; Jericho Excavation Fund, London 24 top right; A F Kersting, London 12 top, 105 bottom, 124 bottom, 198, 204, 216 bottom, 218 top, 218 bottom, 219 top, 229 top, 241 top, 249 bottom, 255 top, 261 top, 264 bottom, 268 bottom, 270 bottom, 273 top, 275 bottom, 289 top, 291 top; Paolo Koch, Zollikon 153 top, 153 bottom, 154; Eugen Kusch, Nuremberg 191 top; R J Mainstone, St Albans 77, 79 top, 79 bottom, 80 left, 80 right, 85 top, 86 bottom, 87 top, 89 bottom, 92 top; Mansell Collection, London 264 left, 281 bottom, 289 bottom; Bildarchiv Foto Marburg, Marburg-Lahn 25 bottom, 33 top, 33 bottom, 40 bottom, 44, 55, 72, 81, 108 top, 185 bottom, 209, 210, 221 top, 221 bottom, 225 bottom, 229 bottom, 235 bottom, 288 bottom, 298 centre; Mas, Barcelona 197 top, 205 top, 240 top; John Massey-Stewart, London 158–9; Metropolitan Museum of Art, New York 50 bottom; Mexican National Tourist Council, London 184 top; Middle East Photographic Archive, London 33 centre, 97, 106 right, 113 bottom; Marion and Tony Morrison, Woodbridge 188 top, 188 bottom, 188–189, 189, 190 bottom, 191 bottom; Musées Nationaux, Paris 248 top; Museo Civico, Como 298 top; Museum of Finnish Architecture, Helsinki 303; National Monuments Record, London 290 top left; Novosti Press Agency, London 301 bottom; Bildarchiv der Österreichischer Nationalbibliothek, Vienna 225 top; Antonello Perissinotto, Padua 116; Popperfoto, London 160; Josephine Powell, Rome 25 top, 58, 70 top, 70 bottom, 82 top, 120 bottom, 125, 127, 132–3, 140, 141; Press Association, London 265; RIBA Drawings Collection, London 57, 253 bottom, 290 bottom; Rapho, Paris 107; Jean Roubier, Paris 201, 212, 213 top, 213 bottom, 216 top, 242; Sakamoto, Tokyo 163 bottom, 168, 170 top, 170 bottom, 172, 173, 176 bottom; Scala/Robert Emmett Bright 253 top, 304 bottom; Robert Skelton, London 128; Edwin Smith Collection, Saffron Walden 193; Sir John Soane's Museum, London 280 top; Michaela Soar 124 top; Spanish National Tourist Office, London 238 bottom, 247; Sean Sprague, London 181 top, 181 bottom, 185 top; Henri Stierlin, Geneva 104 top; Ezra Stoller Associates, New York 305 bottom; Wim Swaan, New York 104 bottom, 144 top, 144 bottom; William Taylor, Oxford 44A, 44B, 45 top, 48 left, 48 right, 49 top, 49 centre, 49 bottom, 52 bottom, 53 left, 53 right, 54, 56A, 56B, 56C, 64 bottom; Ullstein Bilderdienst, Berlin 301 centre; Roger-Viollet, Paris 105 top, 109 bottom, 118, 120 top, 130 top, 130 bottom, 132 bottom, 143 top, 145 top, 158, 186 bottom, 200–1, 212–3, 224 bottom; John Warren, Horsham 96 bottom, 103 top right, 103 bottom, 112 top, 117 left; Roger Wood, London 117 bottom.

Illustrations from publications

Page 160A and B from Andrew Boyd, *Chinese Architecture and Town Planning*, Alec Tiranti, 1962. Page 45 bottom from A Fürtwangler *et al*, *Aegina: das Heiligtum der Aphaia*, Munich, 1906. Page 288 top right from J-L-C Garnier, *Nouvel Opéra de Paris*, 1878–81. Page 85 bottom from A C Headlam, *Ecclesiastical Sites in Isauria*, 1895. Page 255 bottom from Eberhard Hempel, *Geschichte der Deutschen Baukunst*, Munich, 1956. Pages 163 top and 164A, B and C from *Nihon no Kenchiku: I Kodai*, Dai-ippoki Shuppan, Tokyo. Page 67 bottom from T Wiegund *et al*, *Baalbek*, 1898–1905.

The following illustrations are reprinted by permission of Penguin Books Ltd: page 71 from Axel Boethius and J B Ward-Perkins, *Etruscan and Roman Architecture*, Pelican History of Art, 1970, © the estate of Axel Boethius and J B Ward-Perkins, 1970: figure 93, page 222; page 204A and B from Kenneth John Conant, *Carolingian and Romanesque Architecture 800 to 1200*, Pelican History of Art, second revised edition 1966 © Kenneth John Conant 1959: figure 59, page 242; figure 28(5), page 94; page 217C from Paul Frankl, *Gothic Architecture*, Pelican History of Art, 1962 © the estate of Paul Frankl, Princeton University, New Jersey, 1962: figure 41, page 155; pages 84 top, 85 bottom, and 91 from Richard Krautheimer, *Early Christian and Byzantine Architecture*, Pelican History of Art, 1965 © Richard Krautheimer, 1965: figure 44, page 112; figure 70, page 179; page 360; pages 166A and B, 167, 169 top left, 172 top, and 173 top from Robert Treat Paine and Alexander Soper, *The Art and Architecture of Japan*, Pelican History of Art, second revised edition, 1974 © the estate of Robert Treat Paine and Alexander Soper, 1955, 1960, 1974: figure 2A, page 174; figure 3A, page 175; figure 7A, page 186; figure 6A, page 185; figure 29B, page 236; figure 32B, page 244; pages 122, 123 bottom, 128 right, 136 top, 137 bottom, and 148 bottom from Benjamin Rowland, *The Art and Architecture of India*, Pelican History of Art, third revised edition, 1967 © 1953, 1964 Penguin Books Ltd: figure 42, page 237; figure 17, page 133; figure 30, page 194; figure 4, page 50; figure 7, page 70; figure 48, page 263; pages 204C and 217B from Geoffrey Webb, *Architecture in Britain: The Middle Ages*, Pelican History of Art, second edition 1965 © 1956 Penguin Books Ltd: figure 23, page 37; figure 46, page 78; page 249 top from Rudolf Wittkower, *Art and Architecture in Italy*, Pelican History of Art, second revised edition, 1965 © Rudolf Wittkower, 1958: figure 15, page 251.

315